Archaeogaming

Archaeogaming

An Introduction to Archaeology in and of Video Games

Andrew Reinhard

berghahn
NEW YORK · OXFORD
www.berghahnbooks.com

First published in 2018 by

Berghahn Books

www.berghahnbooks.com

Library of Congress Cataloging-in-Publication Data

Names: Reinhard, Andrew, author.
Title: Archaeogaming: An Introduction to Archaeology in and of Video Games
/ Andrew Reinhard.
Description: New York: Berghahn Books, 2018. | Includes bibliographical
references and index.
Identifiers: LCCN 2018005079 (print) | LCCN 2018005777 (ebook) |
ISBN 9781785338748 (Ebook) | ISBN 9781785338724 (hardback: alk.
paper)
Subjects: LCSH: Virtual reality in archaeology. | Imaging systems in
archaeology. | Archaeology—Computer simulation. | Video games—
Technological innovations.
Classification: LCC CC79.I44 (ebook) | LCC CC79.I44 R45 2018 (print) |
DDC 930.10285—dc23
LC record available at https://lccn.loc.gov/2018005079

British Library Cataloguing in Publication Data

A catalogue record for this book is available from the British Library

ISBN 978-1-78533-872-4 hardback
ISBN 978-1-78533-873-1 paperback
ISBN 978-1-78533-874-8 ebook

For my dad, who introduced me to
Homer's Odyssey *and Nishikado's* Space Invaders

.

Contents

Illustrations

Acknowledgments

I would still be a level 1 n00b if it were not for the patient people in my archaeogaming guild who have taken time away from their own quests to assist me in mine. That is what good guildies do, and I hope to return the favor one day. Modern writing is an eSport, and I am lucky to be on the team with these players: From the University of York's Centre for Digital Heritage, Meghan Dennis, Emily Johnson, Colleen Morgan, and Sara Perry. From the Atari excavation: Bill Caraher, Raiford Guins, Richard Rothaus, Bret Weber, and Zak Penn. Thanks to Theresa, Cath, Hailey, and Justin for reading early drafts of this manuscript, and to Anna, Viktor, and Maia for encouraging my strange obsession. Thanks also go to Stu Eve for suggesting sections on further reading at the end of each chapter, and to Sian Beavers for sharing her DiGRA presentation with me on historical video games. Thanks to Megan von Ackermann for her last-minute photography of Sore Thumb Games in York.

Thanks to John Aycock and Katy Meyers Emery for grouping with me on archaeogaming articles, and to the editors of *Internet Archaeology*, *Public Archaeology*, *SAA Archaeological Record,* and the *Journal of Contemporary Archaeology* for publishing early peer-reviewed articles on archaeogaming. I want to also thank Jonathan Ore, Robert Rath, Sarah Bond, Jordan Oloman, Carly Silver, Douglas Heaven, Jennifer Lepies, Damion Collins, Andrew Pallett, Luke Plunkett, and Kathleen Caulderwood for taking a chance on writing about my work for general audiences on the weirdness that is video game archaeology, and to Eleanor Flegg, Chris Webster, Chris Sims, Nora Young, Marc Barkman-Astles, Cobra Smith, Sera Head, Alli Gold, Jen Jamula, and Tristan Boyle for having me on their podcasts and radio programs to talk about archaeogaming.

Thanks to the VALUE Project at the University of Leiden for hosting the first-ever international conference on archaeogaming (2016), The Interactive Past, and for bringing me along for the ride. Thanks also to the University of Umeå's HUMlab for their enthusiasm for video game archaeology, for their "Challenge the Past" conference (2015), and for being such a welcome host. The Norwegian University of Science and Technology hosted the "Greek and Roman Games in the Computer Age" conference (2009), which introduced me to Classical reception in video games (and its grand master Dunstan Lowe) and set me on my way to thinking about video games archaeologically.

Special thanks go to Tara Copplestone, Shawn Graham, and Lorna Richardson for pushing me, asking the difficult questions about the meaning and purpose of video games when studied archaeologically. If it were not for you, there would be no archaeogaming (or at least my flavor of it).

Thanks to my editor, Caryn Berg, for being open to the idea of video games as built environments worthy of archaeological study and for bringing my manuscript to Berghahn Books, and to my friend and agent David Hendin for helping me seal the deal. Thanks also to the three anonymous readers of the initial manuscript whose comments made the final product worlds better.

Thanks to Ute Wartenberg for helping me achieve my dreams.

Thanks to my family for their love and support, especially Cleo who sat on my shoulder throughout and whispered in my ear while I typed.

Some sections of this book first appeared in draft form on my blog at archaeogaming.com, and earlier versions of my thinking on archaeological tools/methods and game-sites appeared in the *SAA Archaeological Record* and *The Interactive Past*, which have been updated for this volume. Any mistakes in this book are solely my own, and the above guild members shall remain blameless. I owe you all rounds of Thunder Ale in Orgrimar.

—Andrew Reinhard
May 2018

Introduction

Prologue

It's 2014, and a team of archaeologists arrives in the desert of Alamogordo, New Mexico, to watch as a bucket auger drives thirty feet into the earth to retrieve evidence of a 1983 burial. After a few test holes, the auger recovers printed cardboard and a few pages of what appears to be an instruction manual. This is all the proof needed to mark the spot with an "X." The salvage excavation begins the next day, a backhoe puncturing the ceiling of a landfill cell in search of the largest (and possibly only) assemblage of video games ever dumped. On the third day of digging, hundreds of Atari cartridges and boxes surface, and the archaeologists catalogue and photograph these artifacts of Late Capitalism, part of a generation's material culture and digital heritage.

It's 1996, and I am working my way through the monastery of St. Francis in Greece, having solved several puzzles, nearly falling to my death on several occasions, searching for the tomb of a ruler of Atlantis. I've just earned my masters in archaeology, and it feels good to blow off steam playing as Lara Croft for the very first time, although I'm conscious that this is definitely not representative of archaeology or of how archaeologists behave. Still, it's fun to raid these tombs (and to critique the game while I play).

It's 2017, and I have just learned about a climate-induced mass migration of thousands of people. I wonder who they are and what they left behind in their haste to evacuate the planet for another star system. Over the next few days I make my way to their abandoned, icebound homeworld and see the memorials they left as they said goodbye. *No Man's Sky* is the first video game to feature an accidental catastrophic event that forced human players to flee *en masse,* and now archaeologists can conduct archaeological investigations into how a digital Vesuvius compares to the historic one and if people reacted similarly in the natural and synthetic worlds.

These scenarios are examples of "archaeogaming."

What Is Archaeogaming?

Archaeogaming, broadly defined, is the archaeology both in and of digital games.[1] Archaeology is the study of the ancient and recent human past through material remains in pursuit of a broad and comprehensive understanding of human culture.[2] In archaeogaming, archaeology is not used as an analogy or metaphor for a certain kind of analysis. As will be described in the following chapters, digital games are archaeological sites,[3] landscapes, and artifacts, and the game-spaces held within those media can also be understood archaeologically as digital built environments containing their own material culture.[4] The gaming archaeologist (or archaeogamer) understands that all games can be explored on two levels: in-game (synthetic world) and extra-game (natural world), existing at the same time, using hardware as a nexus connecting the two. Archaeogaming does not limit its study to those video games that are set in the past or that are treated as "historical games,"[5] nor does it focus solely on the exploration and analysis of ruins or of other built environments that appear in the world of the game. Any video game—from *Pac-Man* to *Super Meat Boy*—can be studied archaeologically.

All archaeogamers are players, and some are developers.[6] Millions of people interact with games both in-world[7] and out, occupying them as sites and manipulating them as artifacts when they play, study, and live. Video games, created directly by people (or indirectly by machines or routines created by people), contain their own real-world player- and developer-cultures (e.g., the player culture of eSports [competitive gaming] teams/leagues/spectators and the development culture of Atari programmers in the early 1980s) and can contain their own manufactured cultures (e.g., the race of Draenei in *World of Warcraft*), which exist solely within the game-space.[8] Because of this creation and occupation in the natural and synthetic worlds (i.e., "meatspace" and "metaspace"), games merit archaeological study. This study differs from media archaeology and game studies as will be explained below, but suffice it to say that archaeogaming is the literal interpretation of games as sites, built environments, landscapes, and artifacts, no different than any place on Earth that has been manipulated, managed, and transformed by people past and present.[9] "Video games," Colleen Morgan writes in her introduction to the special archaeogaming issue of the Society of American Archaeology's *Archaeological Record,* "provide landscapes and objects that are productive for archaeological investigations of digital materiality" (Morgan 2016: 9).

Figure 0.1 is a map/chart of archaeogaming as I see it, and largely reflects what my colleagues and I are doing in the field right now. There are five main themes, each with room for growth and participation:

1. Archaeogaming is the study of physical video games as well as the metadata surrounding the games themselves. This is the media archaeology approach, which views a game as a physical artifact, looking at the box, the manuals, the disks/cartridges, exploring its history of use on a personal level as well as at its commercial level and everywhere in between.[10] The Atari excavation in 2014 (see chapter 1) took this idea most literally. The video game archaeologist can now study hardware and software and how they combine for gameplay. Archaeogamers can compare gaming on physical media to downloading the same content from places such as Steam, a computer-based video-game-delivery platform, store, and community. We can explore modding communities (creating modifications to games) and how games change through ownership. We can explore how games change within a series and how they influence other games in a long tradition of flattery and theft. We can reverse engineer games to understand the underlying code and structures and the materials that house them.

2. Archaeogaming is the study of archaeology within video games. This is the reception studies approach where we see how games, game developers, and players project and perceive who archaeologists are and what they do. We can explore the phenomenon of looting and the emerging field of archaeological ethics within games. We can see how games actively enable players to conduct archaeological study. We can examine the tropes of popularized archaeology and how they contribute to the gameplay experience.

3. Archaeogaming is the application of archaeological methods to synthetic space. This is where we do our in-game fieldwalking, artifact-collecting, typologies, understanding of context, even aerial/satellite photography. Instead of studying the material culture (and intangible heritage) of cultures and civilizations that exist in "meatspace," we instead study those in the immaterial world.

4. Archaeogaming is the approach to understanding how game design manifests everything players see and interact with in-world.

5. Archaeogaming is the archaeology of game mechanics and the entanglement of code with players. Video games are multisensory collections of interactive math, so what deeper meaning(s) can the video game archaeologist infer from these new kinds of archaeological sites and how players engage with them?

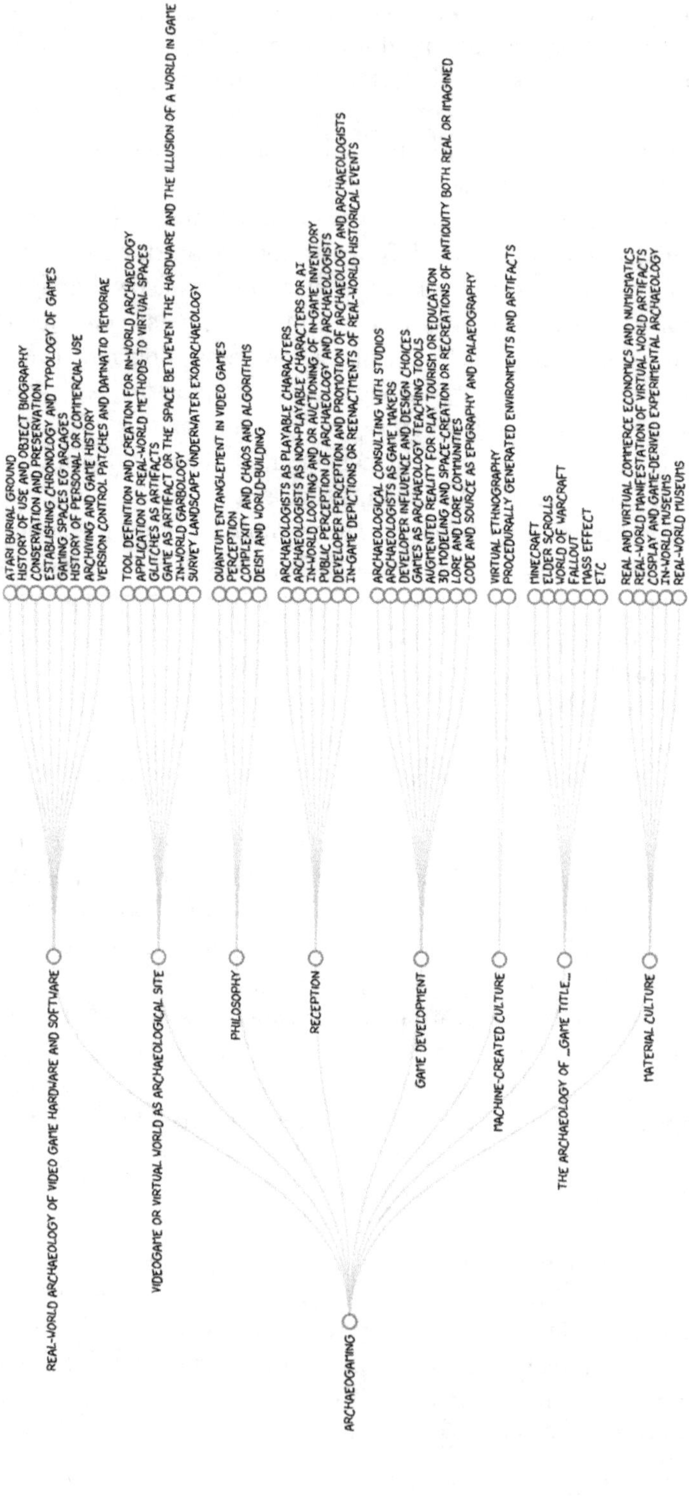

ARCHAEOGAMING

REAL-WORLD ARCHAEOLOGY OF VIDEO GAME HARDWARE AND SOFTWARE
- ATARI BURIAL GROUND
- HISTORY OF USE AND OBJECT BIOGRAPHY
- CONSERVATION AND PRESERVATION
- ESTABLISHING CHRONOLOGY AND TYPOLOGY OF GAMES
- GAMING SPACES EG ARCADES
- HISTORY OF PERSONAL OR COMMERCIAL USE
- ARCHIVING AND GAME HISTORY
- VERSION CONTROL PATCHES AND DAYNATIO MEMORIAE

VIDEOGAME OR VIRTUAL WORLD AS ARCHAEOLOGICAL SITE
- TOOL DEFINITION AND CREATION FOR IN-WORLD ARCHAEOLOGY
- APPLICATION OF REAL-WORLD METHODS TO VIRTUAL SPACES
- GLITCHES AS ARTIFACTS
- GAME AS ARTIFACT OR THE SPACE BETWEEN THE HARDWARE AND THE ILLUSION OF A WORLD IN GAME
- IN-WORLD GARBOLOGY
- SURVEY LANDSCAPE UNDERWATER EXOARCHAEOLOGY

PHILOSOPHY
- QUANTUM ENTANGLEMENT IN VIDEO GAMES
- PERCEPTION
- COMPLEXITY AND CHAOS AND ALGORITHMS
- DESIGN AND WORLD-BUILDING

RECEPTION
- ARCHAEOLOGISTS AS PLAYABLE CHARACTERS
- ARCHAEOLOGISTS AS NON-PLAYABLE CHARACTERS OR AI
- IN-WORLD LOOTING AND OR AUCTIONING OF IN-GAME INVENTORY
- PUBLIC PERCEPTION OF ARCHAEOLOGY AND ARCHAEOLOGISTS
- DEVELOPER PERCEPTION AND PROMOTION OF ARCHAEOLOGY AND ARCHAEOLOGISTS
- IN-GAME DEPICTIONS OR REENACTMENTS OF REAL-WORLD HISTORICAL EVENTS

GAME DEVELOPMENT
- ARCHAEOLOGICAL CONSULTING WITH STUDIOS
- ARCHAEOLOGISTS AS GAME MAKERS
- DEVELOPER INFLUENCE AND DESIGN CHOICES
- GAMES AS ARCHAEOLOGY TEACHING TOOLS
- AUGMENTED REALITY FOR PLAY TOURISM OR EDUCATION
- 3D MODELING AND SPACE-CREATION OR RECREATIONS OF ANTIQUITY BOTH REAL OR IMAGINED
- LORE AND LORE COMMUNITIES
- CODE AND SOURCE AS EPIGRAPHY AND PALAEOGRAPHY

MACHINE-CREATED CULTURE
- VIRTUAL ETHNOGRAPHY
- PROCEDURALLY GENERATED ENVIRONMENTS AND ARTIFACTS

THE ARCHAEOLOGY OF _GAME TITLE_
- MINECRAFT
- ELDER SCROLLS
- WORLD OF WARCRAFT
- FALLOUT
- MASS EFFECT
- ETC

MATERIAL CULTURE
- REAL AND VIRTUAL COMMERCE ECONOMICS AND NUMISMATICS
- REAL-WORLD MANIFESTATION OF VIRTUAL WORLD ARTIFACTS
- COSPLAY AND GAME-DERIVED EXPERIMENTAL ARCHAEOLOGY
- IN-WORLD MUSEUMS
- REAL-WORLD MUSEUMS

Figure 0.1. Archaeogaming map created by the author (text) and Shawn Graham (design).

How Is Archaeogaming Archaeology?

Archaeology is perhaps uniquely qualified as a discipline to document (on a rolling basis) the human experience through its materiality. Although archaeology is historically understood as dealing with the deep past, in recent decades archaeologists such as Bill Caraher, Cassie Newland, and Michael Shanks have plied their trade on the near-immediate. There is a logic to this: in the pre-Industrial past, technological innovation and the understanding of material science occurred at a rate much slower than what is observable today. Upon understanding and exploiting electricity for the purposes of labor, the pace of science, technology, and innovation (not only in things like manufacturing but also in the creative arts) increased exponentially, thereby creating more "stuff" than the world had ever seen before. Archaeologists of the recent past and of Late Capitalism must race to keep up with planned obsolescence, with annual typologies and seriation, on a volume and scale requiring an understanding of Big Data and a globalized, shared market of billions of living people, all of whom continue to make, accumulate, and discard things. Archaeologists of the present (and future) have their work cut out for them.

The past sixty years have seen the creation of an invisible shroud of computer-created data and connectivity, which has largely buried earlier invisible communication networks between people and the environment. New communication technologies and computing power merged with human creativity to make new worlds to inhabit intellectually. What used to be the sole province of printed fiction, which offered a univocal entry point to imagined spaces, we now have fully realized, interactive, digital built environments to help us create our own stories within the context of these new, virtual worlds.[11]

As will be discussed in more detail below, these digital built environments are the new constructions of the late twentieth and early twenty-first centuries. For thousands of years we have occupied houses we have made of mud, brick, wood, stone, and steel, organized together to form temporary settlements and permanent cities. In the space of the past forty years we have created entire hitherto-unseen universes of very real human occupation replete with their own material culture. This digital material culture precipitates a new kind of archaeology, one that seeks to understand human-computer interaction (and human-human and human-nonhuman interactions) in incorporeal spaces (see Mol 2014).

Many of the digital spaces created over the past forty years fall under the category of digital entertainment, namely video games. Of those games that use the Earth as a setting for play, many appropriate cultural iconography/tropes in order to communicate with the player by visual shorthand that they are in ancient Egypt (e.g., *Tomb Raider*), Paris (e.g., *Assassin's Creed: Unity*), the old American West (e.g., *Red Dead Redemption*), or the entire history of the World (e.g., *Civilization VI*) (Mol et al. 2017). These games contain a visual archaeological/heritage component, an interpretation of past places and civilizations by one or more creators who revise the world to impose new rules for the purpose of engaging an audience. It's a kind of cultural appropriation, remixing a physical reality and creating new narratives from it. This is not unlike archaeological storytelling published by archaeologists as they interpret past worlds as they have found them based on the data retrieved and interpreted from the archaeological record.

Over the past few years, a new trend in digital built environments has emerged. Creators of born-digital worlds (mostly video game developers) are abdicating their role of hands-on creation to mathematical algorithms. These algorithms take coded instructions from human makers (for now), and then interpret them to create variations of things on their own. Dubbed "procedural content generation" (PCG or ProcGen), these algorithms populate environments with nearly countless variations of objects, which can include, but are not limited to, structures and artifacts. Current (2018) games now go so far as to use PCG for the spontaneous creation of landscapes as well as soundscapes (e.g., *No Man's Sky*), populating worlds with complex, fully realized cultures that have never been seen before yet have their own readymade history and ways of interacting with players and with each other (e.g., *Ultima Ratio Regum*).

While conducting archaeological investigation into traditional digital games where the designer's hand is always present in every detail, PCG games have the potential to display emergent, culturally significant behavior independent of exact design choices, mimicking how evolution works, or at least how mutations can create interesting artifacts that enable us to comment on them as well as the environment that created those mutations. As archaeologists, how can we document, preserve, and understand these new cultures, and do we need to reconsider our definitions of culture and of material culture?

In a digital built environment, it may be easy for some of us to fall into the trap of doing "dirt archaeology" because we carry our assumptions and real-world experience with us into the spaces in games. Archaeologists who study synthetic worlds must suspend their belief that things in games should work as they do in nature. In games, everything is manufactured, even gravity. The normal rules do not apply.

There is no difference between earth and sky; the horizon line is artificial. It is all pixels and code. When video game archaeologists bring themselves to this understanding, patterns emerge within the structure and execution of the game itself. Culture is a construct. Taking this one step further, what twenty-first-century humans are encountering—especially those who regularly use digital/communication technology—is a blended reality. Digital devices exist in the real world and connect us to others in the real world by way of mediation. The digital artifact is the catalyst for this kind of "out-of-body" travel where people project themselves through devices. It's a new kind of telepresence. In the past, one could operate a joystick on a video game console in order to direct a ball's movement on a screen. Now it is commonplace for a game-space to host numerous live players whose interactions and emotions remain quite real, even if mediated through the digital environment. Archaeologists are beginning to encounter blended reality, which contains not only the physical artifacts of mobile phones and computers but also born-digital artifacts that reside within spaces we cannot see without the aid of hardware, artifacts within artifacts.

The obvious question about archaeogaming is whether or not it really is archaeology as opposed to playing at archaeology. Starting with Colin Renfrew and Paul Bahn's glossary definition, "archaeology involves the study of the human past through its material remains" (Renfrew and Bahn 1991). Archaeogaming fits within that rubric, as games are part of the material culture of the recent past, that which has existed within the past fifty years. Compare that with Foucault (1972: 138–39), who sets out the underpinnings of archaeology: (1) archaeology tries to define discourses that follow certain rules; (2) archaeology defines discourses in their specificity to show the way the set of rules they put into operation is irreducible; (3) archaeology is a rewriting, a regulated transformation of what has already been written, a systematic description of a discourse-object. Archaeologists work on the things that have already been said (materially) and offer their most practical interpretations of these things. What Foucault wrote is as valid in archaeogaming as it is in dirt archaeology. The archaeology of synthetic worlds is much more dependent on detecting, understanding, and operating within the rules created by the makers of these digital built environments, so Foucault might be even more important to archaeology within synthetic worlds.

Thinking about the archaeology of the new generally, and of digital built environments specifically, one recalls Cornelius Holtorf in his 2011 dialogue with fellow archaeologist Angela Piccini (Piccini and Holtorf 2011: 9) about the nature of contemporary archaeology: "There is no reason why archaeologists, studying material remains, should not be studying objects from the recent pasts of the 20th and 21st centuries. Our surroundings are literally made of artifacts, sites and monuments from this period."

For archaeologists (including archaeogamers), archaeology must also attempt to interpret things as they were (reconstructing patterns of cultural descent) while proposing and testing explanations for the forces that have shaped such patterns (Shennan 2012: 23). How did we get here from there? Why do certain shapes of drinking vessels evolve over time to specialize for the liquids they contain? Archaeologists must ask what caused divergences and attempt to reverse engineer the thought processes behind these design decisions. In this respect, archaeogaming is a kind of cognitive archaeology as most fully described by Colin Renfrew (Renfrew 1994). We are attempting to understand the minds behind the creation of the things they built and left behind. This becomes increasingly more difficult when considering machine-created culture.

In New Archaeology, archaeologists emphasize cultural evolution and look for generalities and emphasize systems thinking (Johnson 2010: 23). The turn from the culture historical approach came about in the 1960s with Lewis Binford as its champion; the approach was refined in 1972 by James Deetz, who sought to apply a scientific method to archaeology while also focusing on the cultural process(es) behind the creation of an artifact. All of a sudden the "why" of an artifact finds precedence over the "when." Archaeogaming mixes both the why and the when. Finding each provides valuable contextual information that cannot be disentangled. We can ask the "why" questions to determine reasons behind design decisions, sales, popularity, playability, even complexity, but the "when" allows us to reconstruct a chronology of events that help generate these "why" questions. In archaeogaming there is no "why" without "when." Video game development (and the creation of virtual worlds) is iterative. Archaeogaming breaks with Ian Hodder's postprocessual archaeology (where archaeological interpretations are subjective) by maintaining a positivistic distinction between material and data, but it also takes postprocessualism further by acknowledging at least three actors (the developer, the player, and the player's avatar) as well as three separate contexts that are intertwined (the game media, the player's environment, and the game-space itself). Archaeogaming also accepts the core tenet of behavioral archaeology, which "redefines archaeology as a discipline that studies relationships between people and things in all times and all places. . . . The relationships between people and artifacts are discussed in terms of regularities discerned in processes of manufacture, use, and disposal that make up the life histories of material things, as in flow models and behavioral chains" (Johnson 2010: 65).

Archaeogaming as a subdiscipline of archaeology still has far to go in justifying its existence not only to the academy and to more traditional archaeologist colleagues but also to the general public. As Holtorf (2005: 6) describes, "Archaeology remains significant, not because it manages to import actual past realities into the present but because it allows us to recruit past people and what they left behind for a range of contemporary human interests, needs, and desires." In *Archaeology Is a Brand,* Holtorf posits several theses about contemporary archaeology:

- Archaeology is mainly about our own culture in the present.
- The archaeologist is being remade in every present and is thus a renewable resource.
- The process of doing archaeology is more important than its results.

Archaeogaming fits the above definitions neatly. Archaeology, although largely focused on the past, is really about the present, and archaeologists must keep the current audience in mind when conducting and publishing their work. With archaeogaming, archaeologists are perhaps better positioned to connect with a curious public (many of whom play games) about what archaeologists are and what we do, transferring lessons learned in-game to real-world sites and projects, starting from a common vocabulary of play, ultimately leading to diverse interests in what is happening *outside* of the box.

This connection with the public benefits both the audience and the archaeologist. As Kathryn Fewster writes, "The researcher alone cannot interpret the action of the people in the present with regard to their material culture without listening to the people themselves. . . . It gives the researcher more clues about the significance of modern material culture to wider processes of social life and social change and facilitates an archaeology of practice" (Fewster 2013: 32). Martin Heidegger agrees, stating in 1973 that "humans are situated in and inseparable from the world that is around them and into which they are thrown and dwell." Video games are a very large part of our contemporary culture and as such are deserving of archaeological study. Shawn Graham (2016: 18) reminds us that

> archaeogaming requires treating a game world, a world bounded and defined by the limitations of its hardware, software, and coding choices, as both a closed universe and as an extension of the external

culture that created it. Everything that goes into the immaterial space comes from its external cultural source in one way or another. Because of this, we see the same problems in studying culture in games as in studying culture in the material world.

Strangeness created from the blurred boundaries of the natural and the synthetic mediated by digital technology lends itself to new research questions, and archaeology is pulled further into the future. As in some games where players can create and destroy, such is the case with any kind of archaeology: we create new ways of looking at material culture while destroying old theories that no longer hold when considering these new classes of artifacts. One main difference between "real-world" archaeology and archaeogaming is that in the former the site is methodically destroyed: archaeologists have exactly one chance at recording as much information as possible as excavation proceeds. In video games, however, archaeologists often have access to multiple copies of the same game or can restore their progress from save points in the event of a misstep or missed opportunity.

Archaeology is a combination of the academic and the social. Archaeology is almost guild-like in how it mixes applied knowledge with learned behavior. Michael Shanks championed this definition of archaeology in 1995, stating that "archaeology is largely a set of experiences." Holtorf takes this one step further in the cases of simulated environments (think roadside attractions like Carhenge near Alliance, Nebraska, that mimic original buildings or spaces but in far-flung locations using different materials). Even these facsimiles "can provide us with fabricated, but nonetheless real, experiences of both the 'authentic' past and archaeology. Their realism is not that of a lost, real past but of real sensual impressions and emotions in the present, which engage visitors and engender meaningful feelings" (Holtorf 2005: 135). For both Holtorf and Shanks, the experience of a perceived past is just as important as an academic analysis of "proper" sites and artifacts. As will be seen in chapter 4, designers of historical video games aspire to recreate representations of real-world built environments as they might have been, including these buildings to enhance the player's experience. The design is both practical and emotional, shared among many communities of developers and players responsible for both creating and inhabiting the game-space.[12]

Artifacts, however, are just things. They cannot explain themselves (although they occasionally get help from mentions in primary text, which in the case of video games are instruction manuals, design notes, and code), and require the archaeologist to serve as a kind of temporal interpreter between the past and the present. As Matthew Johnson wrote, "Artefacts actually belong in the present and tell us nothing about the past in themselves . . . the past exists only in the things we say about it" (Johnson 2010: 12). An archaeologist is needed as an interpreter between past and present mediated by artifacts.

Most of archaeology could be described as the history of technology. Claus Pias defines technology as "a relay between technical artifact, aesthetic standards, cultural practices, and knowledge. Technology does something, not is something" (Pias 2011: 180–81). As Olli Sotamaa wrote, "The known history of games is a history of artifacts" (Sotamaa 2014: 3–4). Technology is an artifact-creation tool, itself a creation of people. Wolfgang Ernst said, "[Archaeologists] are dealing with the past as delayed presence, preserved in technological memory. We are not communicating with the dead" (Ernst 2011: 250). Moshenska notes that "the archaeology of digital technologies is a foundational and ever-growing element of the archaeology of the modern world" (Moshenska 2014: 255). Video games, as with other software, are therefore not only artifacts (and sites) but also sources of preservation. When we play the games, the games are as in-the-moment and active as they ever were, ignorant that any time has passed, performing just as they were programmed to perform. Games—at least in 2016—remain unaware of themselves, just dumb output from smart people, like any other artifact, or as Hodder calls them, "things" (Hodder 2012).

Video games are things. They are often created out of a suite of needs that include a desire to be entertained, challenged, and to make money. In Goldberg and Larrson's introduction to *State of Play*, they note that games have traditionally been engaged with and discussed as products of technology rather than products of culture (Goldberg and Larrson 2015: 8). The road to the serious study of video games as well as their scrutiny as forms of entertainment have most often come from outside gaming culture (both those of developers and players) (Goldberg and Larrson 2015: 12). Goldberg and Larrson see contemporary games as transcending their perceived definition of artifacts of technology into something more (Goldberg and Larrson 2015: 13). This assessment supports archaeogaming's premise that games cannot be disentangled from the context and culture in which they were made, and that games as both sites and artifacts contain far more than whatever manifests onscreen. "Like films and books, video games are cultural texts. They say something about the society in which they were made" (Knoblauch 2015: 187).

State of Play becomes a transitional text in understanding video games outside of positivism. "A video game is a creative application of computer technology" (Golding 2015: 130). "Games are a pursuit of order" (Ellison and Keogh 2015: 144). Cara Ellison and Brendan Keogh later summarize the career of one of gaming's greatest auteurs, John Romero (cofounder of id Software, maker of the classics *Wolfenstein 3D, Doom,* and *Quake*) who famously stated his Tidiness Theory, saying that all games are about cleaning up. As players, we collect, we construct, we destroy all enemies, we complete quests, we reach the level cap, we unlock all points on the map. Gaming then is parallel to archaeology, which is also about tidying, about looking at messy information and making something out of it, bringing order to chaos.

Archaeogaming, Media Studies, and Media Archaeology

Archaeogaming, in its interdisciplinary approach to the archaeology of the recent past, incorporates the object-oriented aspects of media studies, especially when it comes to AAA (i.e., blockbuster) games, mass media purchased by (for some games such as *Tomb Raider*) millions of players. What studios made the games, and how many units were produced, sold, returned? Who played the games and why, and what happened to the games after they were consumed, when the endgame was reached, when the novelty wore off, or when frustration set in? These questions differ little from those that deal with ancient manufacturing and can compare with the study of Roman *sigillata* (fancy pottery) production throughout the empire, which includes branding and large-scale distribution. A lot of archaeogaming is "new wine in old bottles," although, as later chapters will demonstrate, there is more to be said, especially when it comes to archaeology done within the games themselves.

Archaeogaming differs from media studies—and more specifically media archaeology[13]—in two major areas: in its focus on artifacts and on the built environment. Archaeogaming concentrates on individual artifacts, as well as the content held within video games, their creation and use, how that content changes over time, and the mechanisms that drive that change. Jacques Perriault in 1981 was the first person to coin the term "media archaeology" when dealing specifically with media artifacts (anything from typewriters to reel-to-reel tapes), exploring "use function" and "social representation" while comparing past and contemporary use of that media (Huhtamo and Parrika 2011: 3).

The two biggest voices of media archaeology, Erkki Huhtamo and Jussi Parikka agree with him: "Media archaeology should not be confused with archaeology as a discipline. Media archaeology rummages textual, visual, and auditory archives as well as collections of artifacts, emphasizing both the discursive and the material manifestations of culture" (Huhtamo and Parrika 2011: 3).

Archaeogaming also considers video games to be "built environments." To traditional archaeology, a built environment is something created by people that has the elements of both space and culture in which people regularly live, work, and play. This definition lends itself not only to physical structures but also to synthetic worlds, which do, by any definition, incorporate space and culture for both work and recreation for many people to engage with for hours every day.

Ernst adds an interesting wrinkle, however, stating that "media archaeology discovers a kind of stratum—or matrix—in cultural sedimentation that is neither purely human or purely technological, but literally in between" (Ernst 2011: 251). It is this in-between, crossover space that concerns the archaeogamer, the crossover from natural to synthetic and back again, with the artifact of the game enabling this movement. For the purposes of archaeology, people cannot be separated from their things. The story of humanity is the story of adaptive technology.[14] Following Ernst's analogy, if humanity is the matrix (soil), then examples of our technology are the inclusions (pebbles, artifacts, etc.) in it.[15]

Archaeogaming and Game Studies

Archaeogaming could be considered a part of video game studies just as it is a part of archaeology. Game studies examines games, who plays them, how they are played, and how they are made, in addition to gaming culture (typically evolving from specific game platforms, game series, and individual games). The main difference between archaeogaming and media studies is the attention paid to the material culture of video games themselves, the use of hardware and software, and the material culture of virtual spaces created when the software is run. While game players and gaming culture certainly inform archaeogaming to some extent, they are not the end goal for archaeological research but rather a means to an end, especially when describing an object's biography, its history of use. Understanding how a culture comes to create a video game (and why), or how a community chooses to spend discretionary time and income on some games and not others, is important to put a game into a sociocultural context but ignores the artifact of the game itself, and of the creation of the virtual world and culture(s) held within as created by code.

The International Communication Association's Game Studies division defines game studies this way.[16]

> The study of games offers the opportunity to investigate human communication involving multidisciplinary approaches. The scope is not bound to studies of games but includes simulations and virtual environments (VEs) in general. Disciplines of communication and media studies merge with cultural studies, social sciences, computer sciences, design, cognitive sciences, engineering, education, health studies, and information technology studies.
>
> - the social and psychological uses and effects of video games, simulations, and VEs in general
> - the cultural affordances, uses, and meanings of games, simulations, and VEs
> - games, simulations, and VEs as training or instructional media
> - comparative media analyses involving games, simulations, or other VEs
> - human-computer interaction in games, simulations, and VEs
> - design research in the context of games, simulations, and VEs
> - users' motivations and emotional, cognitive, and psychophysiological experiences in games, simulations, and VEs

Three of the above points qualify as archaeogaming, namely using games as trainers for archaeologists, human-computer interaction in games, and design research. Archaeogaming concerns itself with how gaming technology is received by people, as well as the genesis of those games, their cultural and historical impact, how they portray actual history, and their eventual disposition.

Archaeologists as Game-Makers

Archaeologists can interpret video games as both sites and artifacts. They can explore how the archaeological profession is understood and adopted by game-makers and players for the purposes of entertainment and narrative. But archaeologists can also be proactive in creating their own narratives and in having a seat at the game-development table, either by invitation to established studios or by forging ahead to create their own games from the ground up. There is a space in between where archaeologists can contribute to game creation, not just as ethical or professional advisers but also as active participants in lore communities and in the creation of virtual reconstructions of actual monuments and sites, and by bringing archaeological voices to augmented reality, participating in the storytelling while encouraging both developer and player engagement with the subject matter and the environment.

The creative, professional output for archaeologists often rests with the published synthesis of excavated material done in the form of a preliminary report, peer-reviewed journal article, and/or monograph. The creativity not only comes in the form of writing but is perhaps more present in the critical thinking that makes connections between bits of data and observations in an attempt to draw a conclusion about the history of a site, the manufacture and purpose of an artifact. These conclusions are often preliminary, or are almost always presented with some doubt. Archaeologists know that there is likely additional evidence unknown at the time of publication that might change a theory, or that future thinking might reinterpret existing data.

During the excavation season, and later when considering the recovered archaeological material, the archaeologist will play with ideas and consult with others on issues of interpretation. Until recently, game-making was left to developers and coders, professionals and hobbyists. But now some archaeologists are making games. One purpose of building a game or a reconstruction in a virtual world is to explore a question in an archaeologist's research (see Morgan 2009). Morgan reflects on her Çatalhöyük reconstruction project, stating that it "made me truly engage with some of the questions that as an excavator I had pondered only in passing while filling out my data sheets" (Morgan 2009: 471). Other archaeologists make games in an attempt to control an archaeological narrative told from the archaeologist's perspective.[17] This includes games on how to excavate and how to ethically deal with artifacts. This also includes games on what it means to be an archaeologist. The act of creation often helps clarify thinking about one or more questions, including a narrative aspect or the reflexive exploration of a mechanic in a serious game. Ian Bogost calls this exercise "carpentry" (Bogost 2012: 92).

Andrew Gardner agrees with the prospect, writing that "the possibility . . . of archaeologists being involved in design, such as a (historical) game, where the player could at least for a while live as a farmer in central Italy (rather than Tatooine) is enticing" (Gardner 2007: 272). Games can allow archaeologists to reconstruct/reimagine the past. Because games by their nature are intended to be engaged with by a wider audience (as opposed to a journal article, which might be read by a handful of people), Gardner also believes that "archaeologists might yet find a valuable tool to aid them in the task of creating challenging pasts for wide audiences" (Gardner 2007: 272). Ethan Watrall seconds the idea in one of the first (if not *the* first) articles on video game archaeology, "Interactive Entertainment as Public Archaeology," in the March 2002 issue of the *SAA Archaeological Record* (Watrall 2002: 579.) However great the desire and potential public audience, there remains the significant issue of translating ideas and art into code. Brittain and Clack agree. "The expertise needed to design and function digital technology, and dominant programming systems required for their function is addition to their cost, could prove to marginalise rather than empower multiple communities around the globe" (Brittain and Clack 2007: 65). Archaeologists need a high level of digital literacy not only to realize the games they want to make but to even ask basic questions or understand the basic steps in actually planning the development of a game, however small.

There is a handful of archaeologists who have created games all the way to completion and distribution, but that number will grow thanks to the phenomena of "game jams," coding marathons that facilitate the rapid creation of games, which are rewarded not only for design but also for story and characterization. Since 2014, the University of York's Department of Archaeology has hosted an annual Heritage Jam featuring the work of international archaeologists interested in using digital visualization (including games) as entertainment and communication tools for exploring archaeology (see Figure 0.2).[18] The 2014 event featured seventeen entries ranging from mapping projects to augmented reality to 3D model-ing. Winning projects included augmented reality,[19] interactive fiction,[20] role-playing,[21] and exploration within a museum setting.[22]

Figure 0.2. Image from the ergodic literature game *Buried* (Tara Copplestone and Luke Botham), a winner of the 2014 Heritage Jam. Used with permission.

The process of creation has allowed each of the participants to grow as designers in order to more broadly communicate what they are working on, but in a way that is arguably more accessible than standard print publication. Archaeology is about engagement and interaction, and all of these visualization projects meet those criteria.

The only commercial game studio created and managed by an archaeologist (who also designs the games) is Dig-It! Games, headquartered in Bethesda, Maryland (also home to game giant Bethesda Softworks, makers of the *Elder Scrolls* and *Fallout* series of games, among others), founded by Suzi Wilczynski. Taking a game-based learning approach to pedagogy, Wilczynski designed *Roman Town,* an archaeological excavation simulator for children to help teach them about the art, history, and archaeology of a town destroyed in the eruption of Mt. Vesuvius in CE 79, while integrating puzzles to help teach critical thinking. Later games incorporate ancient and archaeological themes as a backdrop for learning math, science, and language arts. Wilczynski, an archaeologist with nearly ten years' experience in the field in Greece and Israel, is also a social studies teacher who taught herself how to write games as a way to help her students learn and engage with the material.[23] Now into its twelfth year, Dig-It! Games continues to thrive. Most of the games do not have archaeology as their core mechanic, however, which makes one wonder if there ever will be titles, either indie or AAA, that will be strictly archaeological or will apply an accurate archaeology mechanic within the gameplay of something designed as entertainment.

Games have a long tradition of being used for education, or have been specifically developed for the purpose of education. When considering games as archaeological teaching tools, it is a bit like teaching how to make a film by watching movies. We can critique the good and bad, what works and what does not, what is realistic and what is fantastic. Is it enough to play through a *Tomb Raider* title and talk about the lack of real archaeology that actually happens in the game or about the ethical disposition of the artifacts that Lara Croft collects? Are there games on the market or in the wild (or already in the archive) that can actually instruct players on practical archaeology in the field and in the lab? If not, archaeologists need to reach out to game studios to lobby for the inclusion of various archaeological mechanics without sacrificing the intended entertainment value of any game.

Chapter Summaries

This book is organized into four chapters following this introduction that explore the major branches of archaeogaming, followed by a conclusion offering a glimpse into the future of archaeology both in and of video games. Each chapter features one or more in-depth examples of conducting archaeological investigation within contemporary video games and concludes with a brief bibliography for further reading.

Chapter 1 covers the real-world archaeology of video game hardware and software, including a summary of the 2014 excavation of the Atari Burial Ground in Alamogordo, New Mexico. Video games are artifacts, which have a history of use, an object biography. As with more traditional artifacts, video game conservation/preservation/archiving must also be considered, heading toward the creation of formal video game chronologies and typologies. Gaming spaces (e.g., arcades, game development studios, and retrogaming stores) are also discussed as contemporary ritual and secular sites, as well as abandoned places.

The gaming public and video game developers appear to have set ideas on how to portray archaeology and archaeologists (gender, clothing, and accoutrements). Chapter 2 focuses on archaeologists as both playable and non-player characters (NPCs). Game mechanics such as excavation and looting lend themselves to a discussion of in- and extra-game ethics.

Definitions of archaeological sites, landscapes, and built environments are applied to video games in chapter 3. Game-generated glitches are the new artifacts. Tools for conducting archaeology in-game are defined, applying real-world methods to synthetic spaces. Also introduced: augmented reality, in-world garbology, and survey, underwater, and exo-/xenoarchaeology, all conducted within a game, including a proof-of-concept archaeological investigation of an open-world video game, the *No Man's Sky* Archaeological Survey.

Chapter 4 examines the crossover of natural and synthetic worlds, real-world manifestations of game-world artifacts, video game cosplay, and game-derived experimental archaeology. Players interpret video game recipes to make real-world food and design and sell game-derived clothing, armor, and weapons, creating a parallel archaeological record. Museums mark the final crossover between video games and the real world, including the Vigamus museum in Rome and virtual museums within games such as *Skyrim*.

This book concludes by pondering the future of video game archaeology. Archaeogaming is wide open, with virtual ethnography as one of the main avenues of research. Archaeogaming makes an early effort to prepare future archaeologists for purpose-built, digital-only environments and how to study them. A handful of international scholars are making headway in describing what it means to study video games archaeologically as the discipline continues to grow and change.

The ethics guidelines for the *No Man's Sky* Archaeological Survey, written by Catherine Flick (De Montfort University) with contributions from L. Meghan Dennis (University of York) and myself, occupies the appendix and is reproduced here by permission. These guidelines can (and should) be adapted by other archaeologists as they research video games, the cultures within them, and the people who play them.

A short glossary of archaeological and video game terms used in this book and a "ludography" of games cited in the text round out the volume.

What This Book Is Not

This book is intended to be an introduction to the field of archaeogaming, and as such it does not dive as deeply as an academic monograph might. Instead, it introduces the major themes that comprise the archaeology in (and of) video games that merit future discussion and research at a very fine grain. I have chosen to focus exclusively on digital games, leaving out tabletop (board/dice/pen-and-paper) games as well as non-game virtual platforms/communities such as *Second Life,* and the now-defunct *Multiverse, Habbo Hotel,* and others for which there is already a massive amount of published scholarship. Also, each chapter and section contains some examples taken from video games both old and contemporary to illustrate various points often with humorous or unanticipated results. This book is not encyclopedic in its cataloguing of games, and while I did my best to use the games that I felt were most relevant to the topics at hand, there are many, many other examples that could have been used (including a wealth of indie games). It is my hope that the readers of this book will take the theories and methods described in each chapter and apply them to digital games big and small wherever possible, creating a corpus of knowledge that will be shared with everyone. All digital games are archaeological sites. Archaeogaming allows archaeologists to work in the open on these sites, engaging with the public as they do.

Notes

1. I primarily use the term "video games" throughout this book because of its dominance in the vernacular when discussing interactive entertainment accessed by screens. Scholars of game and media studies prefer "digital games," which casts a wider net to include interactive entertainments that do not necessarily have a visual component and get away from the immedi-

ate connection between "video games" and nostalgia when using the term. "Egames" has also found favor in scholarship and is on public view at the Strong National Museum of Play in Rochester, New York, the second floor galleries of which are largely dedicated to egame history.

2. Society for American Archaeology, "What Is Archaeology?," http://www .saa.org/ForthePublic/Resources/EducationalResources/ForEducators/ ArchaeologyforEducators/WhatisArchaeology/tabid/1346/Default.aspx (retrieved December 6, 2016).

3. Adam Chapman lists one of the functions of games as being "heritage sites by functioning as a form of 'living history'" (Chapman 2016: 176).

4. Colleen Morgan hinted at this potential (especially within the context of MUDs [multi-user dungeons], MOOs [MUDs, object-oriented], and MMOs [massively multiplayer online games]) in 2009, stating that "most of these gaming formats remain largely unexplored within academic archaeology" (Morgan 2009: 471). Ethan Watrall published the first article on video games and archaeology in 2002, "Interactive Entertainment as Public Archaeology" (Watrall 2002), laying the foundation for what would eventually become archaeogaming.

5. For an extensive treatment on how video games treat actual historical events, see Adam Chapman, *Digital Games as History: How Videogames Represent the Past and Offer Access to Historical Practice* (2016).

6. See Tara Copplestone, "Designing and Developing a Playful Past in Video Games" (2016). The focus of Copplestone's research is in archaeologists creating video games in order to work through archaeological problems.

7. In this book, "in-world" and "in-game" are synonymous meaning that a person is actively engaged in gameplay, immersed in a game's environment.

8. I use "player" instead of "gamer" following on Therrien's distinction: "Gamer: plays to complete objectives and win. Player: Defines own objective, with no clear valorization of outcomes" (Therrien 2012: 23). Ever since Gamergate began in 2014, "gamer" has taken on political and emotional baggage (see https://en.wikipedia.org/wiki/Gamergate_controversy). "Player" is more neutral while still defining a person who interacts with games.

9. "Meatspace" was introduced to the vernacular by William Gibson in his 1984 novel *Neuromancer* (p. 6 in the Ace paperback edition) and was later adopted by Usenet groups and other denizens of the young internet to differentiate between the real and the virtual (aka cyberspace). I use "metaspace" in this text as a pun/anagram of "meatspace" to designate the virtual world. Nardi in her 2015 article "Virtuality" notes that "'real world' is a folk term in gamer (and other) discourse, and its consistent use in an established lexicon recommends it in the absence of a better academic term" (Nardi 2015). I will also use the differentiation of "natural" and "synthetic" worlds as proposed by video game economist Edward Castronova (Castronova 2005).

10. The actual archaeology of digital media finds precedent in Gabriel Moshenska's excavation, conservation, and examination of a USB stick (Mo-

shenska 2014). See also Perry and Morgan's systematic archaeological excavation and mapping of a recovered hard drive (Perry and Morgan 2015).

11. Archaeologists continue to update tools and methods to conduct archaeological investigations into these digital spaces. See Huggett 2017 and Edgeworth 2014.
12. See King and Borland 2004 for a thorough treatment of these gaming communities.
13. For good introductions to what media archaeology is, see Brittain and Clack 2007; Huhtamo and Parikka 2011; Parikka 2012.
14. Summarizing William Sewell (1997): the design of tools shapes their use, and the use of them leads to new changes to them.
15. The play on the word "matrix" is intentional. The cultural resonance of the eponymous film trilogy blends the technical real/virtual dualism with the archaeological use of the same term, which is shorthand to describe the type of earth being dug within a particular unit.
16. https://www.icahdq.org/group/gamestds (retrieved February 15, 2018).
17. See Tara Copplestone's *Buried* for an example: http://www.taracopplesto ne.co.uk/buriedindex.html (retrieved December 10, 2016).
18. http://www.heritagejam.org (retrieved December 10, 2016).
19. http://www.heritagejam.org/jam-day-entries/2014/7/12/voices-recognit ion-stuart-eve-kerrie-hoffman-colleen-morgan-alexis-pantos-and-sam-kinc hin-smith (retrieved December 10, 2016).
20. http://www.heritagejam.org/exhibition/2014/7/11/buried-an-ergodic-lit erature-game-tara-copplestone-and-luke-botham (retrieved December 10, 2016).
21. http://www.heritagejam.org/2015onthedayentries/2015/10/4/happy-gods-edwige-sam-matthew-juan (retrieved December 10, 2016).
22. http://www.heritagejam.org/2015exhibitionentries/2015/9/25/cryptopor ticus-anthony-masinton (retrieved on December 10, 2016).
23. Read an interview with Dig-It! Games' founder here: http://dig-itgames .com/digital-learning-day-qa-with-suzi-founder-of-dig-it-games-from-fa blevision-studios/ (retrieved December 10, 2016).

Further Reading

Averett, E. W., J. M. Gordon, and D. B. Counts. 2016. *Mobilizing the Past for a Digital Future: The Potential of Digital Archaeology.* Grand Forks: The Digital Press at the University of North Dakota.

Aycock, J. 2016. *Retrogame Archaeology: Exploring Old Video Games.* New York: Springer.

Boellstorff, T. 2016. "For Whom the Onotology Turns: Theorizing the Digital Real." *Current Anthropology* 57(4): 387–407.

Boellstorff, T., B. Nardi, C. Pearce, and T. L. Taylor. 2012. *Ethnography and Virtual Worlds: A Handbook of Method.* Princeton, NJ: Princeton University Press.

Copplestone, T. 2017. "Designing and Developing a Playful Past in Video Games." *The Interactive Past: Archaeology, Heritage, and Video Games,* edited by A. Mol et al., 85–97. Leiden: Sidestone Press.

Edgeworth, M. 2014. "From Spade-Work to Screen-Work: New Forms of Archaeological Discovery in Digital Space." In *Visualization in the Age of Computerization,* edited by A. Carusi et al., 40–58. New York: Routledge.

Graves-Brown, P., R. Harrison, and A. Piccini, eds. 2013. *The Oxford Handbook of the Archaeology of the Contemporary World.* Oxford: Oxford University Press.

Huhtamo, E. 2016. "The Four Practices? Challenges for an Archaeology of the Screen." In *Screens: From Materiality to Spectatorship—A Historical and Theoretical Reassessment,* edited by D. Chateau and J. Moure, 116–24. Amsterdam: Amsterdam University Press.

Huhtamo, E., and J. Parikka, eds. 2011. *Media Archaeology: Approaches, Applications, and Implications.* Los Angeles: University of California Press.

Ingold, T. 2013. *Making: Anthropology, Archaeology, Art, and Architecture.* New York: Routledge.

Lucas, G. 2013. "Afterword: Archaeology and the Science of New Objects," In *Archaeology after Interpretation: Returning Materials to Archaeological Theory,* edited by B. Alberti, A. M. Jones, and J. Pollard, 369–80. Walnut Creek, CA: Left Coast Press.

Mäyrä, F. 2008. *An Introduction to Games Studies: Games in Culture.* Los Angeles: SAGE Publications.

Mol, A. et al. 2017. *The Interactive Past: Archaeology, Heritage, and Video Games.* Leiden: Sidestone Press.

Parikka, J. 2012. *What Is Media Archaeology?* Cambridge: Polity.

Wolf, M. J. P., and B. Perron, eds. *The Routledge Companion to Video Game Studies.* New York: Routledge.

Chapter 1

Real-World Archaeogaming

Exhuming Atari

Archaeology shows us things we are not normally supposed to see.
—Laurent Olivier, *The Dark Abyss of Time*

Alamogordo, New Mexico, with a population of just over thirty thousand, is famous because of what it is near: White Sands National Monument, the Trinity atomic bomb testing site, and Roswell. It is also home to the New Mexico Museum of Space History with its marker honoring Ham the space chimp, whose toe is buried there. Alamogordo, an otherwise typical New Mexico town, is in the epicenter of weirdness, contributing to the aura by the grace of a video game legend that should not have been a legend at all.

In April 2014, a documentary film crew helmed by Zak Penn, director of *Incident at Loch Ness* and screenwriter for *Ready Player One*, joined forces with an amateur historian, a group of city workers, and a team of archaeologists to excavate the so-called "Atari Burial Ground" in front of an audience of hundreds of nostalgic gamers, video game media journalists, and industry professionals.[1] The urban legend stated that in 1983, Atari, Inc. trucked millions of copies of *E.T.: The Extraterrestrial*, the "worst game ever made," to the Alamogordo city landfill, dumping them, crushing them by driving over the cartridges, and then covering them with a slab of concrete followed by backfill, making it impossible for the games to be recovered. Penn's team, Lightbox, the entertainment division for Microsoft's Xbox, secured exclusive rights to dig, finding a partner in Joe Lewandowski, a waste management expert for the city who was present at the initial dumping and who later spent years trying to pinpoint the location of the cell (landfill pit) in which the games were buried. The archaeologists (including myself) were invited almost as an afterthought, but we became instrumental in helping to plan and execute the dig.

This would be the first-ever video-game-only archaeological excavation in history (see Figure 1.1). On the surface, the main reason given for the dig was either to prove or disprove the urban legend of the burial. Did Atari really bury the games? Was it just *E.T.*? How many games were buried? Would the games still be playable? The archaeologists had deeper questions (pun intended) that went beyond the myth into understanding mass-produced entertainment, e-waste, and the current culture driven by nostalgia for what was unequivocally discarded as trash.

It should not have been a legend at all. Both the *New York Times*[2] and the *Alamogordo Daily News*[3] ran stories when the dump happened, but this was pre-internet, and the articles were largely lost to time. The story eventually circulated through Usenet groups and chatrooms with the articles resurfacing online as scans to be debated as real or fake, and if real, how to locate the exact spot to dig, knowing full well that the games were possibly thirty feet down and perhaps under a layer of cement of unknown thickness.

The Atari excavation marked a convergence of nearly every pop culture trope associated with how the general public perceives archaeology: a legend (possibly apocryphal), a ragtag team in the desert, a local informant who knows where to dig, treasure (the games), and a curse: over the course of two days of digging, two of the six archaeolo-

Figure 1.1. Excavation photo from the Atari Burial Ground, Alamogordo, New Mexico. Photo by the author.

gists were hospitalized, and the dig was effectively shut down by a late afternoon sandstorm, the worst the town's residents had seen that year. Spielberg could not have scripted it better.

The games were found, with over thirteen hundred recovered (out of approximately eight hundred thousand total games dumped, or roughly 0.002 percent). *E.T.* only accounted for roughly 10 percent of the recovered cartridges, with over forty other separate titles catalogued. The myth of the concrete cap was dispelled, but the team did find evidence of cement slurry attached to some of the games. The team was also able to answer a number of other questions: What happens to video game cartridges (and other consumer electronics) when buried in a desert landfill for thirty years? Answer: not much. Many of the cartridges were unbroken and looked playable (but none were). What can the assemblage of games tell us about corporate culture, the video game crash of 1983, of postconsumer waste and how people treated their entertainment commodities? Answer: new inventory always takes precedent over old, and dumping was, for Atari at the time, the cheapest way to make space in their warehouse.

Olivier notes that archaeological time does not stop when sites are abandoned. Time continues to work away at the component matter, which is then assimilated into another environment where, imperceptibly, it holds the memory of other eras (Olivier 2015: 58). This is as true with ancient sites as it is with modern ones. For the myth underlying the dig (or any dig for that matter), it is almost as if archaeological excavation is a Schrödinger's Cat problem: there could be anything down there. Archaeologists might have a pretty good idea about what to expect through research, guidance from primary sources, speaking to local residents, conducting archaeological surveys, and remote sensing. As Olivier writes, "Everything in the earth is floating in uncertainty, in a realm of maybe. Every dig is a necessarily false proposition, for the act of extraction is the act of amputation, of simplistic elimination" (Olivier 2015: 181). To dig is to discover, both to confirm and deny, creating data from the very destruction of the source. And still, exploring the myth was a heroic act (in the Classical sense), delving into the Underworld, a descent, searching for perceived "hidden treasures" (Holtorf 2005: 16–38).

Apart from the fantasy of archaeology that was filmed for the documentary *Atari: Game Over,* the Atari archaeologists were in reality dealing with garbage. The Atari assemblage, buried in a landfill, marked the cartridges' entrance into suspended animation as they waited to be recovered. Garbologist Josh Reno calls this a "reactivation" of the items, regaining meaning (albeit different from the original intent of an artifact's makers) through excavation (Reno 2013: 267). Because burial happens in a landfill, whatever is dumped becomes collectively labeled "trash." Each dumping is an assemblage of artifacts from one place at one point in time. As such, Reno notes that a landfill becomes an ideal archaeological setting, representing almost an entire cultural formation process (how a site is created by human action) with the trash being a behavioral outcome (Reno 2013: 263–64). There is almost order in the dumping, and in Atari's case there was, with a specific cell dug solely for the warehouse goods brought by the truckload over a few days. Everything was dumped from one place into a single pit then covered with cement slurry, a layer of earth, and then gradually with other non-Atari household waste.

Traditional landfills can tell the social and environmental story of a municipality and its people, but with the Atari dump the landfill now tells a crucial part of corporate history (Atari's) as well as adding content to the history of the so-called video game crash of 1983. It confirmed and also disproved parts of the Atari dumping myth. Holtorf recalls Rathje's Garbage Project, which convincingly showed how material evidence can correct other kinds of evidence such as interview surveys (Piccini and Holtorf 2011: 11). Memory is imperfect, and as the Garbage Project proved, people will say what is socially acceptable when talking about what they throw away. Gaining access to the landfill was crucial for the Atari story for this reason. Atari had at first denied the dumping outright; it then later stated that it had only dumped defective merchandise. But by digging through their garbage, we proved that this was not the case at all. There were hundreds of unsold, unopened games. If we had not been given access to the site, these facts would literally have remained buried, possibly forever. Reno states that garbage reveals the "hidden self" ownership of waste and that control of access to waste sites can be highly contested (Reno 2013: 266–67).

In this instance the archaeologists became garbologists, who, as Reno says, "offer unique contributions to a future-oriented archaeology as well as opportunities to reflect on the role of archaeological practice in shaping and living in that world" (Reno 2013: 271). The archaeologists also gained experience with how to interface with a genuinely interested public, balancing archaeology with nostalgia while explaining digging methods, what was found, what was happening. The Atari dig marked a turning point in public archaeology, not just with digging in front of a live audience and on camera (both of which are rare, if not unique occurrences for any field archaeologist) but also in performing a kind of archaeological theater on the world stage via social media where the story of the games' recovery trended globally and literally affected the market, specifically eBay, with prices of the 1980s games going up by a factor of ten (and these were not even the games that were recovered during the salvage).

The 2014 Atari excavation was the first dig that solely featured video games, and as such it drew attention to what archaeology could mean when digging artifacts from the recent past in front of a global, public, connected audience. As Piccini and Holtorf spoke about in 2011, "Contemporary archaeologies marry archaeology in the modern world with the archaeology of the modern world" (Piccini and Holtorf 2011: 14). With Atari's 1983 burial happening in the lifetimes of many of the people who came to watch the dig, as well as those who obsessed over its mythology online since the 1990s, we should have predicted the interest in what we were doing at the landfill. "The empathy of events still moist in recent memory should attract a high level of public interest. . . . It awakens conflicts between professional and amateur as to who should be excavating this past" (Brittain and Clack 2007: 39). This conflict was avoided early on by asking the production company how they would handle the archaeology. They didn't know, and they decided to invite us into the narrative they were creating. What would have otherwise been a treasure hunt instead became a way for archaeologists, the media, and the public to work together on a pop culture project.

Part of our involvement was to help control the narrative—or at least introduce an archaeological one—into the story. Archaeologists, as Andrew Gardner writes in "The Past as Playground," are rightly concerned that "responsible" interpretations win out in the battle for public attention and that seriously distorted visions of whatever historical realities on which we ourselves can agree do not contribute to social problems in the present (Gardner 2007: 256). This kind of work has been defined as "recreation archaeology," something that "customizes archaeology to the public and maximizes public appeal" (Moore 2006).

Imbued by mythology and validated by "real" archaeologists trench-side, copies of *E.T.* that sell at retrogaming shops and online for less than ten dollars, boxed with a catalogue and a coupon for Atari's *Raiders of the Lost Ark* game featuring Indiana Jones, would ultimately fetch over $1,000 at auction on eBay and are now being resold by previous buyers for up to $3,000.[4] The games, artifacts by virtue of being non-natural creations of some cultural importance, became highly valued, almost ritual objects defining a generation of players, placing 1980s pop culture front and center. The excavated games became instant collectibles, extraordinarily rare, and valued for their rarity as part of the handful of games that managed to be extracted before the sandstorm closed the excavation. The irony is that there are at least eight hundred thousand other games buried in that location, which will likely remain underground forever because of expense, local and state politics, environmental restrictions and concerns, and other logistical issues.[5] The sheer size of the assemblage makes it nearly impossible to revisit to excavate completely. Moshenska observed in 2014 that archaeologists of the recent past will be confronted by the problem of scale. "Hardware, software, and content are produced and consumed in mind-bogglingly huge quantities around the world. . . . The detritus of this accelerating process litter the material and digital worlds, and present archaeologists of the modern world with a set of distinct and unusual challenges" (Moshenska 2014: 255). The dig was a once-in-a-generation happening. "The greatest problem facing archaeologists of the digital era will be the incalculable, inhuman enormity of the available material" (Moshenska 2014: 256).

Artifacts have biographies. In the case of an *E.T.* cartridge, we see its creation through the imprimatur of Steven Spielberg in 1982, followed by a deal with Atari, the coding of the game by Howard Scott Warshaw, Atari's Christmas marketing blitz, the resulting sales and then returns of stock, the burial, the excavation thirty-one years later, the dispersal of the assemblage to museums and private individuals worldwide, and even now the resale of some of those same excavated games on auction sites as the original buyers try to flip them for profit. The games are artifacts-as-commodities, but at first they were entertainment and then became trash.

The Atari dig merged history and nostalgia, the reality of a commercial decision, and the shared fantasy of what it was like to play Atari games over thirty years ago. Guins says that game historians "lessen the primacy of nostalgia . . . , resisting the urge to regard this past as hermetically sealed. . . . This allows us to examine the enduring material life-cycles of games that greatly exceed the retro-fascination with ageless games from a historic, idyllic, and more often than not, solipsistic and trivialised past" (Guins 2014: 3). S. C. Murphy recalls that "reading the Atari catalogue was an exercise in consumer anticipation and technological promise" (Murphy 2012: 105). The mystery that helped drive the interest in the excavation was, "How could a beloved company such as Atari ultimately fail?" The answers, as articulated by Atari staff interviewed in the documentary, included sacrificing quality for quantity, glutting the market with badly executed games, and overproducing for consumers and a market that no longer needed or wanted another home console. Atari CEO Ray Kassas destroyed Atari's reputation for quality games, with *Pac-Man* and *E.T.* damaging relationships with retailers (Stanton 2015: 88–90). Ultimately the crash ended in 1985 with the North American release of the Nintendo Entertainment System (NES) (Wolf 2012a: 2). With Nintendo, however, came quality, fun games; Nintendo also controlled the quality itself instead of farming out creative projects to third-party developers. Nintendo, and later Sony, which launched the PlayStation in 1994, also understood their market and how to reach the consumers (Stanton 2015: 185). By 1994, Sony was marketing to players who had nostalgia for the old games but a thirst for new ones, and Atari was reduced to its logo alone.

The dig itself became a symbol. The burial made the *E.T.* game cartridge an iconic gaming artifact and an icon of the North American video game industry crash of the time (Sotamaa 2014: 4). "The idea was always that the landfill contained just *E.T.* cartridges. Now we can see it was, in reality, Atari's grave, too" (Stanton 2015: 93).

The excavation of the Atari Burial Ground stood nascent archaeogaming on its ear, turning the original premise of conducting archaeology within synthetic spaces into an actual real-world dig where physical games were the artifacts. The window in which other, future similar excavations might occur is small, with the physical media of video games quietly phasing out in the 2010s in favor of online play, digital subscriptions, and downloadable content. It is likely that in the next ten years there will be nothing physical with which to interact, the game artifact becoming fully virtual. How archeologists can discover and interpret that material is the subject of later chapters in this book.

The Artifacts of Digital Fiction

All video games are archaeological artifacts. The *traditional* definition holds that artifacts are things of cultural/historical significance made by people. For most non-archaeologists, when they think about artifacts, antiquity is implied: artifacts must be old, lost to history until they are recovered through excavation. Physicality is implied: artifacts create material culture as things that can be manipulated in the natural world. Importance and value are also implied: artifacts are shiny, rare, precious, possess some hidden truth about cultures past, and are worth a lot of money.

A more contemporary approach to artifacts sees them as independent of age, of no particular time, part of a past that persists in the present, mundane in their creation and use, physical or virtual, or special not only in their manufacture (either by people or machines) but also in their relationship to a greater context of personal ownership and interaction with people and with other things, part of a chain of their histories of use.[6]

Video games occupy both interpretations of what an artifact is, merging the natural with the synthetic, connecting that which is able to be touched to that which is able to be experienced. Take any cartridge produced by Atari in the 1970s and 1980s: made of plastic and a chip; labeled; boxed; easy to read, handle, and use. The ubiquity of these cartridges does not diminish their importance as cultural artifacts of their time—it would seem to suggest the opposite: such quantity equates to high demand. Commercially, one can purchase old Atari games on eBay or at flea markets and retrogaming stores for mere dollars, considering many titles retailed for around forty dollars upon release. The games themselves are minor miracles of engineering, and the original and current market prices belie all that went into their creation: development, design, testing, production, marketing, promotion, the work of one creative engineer supported by dozens or hundreds of ancillary personnel. Each cartridge is both sacred and profane, a work of specialized talent and vision, then mass-produced and sold. With that comes data for distribution and sales, reviews, reception, returns; end-of-life for the game and later for the hardware on which it was played; and then a new life for collectors, retrogamers chasing nostalgia or appreciating these games for the miniature masterpieces they were—even the "bad" titles.

Fast-forward to the present, and the majority of games sold/played no longer occupy physical media. The software is ephemeral, run either on dedicated hardware (e.g., Xbox or PlayStation, Mac or PC) or online over the internet with nothing to download. Even though no physical media are present, these games are still artifacts, examples of human creativity and thought complete with histories of ownership and use, from the earliest development stage to their consignment to an archive, or to YouTube and Twitch video-streaming services as memories of what we used to find entertaining and important enough to invest hours of our time in. Video games are our modern epics, our literature, products of our culture, from hobbyists to indie developers to AAA publishers.

Not all artifacts are created equal. Just as there are differences between cooking pots made of coarse clay to elaborately painted fineware, some artifacts are more highly valued (for better or worse) than others, even though the data held within each artifact are arguably equal. As seen with the Atari excavation, value changes when an artifact is invested with myth.

The key to understanding an artifact is in knowing its biography, its history of use. As Olivier describes it, "What we inherit from the past rarely comes down to us as it was. Things are reinterpreted, repeatedly used in unexpected ways, in a present they had not been intended for. They carry into the present where they are reworked and enhanced. Things hold memory" (Olivier 2015: 28). An artifact is forever. The philosopher Walter Benjamin first considered in 1940 that artifacts are a nucleus of time with a fore- and after-history that diverge at the point of discovery. An object is from the past, yet also exists in the present, and will most likely have a future. Digital game historian Raiford Guins states in his book *Game After* that "objects acquire histories of their own as they move through time and space regardless of our affinity for them" (Guins 2014: 3–4). This biography runs independent of any kind of human agency, although it can only be told through the intervention of the archaeologist.

"Archaeology," according to Olivier, "allows us to explore the processes at work in the formation of artifacts" (Olivier 2015: 190). Artifacts are altered, destroyed, buried, and perhaps rediscovered and preserved as objects bearing witness to the past, and they may then be destroyed and "forgotten" all over again. When we study video games, we study their creation and immediate use as media commodities, as entertainments that often reflect the *tempora* and *mores* in which the games were created. In some instances, such as with the Atari Burial Ground, those artifacts were indeed destroyed and forgotten, then rediscovered and "reactivated," ready for a new chapter in their history. Artifacts such as weapons and armor found by people during gameplay can also be created/discovered, used, and destroyed within a game itself, following similar patterns of use as their real-world counterparts.

The context is complex. As Holtorf described in 2005, "The life histories of things do not end with deposition but continue until the present day. The [meanings of things] cannot be reduced to a single meaning or significance in the past" (Holtorf 2005: 80). The things archaeologists study cannot be separated from the assemblage (a group of artifacts sharing the same context) from which they are removed. Contemporary archaeologists study connections between things and the people who create/use them. These connections include exchange, consumption, discard, and post-deposition (Holtorf 2012: 42–43). "Archaeology," Holtorf argues, "reveals what the present quite literally consists of" (Piccini and Holtorf 2011: 14). People live their lives materially, and our things have an active social aspect to them (Piccini and Holtorf 2011: 20).

Video games are active parts of modern and contemporary material culture and as such have a very real social component. Game and even mainstream media announce the release of an anticipated game. Platforms such as reddit (reddit.com) host thousands of discussions about minute details related to any given game. We review games, play them, inhabit them, share them, customize them to make them our own and to share with a community. Our interactions with games help give them life, and our agency allows games to grow and change. What historical conditions led to the creation of these games and their interactivity is an archaeological question, just as it is when considering the production and use of other, nondigital technologies (Barrett 2012: 162).

Archaeogaming is rife with dualism, easily stepping between the natural and the synthetic. Fewster notes that "modern material culture studies and archaeologies of the contemporary and recent pasts have added immensely to the archaeologist's understanding of the dualist nature of human action and material culture with an awareness that material culture is not passive and reflective but can act back upon us in unexpected ways" (Fewster 2013: 34). When thinking about the archaeology of video games in the real world, archaeologists must consider pop culture, multivocality, performance, and storytelling, something archaeologist Ian Hodder calls "ethnoarchaeology" (Hodder 1982). By understanding the environment surrounding the use of an artifact via ethnography (especially in developer and player culture), we gain valuable insight that aids our archaeological interpretation. We then enter the domain of behavioral archaeologists, who define behavior as the interaction of people and objects (LaMotta 2012: 64). This interaction creates memory, something completely subjective, and something that can either cloud or clarify the use of a particular artifact at a given point in time.

Gaming Spaces

Just as there are spaces to explore within games, there are also game-related places and spaces to investigate archaeologically. These brick-and-mortar locations include retrogaming stores, where people can purchase pieces of video gaming history; arcades, where people can engage directly with video games past and present; and the offices of game studios where development teams meet to create their products. Gaming spaces provide a wider, human context to the creation and use of games, the spaces themselves having their own biographies.

Gaming Spaces: Retrogaming Stores

Retrogaming falls under the rubric of archaeogaming, more as an applied science of running original software on original hardware (video games from the 1970s, 1980s, and now 1990s) falls under the rubric of archaeogaming, more as an applied science of running original software on original hardware, replicating the original play experience. While some gaming equipment finds a home in museums such as The Strong: National Museum of Play in Rochester, New York, other "vintage" games and hardware become commodities in retrogaming stores, embodiments of artifactual commerce and nostalgia. One such store is Sore Thumb Retro Games, York, England, about four hundred yards from the University of York's archaeology department.

Sore Thumb immediately appeals to the nostalgic player and to the collector/completionist/fetishist. It is both shrine and shop, a well-lighted cave of organized chaos featuring nothing but console games and equipment. Shelves are packed to the rafters with loose cartridges, boxed games, original documentation, mint condition artifacts, and peripherals (controllers of all kinds), plus plush toys and action figures all related to games and gaming culture (see Figure 1.2). It is the most complete retrogaming store I have ever been in, with an obsessive attention to PlayStation 1 and Sega Dreamcast games (although all retro consoles—including Atari 2600, Intellivision, Colecovision, and others—are well represented).

I have seen something approaching the care of curating salable collections in various antique stores and malls both in the UK and the US, but these places lack a reverence to the items in their care. Retrogame shops are different: they feature nostalgia, but also respect. When I enter a space such as Sore Thumb, I equate it to entering a basilica. One enters, and the transition from the street to the interior is both immediate and pronounced. The doorway serves as *propylaeum,* and one transitions from outside to inside. The atrium comes next, featuring a selection of toys and games, an introduction to what is on offer in the store. You pass the narthex then, the counter at which you pay, transitioning into the nave, the heart of the store, a wide aisle flanked by relics and occasional side aisles leading back to the end of the basilica, the apse, in which one finds reliquaries.

Sore Thumb contains five to six locked glass cases behind which sit perfect examples of games from beloved series from days gone by. The collections are largely complete, like the collected bones of various saints presented to the pilgrim for contemplation and remembrance. There has been trade in holy relics (many of them fake), and there still thrives an active trade in antiquities, both legal and illegal. With retro games, the legality is straightforward (unless someone is selling stolen goods), and provenance (history of ownership) is not important. Archaeological context is largely absent, and collectors know the rar-

Figure 1.2. Inside Sore Thumb Games, York, England. Photo by Megan von Ackermann. Used with permission.

ity of the games in which they are interested. Value has already been assigned by the market, both for nostalgic reasons and for difficulty in acquisition.

When I entered Sore Thumb, the person at the counter greeted me and immediately told me that the good, rare stuff was in the cases at the back of the shop. He checked in on me later, pointing out the new acquisitions, including a Sega Dreamcast game now priced at 220 GBP. Had I been a collector, I could have purchased that or any other game in the shop. But I am not a collector. I am an archaeologist, and it troubles me ethically to purchase the things that I study. To some this might seem ridiculous. But for me, it is enough to know that places like this exist in the world, where I can walk in and see something different from month to month, something I've never seen before, that helps me complete the archaeological record of video games that are, in this instance, treated as artifacts (for sale), providing an instant, visual typology, history of use, and a chronology of development of these digital built environments. Places such as Sore Thumb are equal parts shop, holy place, and museum, fulfilling our various needs of exploration, material acquisition, curiosity, and a positive connection to a presumed better time. Nothing like this existed in antiquity, a place to buy old things one used to care about. Retrogame stores are a new kind of space then, a curiosity cabinet where everything is for sale, and anything over thirty years old is as ancient as mummy powder.

Gaming Spaces: Arcades

Readers of any age will likely recall where they played their first video games, and even what game(s) they played. The nostalgia of place and time merges with one of the most crucial memories anyone can create: being handed the controls to something, transitioning from observer to actor. The feeling is the same as learning how to ride a bike, or learning how to drive, or being allowed to lead a hike. The actor is in control, fate in nervous hands.

I first began playing video games in the late 1970s.[7] My dad used to take me once or twice a month to our local video arcade where, like all good dads, he would play me head-to-head in *Asteroids* (which had just come out in 1979) or we'd take turns at *Space Invaders* (1978). I was terrible at both (then again I was seven), which probably says a lot about how far kids have come between now and back then when throttling a joystick and mashing one button at exactly the right time was the pinnacle of difficulty.

These arcades of my preadolescent memory were dark and noisy and filled with kids (mostly boys) of all ages, waiting on lines to play new games, observing the "quarter rule" of arcade etiquette: put your quarter on the deck of the game to get dibs on playing it next. Once my five dollars was spent (usually within twenty minutes, sometimes half of that), I would hang around and watch kids much better than me playing *Pac-Man, Galaga, Centipede.* You want plot? Forget it—these games were all action. The pinball games remained popular, but all the cool kids were going digital, and the really good ones would draw crowds to watch them at work. Arcades were social spaces in the real world, and we all cheered and gasped as things happened beyond the pane of the screen. High scores appeared on the scrolling banner of the games, initials that would remain until the game was unplugged.

My absolute favorite game was Atari's *Star Wars* (1983), with its color, 3D-like vector graphics. I remember playing it in an arcade and giving it all of my money for the unparalleled feeling of flying an X-wing, blasting the tops of turrets, ducking girders in the final run up to deploying torpedoes into the heart of the Death Star. After moving from one town to the next, I searched for this cabinet like some pilgrim until I stumbled across one plugged in at the Ben Franklin hardware store. I played it every day after school, riding my bike over, playing two quarters, and riding home. To me that hardware store became a kind of sacred site, one with personal importance, and a place where I could play (pray?) in solitude, a suburban Mt. Athos near Houston, Texas.

Back in the present, on occasion you can find the rare video arcade that is not tied to children's birthday parties (e.g., Chuck E. Cheese) or that caters to nostalgic grown-ups who want to play arcade games while drinking cocktails and eating a real dinner (e.g., Dave & Busters). There are a couple of old school arcades on the boardwalk in Atlantic City that my brother and I go to between stops at the casinos (where we play table games and stay away from the digital). These still have the old bubblegum stuck everywhere and the smells of fake buttered popcorn and the loud pop music. All is forgotten as soon as we put our heads in the games: *Afterburner, Moon Patrol, Gauntlet.* We tune out and watch each other play.

Barcades are scattered throughout New York City now, harkening back to when video games like *Pong* were diversions for drinkers and you could set your bottle directly on the glass of table-top games like *Pac-Man.* Retrogaming arcades (such as Robot City Games in Binghamton, New York) that approach interactive museum status are also experiencing a resurgence, catering to people my age and older who play to remember and who also bring their children in to teach them the old ways. The games have become artifacts, and the persistent arcades are now archaeological sites blending the past with the present using players as the connection as they always had. As Kocurek wrote in 2015, "The video game arcade was a visible embodiment of emergent cultural values, the persistence of the video game arcade as privileged cultural site demonstrates an ongoing commitment to these values" (Kocurek 2015: 200).

The social nature of the arcade and the arcade's promise of technological novelty were both huge selling points and kept these spaces popular in the 1970s and early 1980s. The writing on the wall came with the mass deployment of Atari and to a lesser extent Intellivision (a console that my family owned), Colecovision, and others, the first and second generations of consoles for at-home gameplay. All of a sudden, we could play games any time we wanted, and we could play with our friends. There was no more playing surrounded by strangers, and there was no more pay-as-you-go gaming to continue play after a final life was lost in-game. We (or our parents) paid once for a cartridge, and we were set for the weekend or for a year of weekends.

Even as the first cabinets were being installed in arcades in the 1970s, the personal computer market was already positioning itself for home use and ultimately for entertainment. The General Instruments (GI) A4-3-8500 chip aided video game production. In 1977, twenty-two computer systems by fourteen companies were in stores, with over half of these in color. The announcement of the Apple II in 1977 and appearance of TRS-80 in 1977 continued to build enthusiasm for home computing and later home gaming (Wolf 2012b: 83–85). The true impact of home computers and the first consoles (such as the first cartridge-based system, the Fairchild Channel F Video Entertainment System in 1977) would not be felt by arcades for another few years. By the end of 1982, profits in arcade video games began to falter. The United States had ten thousand arcades in 1982; in 1983, eight thousand. This was also the same year in which Atari lost half a billion dollars and when rival Mattel/Intellivision quit the industry (Wolf 2012a: 4). One breath of hope in righting the gaming ship came with the Japanese release of the NES by Famicom. As far as arcades being the main venue of play, this marked the end of an era.

The economy of play then had a very real effect on gaming, as did the advent of being able to actually save your progress. Why go to an arcade to throw money away on a novelty when you could play (and ultimately save) your games and scores? The economy shifted as soon as gaming consoles were introduced, and those gaming palaces were largely shuttered over the following years. The arcade cabinets are still available for purchase on eBay and elsewhere, for collectors and hobbyists and for those hung up on gaming nostalgia. Places such as Vigamus (Rome's Video Game Museum) are now more museum than arcade, offering playability with ample signage, documentation, prototypes, and recorded interviews of designers and players.

In looking at contemporary gaming, especially with the advent of MMOs such as *EverQuest* and *World of Warcraft*, one begins to see a resurgence in social games, the mix of playing with friends and with strangers, and a merging of one-time payment with pay-as-you-go (i.e., monthly subscriptions). With Xbox and PlayStation, we can also now contribute to global leaderboards for scores, and we can play and communicate with anyone during gameplay, merging gaming with strangers with the comforts of home and other gaming friends (even if those friends are countries away). We have moved away from the physical space dedicated to play, these temples of gaming, into a gray space where we meet inside the synthetic world to explore, to compete, and to communicate. For those children of the 1960s and 1970s who were the nerds, phreaks, and geeks, however, online social gaming has paralleled video game history since the mid-1970s with PLATO and ARPANET and later dial-up modem access to Bulletin Board Services (BBSs) and multiuser dungeons (MUDs). Online social play has always been around, but now it is available to everyone, including players who do not need to understand how online communications work.

The archaeology then is of these older gaming spaces (arcades) and understanding why they were abandoned or repurposed. This was a spatial shift as well as an economic one. Play became portable, but the community of the arcade did not disperse. It just found a bigger venue in which to gather. The bricks and mortar became unimportant. The play's the thing.

The archaeological interest in arcades includes questions asked of abandoned sites: What happened to the original owners/occupants (in this case of the old video arcades)? What did they do once they shuttered their businesses? Where did they go? Do they resent the shift that caused their livelihoods to change? Do they care? And how were these spaces reused? What moved in, and do the current owners/occupants even know that their new ventures are sited atop (and within) a space held sacred by kids of a certain age who now, from time to time, want to put down their new toys in favor of their old ones? In the case of Low Hall Mill, an arcade in Leeds, England, the building remains abandoned, its games covered in dust.[8] Galaxy, an arcade in Philadelphia, was purchased and turned into a cheesesteak restaurant, Jim's Steaks, which itself closed in August 2017 for health code violations.[9] Buildings remain, but their interiors change to suit new owners and markets, the memories of past uses residing in those who knew what came before and care enough to leave a comment for an online news story about the fate of a particular place. The archaeologist takes an interest in how buildings are repurposed over time, especially those that are built specifically for one thing and then are rebuilt as something else. Barns become taverns. Churches become hotels.

Gaming Spaces: Game Development Studios

The archaeology of real-world gaming spaces/sites extends beyond the arcades and retrogaming stores and into the game developer studios themselves, which have their own histories and leave the footprint of their foundation behind.

The news of the "proposed" closing of acclaimed Lionhead Studios by parent company Microsoft hit the internet hard on March 7, 2016. Creator of the award-winning god game *Black and White* (2001), Lionhead earned its hall-of-fame status through a series of *Fable* games, which attracted the attention (and cash) of Microsoft who ultimately bought the studio in 2006. The greatly anticipated *Fable Legends* was already enrolling people in its multiplayer beta, but Microsoft scrubbed the title.

As an archaeologist, I had questions, some of which are still waiting to be answered as Microsoft and Lionhead continue to work through the process of terminating the studio. From a software perspective, I am wondering what the fate of the legacy games will be (still unknown at the time of writing). Abandonware? Probably not for a while simply because of each game's popularity. One could assume that Microsoft will continue to sell the active and legacy titles via the Xbox store (the URL for Lionhead redirects to there). *Black and White* is another matter, the title having been developed for PC and Macintosh fifteen years ago and is increasingly hard to find outside of occasional listings on eBay and Amazon. The game is still under copyright but could end up as an orphaned work on an abandonware site.

Second, I am curious as to what will happen to the never-to-be-finished *Fable Legends*. It is likely (but as yet unconfirmed) that Microsoft will mothball its intellectual property much like a film studio will save an unreleased film, doing so either permanently or holding the title until it decides the time is right to resurrect it with another developer. The feasibility of that seems doubtful though, bringing on a new team to go through someone else's code. It still remains a mystery if/

how Microsoft plans on archiving Lionhead's games. Microsoft remains mute on the subject.

Going one step beyond, I also want to know if/how Microsoft plans on archiving Lionhead Studios itself, its email, its files, and its physical ephemera (writing, art, storyboards, etc.), as well as bits of its corporate culture. Lionhead started small but grew to around one hundred employees by the time Microsoft broke the news about *Fable Legends*. What artifacts will remain with Microsoft, and what will Microsoft absorb from Lionhead? How will Microsoft make those decisions? What is necessary to keep and why?

Speaking from a more traditional archaeological perspective, what happened to the physical space that once housed Lionhead Studios? The building is situated on Occam Road about a quarter mile from the University of Surrey in Guildford. It is roughly two miles away from Hello Games (*No Man's Sky*). The three-story building screams "university research park" with its clean lines, relatively recent construction, and mirrored windows. The building should have no trouble finding new tenants ready to move in to a space with enough IT infrastructure to enable the computing/data needs of a Galaxy-class starship.

It will be interesting to visit the building on Occam Road in the years following the departure of Lionhead to talk to its tenants about the building's history (as of this writing, the building remains unclaimed). Architecture has its own kind of memory, so what ghosts did Lionhead leave behind? A colleague of mine (who has asked to remain anonymous because of a possible conflict of interest) returned to Lionhead thirteen months after its closure to see what, if anything, had changed. The building is locked, but looking in the windows revealed *Fable* art still adorning the walls even though the space is no longer used for development. There are no signs indicating that the building is for sale or lease. The studio is in limbo, occupied by elements of its past, but not by its people.

One could also ask the question of whether or not this building is important when considering the output of Lionhead Studios under the Microsoft banner. Can we separate space and structure from the resulting intellectual property? The building is certainly a part of gaming history in the fact that *Fable* titles were produced here, but that importance is dwarfed by the artifacts of the games themselves, from the pre-alpha versions to the finished, patched, latest/final editions.

With this kind of nondescript, nondistinct architecture, one might feel a sense of "who cares," but the space is imbued with history nonetheless. When considering the archaeology of Late Capitalism and of the recent past, these buildings are the norm, not the exception. Archaeologists are faced with corporate designs built for a technology-enabled, fast-moving culture with a demand for huge amounts of data delivered at light speed in a comfortable, well-lit space. It communicates something different than Classical structures that were themselves their own message and monument. We might not see tourists at what was Lionhead Studios, but that should not diminish the importance of place in the history of game design.

It might be that in a corner office somewhere, someone (or many people) left written evidence of this past occupation, not necessarily for others to find but for themselves, to give closure, a farewell from the occupants to the reliable structure they had occupied for years, a thank you (or possibly something nasty pointed at Microsoft), a remembrance that will likely be painted over before the next generation moves in, oblivious.

When Video Games Change

Video games, like archaeological sites in the natural world, grow and change based on human usage and need. New features and functionality are added. Code is rewritten. Bugs are fixed. Because the changes are code based, it is rare that traces of the replaced snippets and routines remain, making it difficult for the video game archaeologist to determine what happened to a game over its active history. There are other ways to track these changes outside of the games themselves, however.

News broke on August 4, 2015, that major game developer Bungie had parted ways with actor Peter Dinklage for *Destiny*'s expansion *The Taken King*, opting to recast the voice of the Ghost with veteran video game talent Nolan North. North (*Uncharted, Assassin's Creed*) was not just picking up where Dinklage left off. Bungie hired the actor to re-record all of Dinklage's lines, effectively removing all traces of the Ghost's original actor from the entire game. The Ghost is the player's helper along the way, feeding the payer data while assisting with complex computing tasks during firefights. It is a major role, and Dinklage, most famous for his role of Tyrion Lannister in *Game of Thrones*, was major talent hired by Bungie for its blockbuster game. The split was amicable; Bungie cited Dinklage's unavailability because of film and television commitments.[10] The irony is that the film industry, having lost so much market share to video games, impacted Bungie's flagship series (following *Halo*), leaving Bungie scrambling to find replacement voice talent.

So how does this fit in with archaeogaming? One need not look too hard at the archaeological record to discover dozens of instances of *damnatio memoriae* (Latin for "condemnation of memory") where emperors and pharaohs would demand that images of their predecessors be stricken from all civic art and monuments and either left in a destroyed state, or recarved with the current ruler's likeness. After the death of the Pharaoh Akhenaten (eighteenth dynasty), who introduced the monotheistic worship of the new god Aten to Egypt, his successor Horemheb, the last pharaoh of the eighteenth dynasty, destroyed all images of his predecessor. A similar instance occurred after the death of the Roman emperor Domitian: his successor Nerva famously had his portrait recut atop Domitian's in the Cancellaria Reliefs. The goal of these defamations was to purge the images and memory of past rulers from the current population's minds, as well as from history.

Fast-forward several centuries, and we have possibly the first instance of *damnatio memoriae* in video games, where the voice of arguably *the* main character in *Destiny* has been completely purged. Players new to *Destiny* will enter the game to the voice provided by North only, and many future players will be ignorant of Dinklage's prior association with the game. They will have little or no idea of who came before. For some, the history of the actual game's production will not matter all that much. But for others, this will remain a memorable event, a kind of deposing, swapping one major talent for another.

Archaeologists have been able to deduce why one ruler defaced the depictions of others, and it is possible we can do the same with media generally and games in particular. The twist with *Destiny* is that North did not decide to replace Dinklage's voice in the game. This was Bungie's decision, a corporation deciding to alter its own history in favor of producing something that they perceived as better while sweeping the past under the rug. In time, few will care about the switch, but it is noteworthy that it did happen, and it opens the door to other companies doing the same thing with other games.

Consider the game as an artifact for a moment. First, although the game is/was available on physical media, applying the expansion pack to the game on a console wipes away Dinklage's work. New purchases will have North's voice applied upon installation. For many players (myself included), the game and expansions were purchased via the Xbox or PlayStation online stores and downloaded directly to the consoles. It is as if Dinklage's voice never existed. The only proof that Dinklage contributed to *Destiny* can be found via legacy gameplay videos on YouTube or Twitch as well as on various news sites reporting on the switch of voice actors.

This then begs the question of if and/or how Bungie will archive Dinklage's version of the game, and how it will preserve his voice as part of the history of the game and of Bungie itself. This also leads to the larger question of video game archiving and preservation, especially when dealing with media that exists only in the cloud and not burned to disk. Who is responsible if it is not the company that created it, and will current copyright law allow for a third party to archive a game even if it is not the rights holder? For the meantime, at least one enterprising soul has saved all of Dinklage's dialogue, which is currently available for free online.[11] At this writing, Bungie still has not publicly commented on any plans to archive different versions of *Destiny* or any of its other games, even after releasing *Destiny 2* in the summer of 2017.

Part of archaeology is conservation, preservation, and archiving of finds, done by professional conservators and published by the excavation's personnel as a way to preserve the data, the catalogues of finds, and the synthetic, interpretive text. As with the movie industry, there is at least one place actively archiving games: the University of Texas Video Game Archive. The problem with games as seen in past decades with film (and also on traditional archaeological sites) is the issue of making the decision of what gets preserved. No one knows how many games have been written, played, and forgotten, and it is unclear if any game archive would preserve just popular AAA titles, indie games, or all games. The Library of Congress's Preserving Creative America Initiative of the National Digital Information Infrastructure and Preservation Program has attempted to save the ephemeral with the Preserving Virtual Worlds I and II projects. Often games are preserved by passionate people, but not in any kind of standardized way, and there is always the question of copyright. As will be seen in chapter 4, there are museums dedicated to video games, which is a start, but game archiving remains in a nascent, unorganized state. On archaeological sites, the site director and team decide on what to keep and what to record and then throw away in the pottery dump. For the sites at which I have worked, we retained all "diagnostic" pottery pieces: rims, feet, handles, sherds with art or writing. The rest were weighed, counted, and noted, then discarded. Perhaps this is the model we will see with games: we will keep the best and most representative samples of games, leaving the rest to history and to collectors.

When considering preservation within actual video games (remember that there are always two levels of archaeogaming, in-game and extra-game), there will likely be (or already are) instances in synthetic worlds that could/should be protected or designated as historically significant—that is to say, perhaps an in-world/in-game version of a UNESCO World Heritage Site. Where would such a site be, and why would it be assigned that status?

It is a deceptively simple question. In meatspace, people are typically not far from some kind of landmark, roadside sign, historic home, or something that some locality (or larger governing body) has designated as being important to either preserve or mark in the earth in a permanent way. I live in the Princeton, New Jersey, area. I can throw a rock and hit a statue, marker, or milestone that dates to the 1700s. My friends in the UK can do a lot better than that. But what about in synthetic worlds?

When I was playing vanilla *World of Warcraft* in 2007 as a Tauren hunter, I encountered an early quest in Mulgore, "Kyle's Gone Missing!" The goal of the quest is to find food for a runaway dog, Kyle, and then put it out for him to lure him back to his owner, Ahab Wheathoof. I remember liking this quest, and I wondered why there was a non-*WoW* name given to the dog (names like "Kyle" violate the original terms of service and did not mesh with the role-playing server I was on). My friend who got me into the game told me that this quest was part of a Make-a-Wish Foundation request. The wish's recipient, Ezra Chatterton, visited Blizzard Entertainment, creator of *WoW*, and designed this quest as his Wish.[12] The quest is available to Horde players on every *WoW* server and serves as a permanent memorial to Chatterton. I would not have known that, however, unless someone had told me the story and I had confirmed it online. It is close to a memorial, but not quite.

I then thought about *Minecraft*. There are a number of reconstructions of the World Trade Center that were built as memorials by players in the game on their own (or shared) servers. I found dozens of different *Minecraft* memorials and reconstructions on Google Images, but these were examples of virtual spaces created to remember a meatspace event. This, too, was not quite what the question of commemoration of virtual world events is after.

Back in 2014 I had a Twitter conversation with @spacearchaeology (Steve Wilson) who told me about the historical events that happen in-game with *Eve Online*. The MMO has been around for over ten years, and the server cluster serves a single universe of players (unlike *WoW* that has groups of players on separate identical servers). The game's tenth anniversary saw a world record sixty-five thousand players logged in all at the same time to participate in in-world events. Those who did received a special ship for their hangars, a commemoration for an in-world activity that crossed between meatspace and metaspace. Related to the game is a book that is being written by Jeff Edwards, which collects player recollections of a massive in-game conflict called "The Fountain War." This book (as described by the author) sounds a bit like Thucydides or Xenophon reporting on the Peloponnesian War. While interesting in a virtual historical sense, it still does not designate any in-game space as a virtual kind of Ground Zero.

I predict that actual, historical designation of something akin to a UNESCO World Heritage Site (or even the actual thing) will appear within the next fifty years, although it might be sooner than that based on the 2017 appointment of Cornelius Holtorf as UNESCO Chair of Heritage Futures at Sweden's Linnaeus University, recognizing in part the need to consider how to preserve current heritage for future generations to study.[13] The first UNESCO digital heritage site will likely appear within a communally shared virtual world (an MMO or whatever's coming next). But what will be the historical event that will trigger this award of status? UNESCO offers ten selection criteria, which I argue can be used in both meatspace and in metaspace:

1. to represent a masterpiece of human creative genius;
2. to exhibit an important interchange of human values, over a span of time or within a cultural area of the world, on developments in architecture or technology, monumental arts, town-planning, or landscape design;
3. to bear a unique or at least exceptional testimony to a cultural tradition or to a civilization that is living or has disappeared;
4. to be an outstanding example of a type of building, architectural or technological ensemble, or landscape that illustrates (a) significant stage(s) in human history;
5. to be an outstanding example of a traditional human settlement, land-use, or sea-use that is representative of a culture (or cultures), or human interaction with the environment especially when it has become vulnerable under the impact of irreversible change;
6. to be directly or tangibly associated with events or living traditions, with ideas, or with beliefs, with artistic and literary works of outstanding universal significance. (The committee considers that this criterion should preferably be used in conjunction with other criteria);
7. to contain superlative natural phenomena or areas of exceptional natural beauty and aesthetic importance;
8. to be outstanding examples representing major stages of Earth's history, including the record of life, significant ongoing geological processes in the development of landforms, or significant geomorphic or physiographic features;
9. to be outstanding examples representing significant ongoing ecological and biological processes in the evolution and development

of terrestrial, freshwater, coastal, and marine ecosystems and communities of plants and animals;

10. to contain the most important and significant natural habitats for in situ conservation of biological diversity, including those containing threatened species of outstanding universal value from the point of view of science or conservation.

UNESCO states that something must only meet *one* out of ten of these criteria. Think about the games created so far and which might have a space (and events occurring within) deserving of universal attention.

Chronologies and Typologies

Archaeologists can be preoccupied with dates or, perhaps more accurately, chronologies. What came before? What came later? What did that period of transition look like? How did that transition compare with a similar one that happened elsewhere, and earlier? What can we find to help us date an archaeological site? The soil strata? A coin? An inscription? Pieces of pottery?

For establishing a chronology, it is often the pottery. Archaeologists have found countless tons of sherds from all different kinds of pots and have studied the clays used to source the raw material, the technology used to make the pot (hand- or wheel-made), the firing of the pots, their shapes, and what other objects they were found with and in what context (funerary, domestic, etc.). Over many years, archaeologists have a very good idea of how to assign at least a preliminary date to a site. That chronology established by pottery has a naming system: chronotypes.

Take a look at Greek prehistory for a moment, and more specifically the Aegean Bronze Age (about 2800 to about 1060 BCE). This age is subdivided into three parts: Early Helladic (2800–2100), Middle Helladic (2100–1550), and Late Helladic (1550–1060). Early and Late Helladic periods are further subdivided into three parts each. And then a few of these subdivisions are further subdivided so that when a scholar reads about a site from the LHIIIB2 period, that period covers a forty-year span.

So what do these pots look like? How did they change from period to period to period in the same place? Consider the amphora, a clay vessel for carrying liquid, typically wine or olive oil. Figure 1.3 is a Greek Early Helladic III (2050–2000 BCE) example from Olympia and Figure 1.4 is a Greek Late Geometric II (730–710 BCE) amphora, about thirteen hundred years later. The shapes and function are similar, but

Figure 1.3. Early Helladic III Late (circa 2050–2000 BCE) Greek amphora. Photo by Dan Diffendale. Used with permission.

Figure 1.4. Late Geometric II (730–710 BCE) Greek amphora. Photo by Dan Diffendale. Used with permission.

the technology of the pot's creation has changed. The ancient Greeks were satisfied with what the amphora could do, but they continued to improve upon how that function was delivered. The clay is finer. The pot is decorated. It has a longer neck. The original functionality and design was—to borrow from the gaming community—modded.

And what then of crossing the streams of traditional archaeology and gaming? What does a simple bowl look like in *Elder Scrolls V: Skyrim*? Figure 1.5 is a example. See also Figure 1.6, a ceramic bowl from *Elder Scrolls III: Morrowind*. Both bowls are made of different materials and come from different times and places. *Skyrim's* bowl has better texturing as could be expected from the later game. And bowls in *Skyrim*? Diversity abounds. Over a dozen bowl types exist, likely more, made of diverse materials and decorated according to the race and region in which the bowl was found.

In playing *Skyrim* (set in a northern climate in a generally medieval-like fantasy age), a sense of neatness and order pervades. Bowls are rarely out of place, carried by an NPC or other traveler from one region to the next. The same is true of *Elder Scrolls Online,* where rubbish is actively destroyed when players discard something from inventory. (See chapter 3 for more on in-game garbology.) But except for the very rare game, players in-world cannot leave materials from one place in another for others to find, which would, in effect, corrupt the in-game pottery chronology for the unwary gaming archaeologist.

We can apply the same observations to video games within the same series. We can first do this generically by title from a single company. Consider the graphics in *Final Fantasy,* first published by Square

Figure 1.5. Bowl, *Elder Scrolls V: Skyrim* (Bethesda Softworks). Screen capture by author.

Figure 1.6. Bowl, *Elder Scrolls III: Morrowind* (Bethesda Softworks). Screen capture by author.

in 1987 for the NES (Figure 1.7). Compare these with the graphics in *Final Fantasy IV* four years later for the SNES (Figure 1.8) and then *Final Fantasy XV* nineteen years later (Figure 1.9). As with pots, gaming technology improves. The function (in this case to tell a story and to entertain and challenge players) remains the same, but how that functionality is delivered has changed greatly. Players can tell roughly when a game is produced, typically by its graphics. The same could be said of archaeologists considering pieces of pottery. Clunky shapes and art come earlier—most of the time. Retrogames such as *Eden* and *Minecraft* and *Undertale* are intentionally clunky and should be viewed as separate from this kind of record, almost like intrusions into gaming strata.

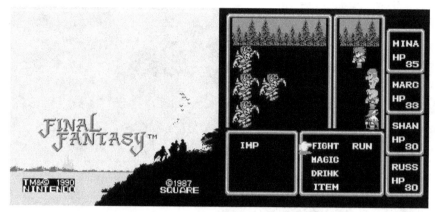

Figure 1.7. *Final Fantasy* for the NES,1987 (Square Enix). Screen capture by author.

But when viewing games in a series such as *Final Fantasy,* players can create a visual chronology based on how the game looks and how it plays, putting it into context.

For games in a series, developers and publishers have established their own chronologies and what to call them. While archaeologists might have LHIIIA, or Late Archaic, or Hellenistic, each qualifier representing dates of production for material made during those eras, so it goes with games. Take a look at the versioning of *Final Fantasy* on its Wikipedia page. Compare that with a chart of the Aegean Bronze Age. There are names and dates. By assigning these version numbers, gamers

Figure 1.8. *Final Fantasy IV* for the SNES, 1991 (Square Enix). Screen capture by author.

Figure 1.9. *Final Fantasy XV* for PlayStation 4, 2016 (Square Enix). Screen capture by author.

have instant recall of the art, music, gameplay, characters, and story, and they add to it the context of where (and who) they were when they played a certain iteration of the game.

Versioning is tied to time, and the gamer-as-archaeologist is in a unique position to be able to travel back to when they first played that game, comparing it with a very human context of playing that game later or with a later version of the game in a series. And for some players whose first experience with an established series might be *Final Fantasy XIII-2*, they can have that added adventure and sense of exploration by going back to the earlier games if they can find the consoles on which to play them, or they can play ports of the game on current technology (e.g., iPhone or iPad).

Going one level deeper, game-versioning further splits into build numbers. Typically a game is released commercially as version 1.0. Pre-release builds are 0.x, and expansions are 2.x, 3.x, etc., with minor patches/fixes making the version numbers creep along between full versions of the game: 1.0.0.1. Many games will display the build number upon launching on consumer hardware, and those builds help developers and players keep track of the version of the game being played. This is no different than checking if one's word processor, virus protection, or operating system is up to date. Software development is iterative, and so is the creation of digital games.

For the archaeologist, build numbers are stratigraphic markers separating layers of the game, one placed atop the next, obscuring earlier builds with later ones. This is arguably where the "real" archaeology happens, getting beyond the somewhat academic exercise of interpreting design of game elements manipulated by avatars and seeing instead how game-space is created and how it evolves with the introduction of new code. With older games, one might only have cartridges released all at once, with no updates following. Post-internet, boxed/installed games could be updated through patches and mods downloaded from the developer or modding community, merging real media with the immateriality of new code. With current games, players can opt in to have updates applied automatically to games downloaded and installed without any physical media. The versions and build numbers increase, but they do so behind the scenes for a seamless playing experience.

To study how a single game changes over time, one then needs a control machine and a variable machine, one with the "vanilla" game as first published and the other with the patched software run on hardware specific to the game's release date. Contemporary hardware might introduce extra complexity into the game, affecting it in ways that would have been unseen by developers and players.

When viewing digital games as artifacts, chronology is supplemented by typology. Returning to the Greek pottery example, there might be a general type of vessel called an amphora, which is used for storing/pouring liquids such as wine or olive oil. Based on place of production and the shapes of the mouth, handles, body, and foot, these are further broken down into types for more exact identification, producing data related to chronology, place of manufacture, place of use, and kind of use. In Roman archaeology, Heinrich Dressel published his amphora typology in 1899, which is still used today with supplemental information added by later archaeologists who discovered additional types of amphoras unknown to him at the time. These amphoras are described as Dressel types, with a number assigned to indicate date of manufacture, shape, and use.

With video games, there needs to be a standardized typology of objects and variants. Game historians and collectors already have these in place for the items they study and collect, publishing these together online: tapes, cartridges, floppy disks, CDs, DVDs, and filetypes, spread across platforms for the same titles on various media. Is *Tomb Raider* the same game when installed from diskettes on a DOS PC as it is when downloaded from a torrent site to run through an emulator on modern hardware? The archaeological context of what version of a game is played on what hardware installed with what media adds critical layers of data for interpreting what is observed in-game, and this context must be recorded/documented as part of the archaeogaming record. The real-world site of Troy is Troy at the macroscopic level, but peeling the layers back, going down through the stratigraphy, yields detail and information on how the site grew and changed over time as the inhabitants "modded" their own city.

In Joachim Fabian's *Time and the Other,* he defines three kinds of time: (1) physical—not subject to cultural variation; (2a) mundane—ages, stages, periods, keeping a cool distance to all times; (2b) typological—intervals between sociocultural meaningful events; (3) intersubjective—emphasis on communicative nature of human action and interaction. Time is recognized as a dimension instead of as a measure (Fabian 2002: 22–23). Time actually becomes political, even colonial, in how it creates distance between cultures (think of how many Western scholars apply BC/AD dates to cultures outside of their own). It is, as Fabian says, a "denial of coevalness," a "persistent and systematic tendency to place the referent(s) of anthropology in a time other than the present of the producer of anthropological discourse" (Fabian 2002: 31). How that relates to creating chronological typologies by definition then "consists of demonstrating synchronic relations of order beneath the flux and confusion of historical events and the expressions of personal experience" (Fabian 2002: 99). As the newer archaeology continues to expand, so does its necessity on relying on context and relationships instead of absolute time. This is applicable for both real and virtual archaeological spaces and artifacts held within. Archaeogaming is an archaeology of the recent past, and as such has multiple time-streams, some of which transcend typical, colonial/political time as applied to Old World sites. "The contemporary period cannot be fixed to a precise chronological bracket, and unusually it might be best to see this as a period defined in reverse, from the present day back to a time when the past seems (subjectively) no longer recent (e.g., 2010–1950)" (Harrison and Schofield 2010).

With a real-world archaeological site, there is no such luxury of preserving it at a single point in time, frozen. Sites, like games, continually evolve, decay, change. Chapter 3 explores the idea of games as archaeological sites, moving from the natural to the synthetic.

A Blended Historical Reality: *Pokémon Go*

Augmented reality (AR) merges the real world with digital data that simultaneously occupies one's senses (audio, visual, or both) in real-time. It differs from virtual reality (VR) because it is not a wholly immersive, otherworldly experience. AR and archaeology already have a rich and varied history as evidenced in the work of Shawn Graham,[14] Stu Eve,[15] and Colleen Morgan,[16] among others, whose work should be considered in detail. Archaeological and historical sites deploy AR as value-added content to the digitally enabled visitor. For those with smartphones, some sites tag areas with QR codes that can be scanned to provide interpretive details, additional images, quotes from primary sources, and more. Other sites go further by providing virtual tours, guiding the guest with GPS. Still others utilize digital overlays where guests can use their phone or tablet's screen as a way to see reconstructions or labels and explanations of the site's features. While all of these are examples of viable and successful deployments of AR in a cultural heritage context, none of them are games. Enter *Pokémon Go*.

Pokémon Go is an augmented reality app released in 2016 for iOS and Android smartphones. It is free to play (although in-app purchases are available), and has a small footprint of around 160 MB so it does not eat up storage. The premise of the game is simple: Pokémon (pocket monsters) are out in the real world, and your phone lets you see and nonviolently capture them, adding to your collection. There are plenty of other things to do (train, battle, level up, etc.), but the basic mechanic is a kind of hide-and-seek, merging a fantasy world with the natural one.

The game is a collaboration between the Pokémon Company and Niantic, Inc. (previously known as Niantic Labs, a Google startup ultimately spinning off in 2015). Niantic's first entry into AR games was *Ingress*, the 2012 augmented reality MMO. Niantic Labs also created *Field Trip*, a free, augmented reality travel app for use with smartphones, tablets, and at one time Google Glass.

What does this collaboration between the Pokémon Company and Niantic do for players? It merges the beloved twenty-year-old Pokémon juggernaut with a smartphone's internal GPS and then uses Niantic's landmarks and maps (also developed and used for their AR game *Ingress*) to create a rich environment of creatures and gyms, integrating them with real-world roads, waterways, greenspace, cities, and landmarks.

Archaeologists who game immediately wondered if there would be Pokémon to catch at local historical sites. When I started playing, I knew of a couple of sites that were a few minutes' walk/drive from my home; I had visited one, but not the other. Given the possibility that Pokémon might be nearby, it gave me the excuse to go touring in my own town. As it happens, I was right.

There is a marker near my home (which I had not yet visited even after living here for over five years) commemorating the route of George Washington's January march by night from Trenton to Princeton where, on the following day, January 3, 1777, he and his army would defeat the British in the Battle of Princeton. A "Pidgey" was waiting for me, and I caught it (see Figure 1.10). *Pokémon Go* goes one step beyond

Figure 1.10. A "Pidgey" superimposed over a historical marker in Robbinsville, New Jersey, during a *Pokémon Go* outing (Niantic Inc.). Screen capture by the author.

monster capture. Because *Pokémon Go* pulls data from Niantic, players can pause to read about places (called "PokéStops") where Pokémon sometimes hide. Players can get basic text or tap for more (including a larger image pulled from older, uncredited, user-uploaded *Ingress* photos) before dismissing the history lesson to return to the game proper.

As players wander, their in-game map displays animated symbols of other nearby landmarks/PokéStops to explore. Sometimes there is a Pokémon present, other times not. But the landmark's data remain accessible through a tap on the screen.

It is not too difficult to make the leap from walking around the neighborhood to actively chasing Pokémon around historic sites. This is where the public archaeology angle comes in: sites and organizations such as Historic Scotland host Pokémon days and activities for players where they can come to a site, look for creatures, and stay to learn more about where they are in the real world. The game is less invasive than geocaching, namely because there is no "geotrash" left onsite, and the presence of Pokémon are variable, meaning that there is no danger of ad hoc trails/desire lines being created or Tupperware or ammo boxes tucked out of sight. Even if there is no formal Pokémon day scheduled, people continue to visit sites and landmarks and will play along, learning about them via Niantic's augmented reality features. Because the app alerts players of nearby Pokémon, travelers can stop at roadside signs to learn a bit more about history that they might otherwise have passed by on the highway.

The game is not without its own ethical problems. Players must exercise tact and common sense when playing. The *Washington Post* reported a story in July 2016 on Pokémon at the Holocaust Museum.[17] The ethics of play also include staying out of restricted or sensitive areas of museums and sites, as well as private property such as residences. For these (and other) reasons, the release of *Pokémon Go* polarized archaeologists. Some embraced the game as a way to bring people to sites, while others lamented that a game would only bring people to sites to catch pocket monsters and not to engage with the site. In an email conversation with Cornelius Holtorf on August 10, 2016, I asked him what his thoughts were regarding *Pokémon Go* and cultural heritage. He admitted to not being a player or "a great phone user," but he replied:

- "Popular culture phenomena like *Pokémon Go* evidently express existing needs and desires of people and should not be dismissed in a patronizing way;

- "Public archaeology is much more than education about the past, and *Pókemon Go* should not exclusively be judged as a device of learning, or of encouraging learning;
- "*Pókemon Go* manifests a novel way in which digital natives engage with places. For an archaeologist (and potentially others), this particular engagement should be interesting in its own right and not only in the way in which it may challenge other engagements they may be more used to."

Why was *Pokémon Go* so successful? First, *Pokémon Go* is built on a brand that was twenty years old at the time of the app's release. Millions of people know what Pokémon is, and a large percentage of those have either played the card games or video games or watched the cartoons. Second, the majority of the digitally enabled population have smartphones or tablets with internet access and on-board GPS. Third, it is human nature to explore and to discover. Fourth, Niantic had already created a successful AR game, *Ingress,* and was able to build on that success, using its lessons learned to create an immersive AR experience. So what can archaeologists learn from such a successful AR deployment in order to create improved AR experiences for visitors to sites?

- Know the audience. Do many of them have technology in their pockets?
- Know the site. Do you want people to be online during their visit?
- Communicate. Let guests know that an AR app is available for download and use. Post this on the site's website as well as at points of entrance/sale.
- Engage. Give technology-enabled users other ways of interpreting the site, but do not penalize or withhold information from those guests who either do not have or choose not to use their devices.
- Brand. It would be more cost-effective and discoverable for a smaller site to partner with an AR service provider to create/distribute an AR app. Larger/famous sites might be successful with creating their own apps based on the current recognition of their brand.
- Be realistic. An app will not save your site, but it does (or should) add value to it.
- Be playful. It is human nature to explore and to discover. Whether or not the AR app becomes a game, make sure to include human stories. The narrative is the most engaging thing of all to the visiting public.

The end goal of any AR heritage project should be to actively engage the visitor with the site. Interaction is key as opposed to treating the app as a passive, one-way conduit of information. Give the viewer choices, and perhaps gamify the experience as other sites have by humanizing it. Create a suite of characters to adopt or assign. Turn the site visit into one of active discovery. Invoke the audible as well as the visual to create the environment. And keep the technology simple. Site staff are not present for technical support. Also understand that many visitors will have no desire to use the app; the site must continue to provide a positive, engaging experience without the need of technology.

One year after the release of *Pokémon Go,* the game itself remains wildly popular, surpassing 752 million downloads, and in-app purchases have topped US$1.2 billion.[18] The popularity of the game's use in the heritage sector is mixed, largely showing a downturn over the past year as the novelty wears off and other museum and site events are planned. Major museums such as the National Museum of the American Indian, the National Air and Space Museum, the National Museum of American History, and the Museum of London all held *Pokémon Go* events in the summer of 2016. The British Museum and Preservation Maryland published *Pokémon Go* guides. Smaller museums and heritage groups such as the Rock County Historical Society (Wisconsin), the Maine Historical Society, and the Fuller Craft Museum held family events and tours tied to the game that first summer as well, and a handful of small museums continue to do so in 2018 (the University Museum of Southern Illinois University at Carbondale and the Lakeshore Museum Center in Michigan).

One major *Pokémon Go* heritage event occurred on the weekend of July 22, 2017, in the historic city of Chester in England. The event partnered the city with Big Heritage and Niantic to promote the game as a way for families to discover heritage hotspots throughout a locality. Big Heritage founder Dean Paton said in the event's press release that "we are so excited about working with Niantic, Inc., who are true innovators in their field, and as passionate as we are about getting people exploring and learning about the world around them. It's a genuine coup for Chester to be the 'test bed' for some amazing new ideas, and we hope we can use the game based on the iconic and beloved Pokémon brand as a tool for helping more people get excited about the past." Hundreds of people descended on Chester for the event, but the real test is to see if the town receives return visitors who come to engage with the heritage, this time without the lure of pocket monsters.

Conclusion

This chapter focused on the archaeology of video games in the natural world, beginning with a literal excavation of games as rubbish and ending with the blurring of natural and synthetic environments via augmented reality. For those who wish to undertake archaeological investigation, gaming spaces abound as we make an effort to interpret the Anthropocene within the past forty years. The role of the archaeologist of the recent past is often misunderstood, even within the academy: why study something if it's less than fifty years old? As will be seen in the next chapter, with archaeogaming archaeologists are developing new ways of thinking about the things we make and how we interact with them, and about how to deal with the massive amounts of things we buy, use, collect, and discard. But before we head into the field, we first need to address the tropes and stereotypes of archaeology and of archaeologists in the games with which we engage.

Notes

1. Carly Kocurek would later write in *Coin-Operated Americans: Rebooting Boyhood at the Video Game Arcade* (2015: xxv) that "perhaps no event has so demonstrated the broad coalition at work in building gaming history as the April 2014 'Atari Dig' in New Mexico."
2. "Atari Parts are Dumped," *New York Times,* September 28, 1983, http://www.nytimes.com/1983/09/28/business/atari-parts-are-dumped.html (retrieved December 7, 2016).
3. "City to Atari: 'E.T.' Trash Go Home," *Alamogordo Daily News,* September 27, 1983.
4. http://www.ebay.com/itm/E-T-Atari-2600-From-The-Alamogordo-Landfill-Ultimate-Gaming-History-Bundle-/172846606583?hash=item283e75e8f7:g:xZUAAOSwr6RZpe-y (retrieved September 16, 2017).
5. I asked if it would be possible to return to excavate the remaining games, if only to properly dispose of them as e-waste after cataloguing the complete assemblage, but was given a very unambiguous "no."
6. See Bjørnar Olsen's excellent short book on "thing theory," *In Defense of Things: Archaeology and the Ontology of Objects* (2010).
7. A full accounting of the arcade culture of the 1970s and 1980s, as well as current retrogaming trends such as the Barcade in New York City, can be found in *Coin-Operated Americans: Rebooting Boyhood at the Video Game Arcade,* by C. A. Kocurek (2015). The earliest published work on the emerging arcade culture was 1983's *Mind at Play: The Psychology of Video Games,* by G. R. Loftus and E. F. Loftus.

8. https://www.derelictplaces.co.uk/main/industrial-sites/9072-low-hall-mi ll-holbeck-leeds-feb-09-a.html#.Wb2ikNOGPVo (retrieved September 16, 2017).

9. http://www.phillyvoice.com/well-known-cheesesteak-joint-closed-20-hea lth-code-violations/ (retrieved September 16, 2017).

10. "Destiny Dropped Peter Dinklage in Part Due to Hollywood Nonsense," *Gamespot*, http://www.gamespot.com/articles/destiny-dropped-peter-din klage-in-part-due-to-holl/1100-6429664/ (retrieved December 7, 2016).

11. https://www.reddit.com/r/DestinyTheGame/comments/3k2e2p/compl ete_clean_peter_dinklage_ghost_dialogue/ (retrieved December 7, 2016).

12. "Blizzard Makes WoW Wish Virtual Reality," http://www.ocregister.com/ news/chatterton-191512-game-blizzard.html (retrieved December 7, 2016).

13. https://lnu.se/en/meet-linnaeus-university/current/news/2017/linnaeus-university-gets-the-worlds-first-unesco-chair-in-heritage-futures/ (retrieved September 18, 2017).

14. See Shawn Graham (2015), "Low-Friction Augmented Reality," https://ele ctricarchaeology.ca/2015/05/20/low-friction-augmented-reality/ (retrieved December 10, 2016).

15. See Stuart Eve (2014), "Augmenting Phenomenology: Using Augmented Reality to Aid Archaeological Phenomenology in the Landscape," *Journal of Archaeological Method and Theory* 19(4): 582–600.

16. See Colleen Morgan (2009), "(Re)Building Çatalhöyük: Changing Virtual Reality in Archaeology," *Archaeologies: Journal of the World Archaeological Congress*, DOI 10.1007/s11759-009-9113-0.

17. A. Peterson, "Holocaust Museum to Visitors: Please Stop Catching Pokémon Here," *Washington Post*, July 12, 2016. https://www.washingtonpost.com/ amphtml/newa/the-switch/wp/2016/07/12/holocaust-museum-to-visito rs-please-stop-catching-pokemon-here/ (retrieved February 15, 2018).

18. https://www.gamespot.com/articles/pokemon-go-passes-12-billion-in-rev enue-report/1100-6451454/ (retrieved September 18, 2017).

Further Reading

Bogost, I. 2012. *Alien Phenomenology, or What It's Like to Be a Thing*. Minneapolis: University of Minnesota Press.

Buchli, V. and G. Lucas. 2001. *Archaeologies of the Contemporary Past*. New York: Routledge.

Jävinen, A. 2009. "Understanding Video Games as Emotional Experiences." In *The Video Game Theory Reader 2*, edited by B. Perron and M. J. P. Wolf, 85–108. New York: Routledge.

Kocurek, C. A. 2015. *Coin-Operated America: Rebooting Boyhood at the Video Game Arcade*. Minneapolis: University of Minnesota Press.

Loftus, G. R. and E. F. Loftus. 1983. *Mind at Play: The Psychology of Video Games*. New York: Basic Books, Inc.

Lucas, G. 2013. "Afterword: Archaeology and the Science of New Objects" In *Archaeology after Interpretation: Returning Materials to Archaeological Theory,* edited by B. Alberti, A. M. Jones, and J. Pollard, 369–80. Walnut Creek, CA: Left Coast Press.

Myers, D. 2009. "The Video Game Aesthetic: Play as Form." In *The Video Game Theory Reader 2,* edited by B. Perron and M. J. P. Wolf, 45–64. New York: Routledge.

Olsen, B. *In Defense of Things: Archaeology and the Ontology of Objects.* Lanham, MD: Rowman and Littefield.

Wolf, M. J. P., ed. 2012. *Before the Crash: Early Video Game History.* Detroit: Wayne State University Press.

Chapter 2

Playing as Archaeologists

You Play an Archaeologist

Lara Croft. Indiana Jones. A big part of archaeogaming is actually playing an archaeologist in a synthetic world. For some players, that means role-playing as archaeologists in games not specifically designed with archaeology in mind. For others, games provide a space for serious archaeological inquiry. And then there are those games that feature at their core a central player who is supposed to be an archaeologist; those games hang their plots on that premise. For many of these games, the choice of casting the main character as an archaeologist seems to be one of convenience, giving the developers a reason for trapping someone in a haunted temple. Other games use the archaeologist as a catch-all for paleontologist, gemologist, or geologist.

Video games enter into the academic field of reception studies (or reception theory), which seeks to understand how an audience interprets something in order to extract meaning from it. For example, within the subfield of Classical reception one can research how ancient audiences might have received the plays of Aeschylus and then investigate how those plays' meanings might change when presented to modern viewers via both traditional and new media. With video games featuring archaeologists, we need to understand how developers and players perceive archaeologists and archaeology and how those assumptions affect game creation and gameplay. How is the popular notion of archaeology received and then used to create interactive digital entertainment, and how do those perceptions differ from actual, real, professional archaeology and its practitioners?

Cornelius Holtorf has made it part of his life's work to study this question, focusing on archaeological communication and media representations of archaeology and archaeologists. "Academic archaeology owes its own existence and establishment to a widely shared popular fascination with archaeology, rather than vice versa. Academic archaeology is one of many systems of meaning" (Holtorf 2005: 12). This is a provocative but not inaccurate statement. How many archaeologists have been asked what they do, and when they say, "I'm an archaeologist," are met with the astonished reply of, "Wow! Like Indiana Jones?" The best known archaeologist in the world is a work of fiction. It would be a safe bet to say that few non-archaeologists could name any nonfictional archaeologists from any point in history, women or men.

It is to the archaeologist's benefit to take the comment "like Indiana Jones" as a compliment and to seize on that initial enthusiasm to gently disabuse the person of the idea of a gun-slinging, Nazi-punching academic, describing instead a little bit about what one does in the field, lab, library, office. But what a "real" archaeologist does is, as Holtorf says above, "one of many systems of meaning." Archaeologists have a very good idea about what they and their colleagues do, which is just as valid as the public perception of what it is archaeologists do. These perceptions often contradict each other, but this can lead to perception and knowledge through dialogue, debate, and public engagement.

Most people when asked to describe an archaeologist will mention clothing, typically gender-neutral and practical. Holtorf observed that "how you dress as an archaeologist will immediately be read as a statement about what kind of archaeology you (want to) do" (Holtorf 2007b: 88). This of course starts with headgear, which changes over time based on how the popular media decides to depict the archaeologist in the field (and it is almost always in the field) (Holtorf 2007b: 86). The hats could be the pith helmet of the British archaeologist in Egypt, or the fedora of postwar America (and Indiana Jones), or perhaps we are finally beginning to see a change with archaeologists in hard hats and Class 2 high-visibility vests getting depicted in modern media, although that has yet to make the jump to video game character design. Other typical clothing includes sturdy trousers and a work shirt, both khaki. Pair these with a fedora or pith helmet for an Instant Archaeologist.

A sense of adventure and discovery invests the idea of archaeology, as if some lost temple is waiting just around the corner. The tropes persist of the archaeologist-as-adventure-hero, dressed in the colonial style. The archaeologist is imagined to be well traveled and to have visited and stayed in exotic locales (Holtorf 2007b: 80). In video games, though, these tropes are a necessity in order to create via uncomplicated, visual language the simplest idea of what archaeology is (Aldred 2012: 100). For video games such as Atari's *Raiders of the Lost Ark,* most players have already seen the eponymous film and know the character of Indiana Jones. The iconography of the character most easily rendered in 8-bit art? His famous hat. For games based on films and other popular media, designers are greatly assisted by earlier reception that can be ported easily into a game-space (although they may not necessarily be able to complete the job of making the game as enjoyable as the film). Divergence between film and video game characters and action may have been ultimately responsible for the limited success they achieved as converged content (Aldred 2007: 102). Players do not get the charm and laughs out of the playable Indiana Jones. Instead, it is all action. Promotional materials for *E.T.* and *Raiders of the Lost Ark* video games show how their central characters came to the game's screen loaded with excess baggage (Aldred 2007: 98). Players already know the back-story and expect to find all of the film's action packed into a playable adventure. There is no archaeology in the original *Raiders* game.

What other games include archaeologists as playable characters? One might expect that many such games would feature white men dressed as Indiana Jones. This is not to be the case. At this writing, most games are played from the first-person perspective so that players do not actually see their character onscreen. However if the game developer creates a playable avatar of an archaeologist, it likely will be male, white, and wearing a fedora (with rare exceptions). At least three games (not including those in the *Tomb Raider* series) have a woman archaeologist as the central character. It might also be surprising for some to learn that many of the archaeologist-driven games are not action-adventure games but instead fall into the category of *Myst* clones, point-and-click puzzle games. Others are casual games, typically of the hidden-object variety. Developers perceive (perhaps correctly) that archaeologists are good at finding things, although the objects the players are sent to find often have no archaeological context at all and no purpose for recovery other than to complete a level.

Below is a short alphabetical list of representative games (and game-types) that feature archaeologists as the main, playable character.[1] The main criterion for selecting the games on this list (as well as game series and one game development company) was that the publisher/creator clearly states that the main player is indeed an archaeologist. The games in the list are from major game developers and from indie houses. The list contains games from 1984 until 2014 developed for various hardware and operating systems. At least one example of interactive fiction is included:

Amaranthine Voyage: The Tree of Life *(Big Fish Games, 2013)*

From the publisher: "During your career as an archaeologist, you firmly believed that the Tree of Life was simply a myth. However, once you uncover a magical artifact, you open brand new worlds of possibility. You are whisked away to a lush world that is slowly being poisoned by a mysterious dark force. Your artifact is the key to restoring this beautiful world, but dark forces stand in your way. Protect the artifact and save this dying world in *Amaranthine Voyage: The Tree of Life,* a thrilling Hidden-Object Puzzle Adventure game."

This is a casual point-and-click hidden-objects game populated by mini-games and completed from the first-person perspective. As will be seen in many games in this section and in the following one on archaeological reception, the archaeologist is defined in name only as a device to activate and advance the game's narrative. No archaeology is really done in the game, but there are places such as temples to explore and artifacts to recover, typically with magical attributes.

Baal *(Psygnosis, 1989)*

From the publisher: "You are an archaeologist of the future (1999) sent in Baal's hideout, a powerful demon, [*sic*] to prevent him from putting his paws on an ultimate weapon, whose parts are scattered around everywhere."

The game's archaeologist in this 2D platformer is of indeterminate gender and race, wearing a red adventure suit and helmet and carrying a very large gun. There is no reason the playable character should be an archaeologist, except that there is work to be done underground and a shattered weapon-artifact to reassemble.

The Ball *(Teotl Studios, 2010)*

From the publisher: "*The Ball* is a first-person action adventure game. The player controls an archaeologist trapped in an underground city, armed with only an artifact that can attract or repel a large metal ball. To progress in the game, the ball must be guided to trigger the puzzle mechanisms, act as a platform in platforming or defend the player in combat. As the player progresses, the ball will gain additional abilities, strengthening its combat ability or allowing the player to progress in platforming and puzzles."

Developed for Steam, this puzzler recalls Valve's *Portal.* As with many other games, the fact that the playable character is an archaeologist only serves to explain why this person is underground and interacting with an artifact, again one imbued with characteristics not easily explained by science.

Buried *(Tara Copplestone and Luke Botham, 2014)*

Free-to-play Twine text-based, in-browser game developed by Tara Copplestone and Luke Botham for the July 2014 Heritage Jam.[2] The player actually plays the role of a real archaeologist making life decisions an archaeologist would make. The game is gender-, age-, and race-neutral. Players can be who they want to be as they balance work with academic and social life within a complex and emotionally invested story. It is arguably unique that one has the ability, unlike in other games, to play an archaeologist with emotional resonance, learning what it is like to inhabit that three-dimensional role.

Dig-It! Games (development studio)

Dig-It! Games has created eight titles (as of 2016) for PC and iOS that combine archaeology with education and include themes such as "beat the looters," repatriation, learning about the Maya, and learning about a Roman village. These are largely point-and-click first-person puzzle games with an educational angle, originally starting with *Roman Town*, an actual archaeological fieldwork simulation, and later branching out more into edutainment with archaeology as a backdrop. Dig-It! Games remains the only developer focused exclusively on archaeological themes for its games.

From the company's website: "In 2005, Dig-It! Games founder Suzi Wilczynski began her quest to create fun, interactive learning experiences for middle school students. As an educator and trained archaeologist, Suzi had used archaeology to bring history to life while calling upon a wide range of skills, including math, science, and language arts. To make these subjects relevant to 21st century kids, Suzi set out to create entertaining, interactive digital games that could be played at school or at home. Her goal was to use games to engage children in an immersive way that goes beyond what they can experience from a textbook, film or lecture. After learning everything she could about game design and playing more games than she cares to admit, Suzi released *Roman Town* in January 2010 to critical acclaim from parents, educators and the education industry. In 2012, Dig-It! Games produced *Mayan Mysteries*, an award-winning puzzle-based adventure game about the ancient Maya. 2013 was all about math at Dig-It! Games, with the releases of math-based games *Loot Pursuit: Tulum*, *MayaNumbers* and *Can U Dig It!*"

Glowgrass (Nate Cull, 1997)

From the developer: "*Glowgrass* is a xenohistorical expedition to recover artifacts of 'the Ancients,' which takes on a surprisingly human and personal tone in this far-future sci-fi story. Simple *Planetfall*-like puzzles, thoughtful prose that establishes moods with parsimony. Short but not rushed."

Glowgrass remains a free-to-play interactive fiction title written in the style of Infocom text games containing puzzles. It is one of the few games that feature archaeology on an alien world.

Hunt the Ancestor (BBC, 2014)

From the publisher: "Time and money are running out and the developer's diggers are wanting to move onto the site of a dig. Experience some of the realities of being an archaeologist by playing *Hunt the Ancestor*."

Players assume the role of dig director (not depicted) and make all archaeological and budgetary decisions on where and how to dig a barrow in England. The game includes archival research, aerial photography, geophysics, and more, and hits quite close to home with budgetary decisions that affect how the excavation ultimately unfolds. The BBC continues to dabble in fun, realistic games such as *Ancient Britain* and *Roman Britain*, adding historical and archaeological verity to short, playable scenarios.

Indiana Jones (series, various publishers, fifteen titles as of 2016)

Raiders of the Lost Ark, Indiana Jones in the Lost Kingdom, Indiana Jones and the Temple of Doom, Indiana Jones in Revenge of the Ancients, Indiana Jones and the Last Crusade (The Action Game and The Graphic Adventure), *Indiana Jones' Greatest Adventures, Indiana Jones and the Fate of Atlantis, Indiana Jones and the Iron Phoenix* (canceled), *Indiana Jones and his Desktop Adventures, Indiana Jones and the Infernal Machine, Indiana Jones and the Emperor's Tomb, Indiana Jones and the Staff of Kings, Indiana Jones Adventure World.*

Players play as Indiana Jones (who happens to be an archaeologist) as he fights his way into tombs and temples in search of artifacts.

Lego Indiana Jones (series, Lucas Arts, 2008 and 2009)

Lego Indiana Jones: The Original Adventures, Lego Indiana Jones 2: The Adventure Continues

As above, players play as Indiana Jones (but can swap to other characters from the films as they play). Again, the character is less of an archaeologist than an adventurer, with the player using a bullwhip and pistol more often than a shovel.

NiBiRu: Age of Secrets *(The Adventure Company, 2005)*

From the publisher: "Martin Holan, a linguistics and archaeology student, finds himself enwrapped in a mystery involving Nazis, Mayans, and extraterrestrials. The full game features 20 to 30 hours of gameplay over 80 different locations."

Martin is played from the third-person perspective, is white, and wears a jacket and jeans. *NiBiRu* is one of the few games that feature an archaeologist who specializes in something, in this case archaeolinguistics. Typically archaeologists in games are painted with a single stroke, but this game adds a bit of depth, which contributes to the game's mechanic.

Oh Mummy *(Amsoft, 1984)*

From the publisher: "You play an archaeologist, looking for treasure, as archaeologists are wont to do. Sadly, mummies are after you. To find the treasure you walk round all 4 sides of the squares while avoiding the mummies to complete. The Streets of Cairo is the theme tune."

The game is a mix of *Pac-Man* and *Concentration,* with the dungarees-clad, white male archaeologist avoiding mummies while walking around blocks to identify treasure. The lead character could be a clown instead of an archaeologist, and it would not make any difference to the gameplay or narrative. But it makes sense to have an archaeologist looking for artifacts in a haunted pyramid. The narrative drives the choice of character. The treasure-hunting trope is addressed in the looting section of this chapter.

Riddle of the Sphinx II *(Dreamcatcher Interactive, 2004)*

From the publisher: "You're an archaeologist whose colleague has just discovered an ancient scroll bearing ominous warnings that prophesy the end of the world. Discover the secret linking ancient civilizations. From Mayan codices to Stonehenge to Easter Island, from the Lost City of Atlantis to additional chambers under the Sphinx, and the mystery of Devil's Triangle, your discovery will bring you to . . . The Omega Stone."

This game is one of several first-person point-and-click *Myst* clones published for Mac and PC. The player assumes the mantle of archaeologist and attempts to act accordingly during exploration of famous archaeological locations while attempting to solve puzzles. While these games are fun (and often befuddling to play), they do not reflect any archaeology conducted in the real world. If only archaeologists could align notches on a dial in order to gain access to a secret room filled with the rescued papyrus scrolls from the Library of Alexandria.

Sphaira *(UBI Soft, 1989)*

From the publisher: "You are an archaeologist who is looking for a lost civilisation which lies underneath the Atlantic Ocean."

One of UBI Soft's (later Ubisoft) earliest games, this puzzle-plat-former is set off the coast of Peru. It runs in MS-DOS and is in French. Ubisoft would later become one of the largest and most successful game developers of all time, thanks in large part to its *Assassin's Creed* series, which places emphasis on the re-creation of historically accurate play environments.

Tomb Raider *(series, various publishers, sixteen titles as of 2016)*

Tomb Raider, Tomb Raider II, Tomb Raider III, Tomb Raider: The Last Revelation, Tomb Raider Chronicles, Tomb Raider: Curse of the Sword, Tomb Raider: The Prophecy, Tomb Raider: The Angel of Darkness, Tomb Raider: Legend, Tomb Raider: Anniversary, Tomb Raider: Underworld, Lara Croft and the Guardian of Light, Lara Croft and the Temple of Osiris, Rise of the Tomb Raider.

Lara Croft is second only to Indiana Jones as being identified as the world's most famous, recognizable archaeologist, albeit still a work of fiction. She remains almost unique in being a female archaeologist in games where players can actually see the avatar they manipulate. While Indiana Jones is a professor, Lara Croft has chosen to pursue archaeology outside of academia (except in *Rise of the Tomb Raider* where she is a PhD candidate), reflecting a life choice most archaeologists are faced with.

With games such as those in the *Tomb Raider* series and in *Indiana Jones*, it is clear that the archaeologist is never really the classical ideal of the hero. Instead, the hero has the profession of archaeology as an attribute, part of the heroic assemblage that comprises the eponymous character (Holtorf 2011: 56).

Uncharted *(series, Naughty Dog, seven titles as of 2018)*

Uncharted: Drake's Fortune, Uncharted 2: Among Thieves, Uncharted 3: Drake's Deception, Uncharted 4: A Thief's End, Uncharted: Golden Abyss, Uncharted: Fight for Fortune, Uncharted: The Lost Legacy.

Nathan Drake is third on the list of video game "archaeologists" behind Croft and Jones, even though he is a treasure hunter throughout the series, albeit one who finds himself embroiled in historical mysteries. As with the later *Tomb Raider* games, *Uncharted* does provide players with some historical information on the things they find.

Archaeologist NPCs

On occasion, games will include characters identified as archaeologists. These non-player characters (NPCs) exist either to give quests to players or to advance the story, and on very rare occasions they do archaeological things. Three notable games feature archaeologist NPCs, although there are a handful to be found in other games.

World of Warcraft arguably has the most archaeologist NPCs of any game. This includes nearly two dozen archaeology skill trainers (eight to nine per faction) such as Harrison Jones, Doktor Professor Ironpants, Belloc Brightblade, and Otoh Greyhide. The race of Dwarves, characterized by their digging nature, have half a dozen more archaeologist NPCs, including Hollee (the only female archaeologist in the entire game), Grof, Flagongut, Andorran, and Chief Archaeologist Greywhisker. Perhaps the funniest (or saddest) manifestations of archaeologist NPCs in *WoW* are the Dying Archaeologists and Enslaved Archaeologists.

The *Mass Effect* series (and particularly *Mass Effect 3* [BioWare, 2012]) features a major NPC, Liara T'Soni, a female Asari archaeologist who, as part of her backstory, visited the Minoan site of Knossos for her research. She is instrumental in the adventures she shares with the lead character Shepard, and she uses her knowledge of ancient technology frequently.

Bungie's 2014 title *Destiny*, a first-person space shooter, features NPCs known as crypto-archaeologists (shortened to "cryptarchs" in the game; see Figure 2.1). As described to the players in *Destiny* when initiating dialogue with these archaeologists, cryptarchs "decode the past and our enemies, seeking new discoveries in matter engrams and artifacts returned by guardians." In *Destiny*, players often discover rare items that must be decoded in order to use. The cryptarch examines each find, revealing its function to the player who can then choose to use, sell, or destroy it. There is no real interaction between the player and this NPC, only one of commerce and information exchange. The cryptarch serves much the same role as an expert on *Antiques Roadshow*.

With the cryptarch we begin to see ethics and politics creeping in to game archaeology. Artifacts are to be used to understand the enemy

Figure 2.1. Cryptarch in *Destiny* (Bungie, Inc.). Screen capture by author.

(making archaeology political), and they can be sold. The next section will discuss the public perception of archaeology and how those attitudes are reflected in games, followed by a note on looting and auctioning artifacts found in-game.

Public Reception of Archaeology

As has been seen earlier in this chapter, archaeology (or the idea of archaeology) can make for a good video game, especially when it involves adventure, danger, locating items, solving puzzles, and saving the world from ultimate evil (or at least from a misused magical artifacts). That archaeological narrative, the idea that archaeologists are well-traveled, think quickly on their feet, care about the sites they visit and the artifacts they find, and occasionally work as part of a colorful team of misfits, can be true to life for many professionals in the field. The fact that evil and/or magic work their way into the games is another matter, but one could argue that if this ever happened in reality, most archaeologists would be up to the task of defeating it.

Archaeology holds a fascination for non-archaeologists just as it does for archaeologists themselves, and some in the profession were likely drawn to the field because of ideas communicated through media, including video games. We return to Holtorf's consideration of the public's perception of archaeology and why it captures the imagination more than most other professions. Holtorf calls archaeologists the "cowboys of science" because there are the elements of surprise and adventure mixed with professional certainty and reassurance (Holtorf 2011: 57). Archaeologists can handle themselves in a crisis, which includes dealing with either Nazis (in fiction) or crumbling balks (trench walls) (in reality).

Holtorf (2005) distills the public's perceptions of archaeology and archaeologists, describing those perceptions as:

- Archaeology is about searching and finding treasure underground.
- Archaeological fieldwork is about making discoveries under tough conditions in exotic locations.
- The archaeologist is a detective of the past.
- Experiencing archaeological practice and imagining the past constitutes the magic of archaeology.

Video games such as those in the *Tomb Raider* and *Indiana Jones* series continue to exploit and prolong these ideas of what archaeology is. Millions of players engage with these games and conceivably come away with a vague notion of what it means to "do" archaeology. The games (and also the films) perpetuate the "archaeological romance of eerie adventures involving exotic locations, treasure hunts, and fighting for a good cause" (Holtorf 2005: 44). Archaeology is a verb, and interactive entertainment confirms the active voice of the discipline. As discussed in the introduction, archaeologists can either accept that games and archaeology will never quite agree or use games to open a dialogue with developers and players to inform them on what archaeology is and how to integrate it into gameplay. Archaeologists can also decide to make their own games and take complete control of the archaeological narrative and mechanic. It is likely that the most successful tack is to combine all three of the above approaches into one.

Archaeology is perceived as fun by non-archaeologists because of the supposed "wow" factor in discovery and problem solving, typically on a grander scale than what is perceived as amazing by professional archaeologists. Both players and archaeologists get similar feelings from similar completed tasks, but in games the rewards are more immediate and tangible (an achievement or trophy or cash as opposed to a publication or tenure). According to research conducted by Brittain and Clack, the most valued archaeologies appear as those who "hold the key to mysteries unsolved, unravelling the truth behind the oldest, grandest, or most splendid of ancient wonders" (Brittain and Clack 2007: 15). It is human nature to be curious and to explore, to finds things, to learn about the unknown. The fact that archaeologists can do this as a career is viewed as lucky, not just for these kinds of opportunities of discovery but also because it is realized how difficult it is to become an archaeologist. But when it comes to communicating plainly what we do as archaeologists, many of us fail. As Holtorf says, "The problem is not one of a lack of public understanding of science, but increasingly one of a lack of scientific understanding of the public" (Holtorf 2011: 58–59).

Because of this lack of proactive communication by archaeologists to the public about what we do, we abdicate that job to media, specifically television. The single most significant source of information about archaeology (for the time being) is TV (Holtorf 2007a: 52). "[On TV], archaeology is portrayed as a process rather than a set of results. Archaeology is about adventure and discovery, it involves explorations in exotic places (near or far) and it is carried out by digging detectives" (Holtorf 2007a: 45). When archaeology happens on television, Holtorf notes that for many archaeologists, "the key issue in this context appears to be that they feel fundamentally misrepresented regarding the depiction of both the existing knowledge about the past and their own occupation. They would like to change the way archaeology is portrayed" (Holtorf 2007a: 105). The question is how. Every archaeologist will have an opinion on how they would like the field promoted to the public, but they need to be able to explain why.

"Engagement with the mass media has precluded a conglomeration of concerns regarding representation of archaeology and archaeologists, accuracy of information and reportage, the 'dumbing down' of information, individual credibility in one's own discipline, and the legitimization of archaeological narratives as recognized by a mass audience" (Brittain and Clack 2007a: 13). The academic appeal of archaeology to many professionals is, as Holtorf puts it, "not obvious to the rest of the population" (Holtorf 2007a: 140). But is it necessary to communicate the academic side of things? It might be enough to encourage the popular idea of archaeology in order to maintain it as a discipline and continue to secure funding for projects. That social enthusiasm is perhaps the most underutilized asset to the professional archaeologist who can perhaps take that goodwill and convert it into preservation, excavation, publication, and more. Holtorf has observed that the "archaeologist cliché has an impact on self-perception of archaeologist, effecting recruitment, specialization and preference for certain professional activities. The archaeologist remains clearly recognizable in pop culture" (Holtorf 2005: 42).

Graduate students at the University of Leiden's archaeology department comprise the VALUE Project, which is dedicated to studying video game archaeology.[3] In 2015 they conducted a survey of department staff and students (169 total respondents) regarding the portrayal and use of archaeology in games and of archaeological/historical games generally.[4] Their findings included the fact that most players associate "history" with games that are set in the past, and "archaeology" with the profession and with methods. History is something you visit; archaeology is something you do. Roughly half of the respondents (51 percent) found archaeology in games to be quite enjoyable, but they felt neutral about archaeology's actual importance within the games being played.

As we think about how archaeology is perceived in video games, there are three models for relations between science and society:

1. Education: collection and dissemination of data by elites to the public;
2. Public Relations: improve image of science in order to increase social and political support for science;
3. Democratic: participatory with non-scientists to emphasize responsibility and sustainability (Holtorf 2007a: 107).

Do archaeologists want to maintain an us/them binary relationship where archaeological ideas and discoveries are handed down from the site? Probably not. Improving public relations will help, possibly by working to break down the barriers between so-called "elites" and the interested public, which leads to the democratic angle. As we found at the Atari Burial Ground, people wanted to help the archaeologists, not only with sharing information but also in the activity of fieldwork. They wanted to participate. It was the thrill of a lifetime for Tony Johnson to share with me the joystick top he found in the Alamogordo desert, and to do that on camera for the documentary. He contributed in a meaningful way to the dig, added to the narrative of the excavation, and will carry that memory with him for the rest of his life.

Archaeology in video games can capitalize on that kind of emotion. Despite the trope that archaeology is "boring" (it's not, and you can read Colleen Morgan's blog to see why[5]), there is emotion tied to the discipline, not unlike the reason anybody pursues their career of choice: it's interesting, and they love to do what they do. For an excavation or survey, "a simulated participation in scientific practice and the magic of encountering enigmatic objects can provide [site] visitors with very powerful experiences" (Holtorf 2005: 155). This could conceivably translate to video games, where the act of digging, of field walking, of research, of labwork can all be done by the player to move the story along and to create both an intellectual and emotional investment in the game while at the same time making archaeology less mysterious, or less predictable, not only for the public but also for archaeologists themselves. Edward González-Tennant concurs: "Walking simulators successfully engage the public's imagination, and not in shallow ways. The topics, narrative style, and emotional impact of these video games can be harnessed by archaeologists for public education and outreach. Crafting virtual worlds based on historical pasts can similarly engage the public's desire for serious content" (González-Tennant 2016: 28).

While public outreach is one obvious avenue in which to exploit games for archaeology, games can also be used for archaeological research, namely as platforms for experimental archaeology, a "fertile environment for archaeological theory testing, for instance into human interaction with space or exchange networks" (Mol et al. 2016: 14–15). Shawn Graham agrees, noting that archaeologists can use game worlds to "reflect on practice, theory, and the perception of our discipline" (Graham 2016: 18). L. Meghan Dennis adds yet another argument for using games to understand and revise archaeological ethics: "Archaeogaming has the opportunity to look at the mistakes made in the past and to counter the errors of colonialism and ethnocentrism that marked the beginning of archaeological scholarship" (Dennis 2016: 29).

However, in order for archaeologists to contribute meaningfully to game development, "we must dispense of the trope that construes archaeology-as-excavation, that relies on the idea of a past that is buried and hidden" (Yaneva 2013: 121). Archaeology-as-surface-survey and as a process of assembly/reassembly are just as valid and important. But as described earlier, this kind of archaeology does not exist in most video games, at least not yet. The conclusion of the VALUE Project's initial survey led the team to write, "We feel that closer collaborations between game developers and archaeologists are needed if video games and archaeology are to be of greater mutual value" (Mol et al. 2016: 15). If Blizzard Entertainment's *Hearthstone* (2014) is any indication of the state of archaeology in games, however, we still have a long way to go.

Archaeological Reception in *Hearthstone*

John Williams–ish *Indiana Jones*–like music welcomes me to *Hearthstone: League of Explorers,* an "archaeology"-themed expansion to Blizzard Entertainment's wildly popular free-to-play online card game (see Figure 2.2). The promise of archaeology is clear from the first screen:

> Scattered across ancient sites of Azeroth are the pieces of a powerful Titan artifact: the Staff of Origination. Join the League of Explorers to acquire it for the museum, and earn 45 cards unique to this adventure.

The League of Explorers is not unique to *Hearthstone* but is itself part of the lore of its parent game, *World of Warcraft*. The League consists of NPC archaeologists and adventurers who scour Azeroth (the world in *WoW*) for Titan (the original, ancient, and mythical race) artifacts relating to the beginnings of the Dwarves. Archaeological tropes abound in the game, mostly drawn from modern media (e.g., Reno Jackson, an "action archaeologist" who draws inspiration from the movie characters Indiana Jones and Remo Williams). The signal tropes are everywhere, from pith helmets to fedoras, utility vests to khaki trousers.

The reward cards that are earned for future use in the main *Hearthstone* game fetishize these elements, skills, and perceived goals of the archaeologist-adventurer. The Explorer's Hat (a *WoW*-style fedora), the Forgotten Torch, and the Jeweled Scarab are a few examples of these. The goal is to collect all of the reward cards, following the trope that archaeologists are collectors, in order to recover the ultimate prize, the Staff of Origination (modeled after the Staff of Ra from *Raiders of the Lost Ark*), which becomes a trophy and collectible card back (the decorative reverse of cards in a deck). This follows suit with other *World*

Figure 2.2. Opening screen to *Hearthstone* (Blizzard Entertainment). Screen capture by author.

of Warcraft artifacts earned in *WoW* itself: some assembled artifacts are trophies, while others do something useful for the player.

I begin the game in the Temple of Osris (not a typo, but playing on the Egyptian god Osiris), which rewarded me with a loading animation of a dotted arrow of travel made famous by the *Indiana Jones* films. I am then informed by the League's librarian/archivist that Reno Jackson is in trouble and needs my help to retrieve part of the Staff protected by a genii who was trapped in a lamp until Reno rubbed it.

Reno and I are formally introduced as soon as I arrive at the card table, which is itself designed to elicit the emotion of archaeology, or what most players feel when thinking about what archaeology might be: ruined columns, a pickaxe, coins, pottery. And there's Reno, "world renowned archaeologist, explorer, and treasure hunter." Throughout the gameplay, Reno regales me with tales of his exploits, including acquiring the Rod of the Sun, which he says is worth "thousands."

Typical to pop cultural perceptions of the adventure of archaeology, the second third of the Temple of Osris adventure takes me into a vault that contains the holy of holies, which we are here to rob. It's never made explicitly clear why we are actually stealing, other than that we need the artifact. The Egyptian-like lingo and art present throughout the adventure adds realism to an otherwise pretend place, allowing the player to populate the game-space with a bit of Egyptian mythology, adding that extra dimension of lore. But generic archaeological tropes continue to fill that space: a collapsing temple, boulders, pit of spikes, carnivorous insects, a cursed tomb. If games are anything to go by, we dig at our peril.

As the game progresses into the mines of Uldaman, I encounter the ugly face of colonialism featuring the subjugation and ultimate genocide of the Trogg race. To begin this part of the game, I meet the founder of the Explorers' League, Brann Bronzebeard. Predictably dressed in khakis and fedora, Brann has a colonial attitude that recalls a nineteenth-century British explorer encountering "savages" whose purpose (to him anyway) is to bar him from taking their cultural heritage. The level concludes in a boss fight with Archaedas, guardian of the Titans. He perpetuates the myth of the ancient/magic protector of a tomb/vault and uses the archaic term for Titans, "makers." Brann takes a moment to reflect on all of the Titan knowledge he's about to lose by killing the only being around who has this data at the ready.

While the Temple of Osris harkened back to nearly every single stereotype contemporary players have come to expect of archaeologists in games, Uldaman raises the darker side that comes with a colonial approach to archaeology. Granted, one could argue that Brann was only reclaiming what was his by the fact that Dwarven archaeologists had the digging rights and that the Troggs were squatters, but the history is that of the Titans, which belongs to Azeroth as a whole.

The third part of the game amplifies colonialism. We are faced with helping the imperial conqueror if we want to complete the game. Sir Finley Mrrgglton is dressed as the prototypical jungle explorer, complete with pith helmet, khaki shorts, backpack, and machete. He's also wearing a monocle, and when he speaks he uses colonial British English affectations. He is a Murloc. Murlocs are original citizens of Azeroth, a race of amphibious creatures with a distinct language consisting of burbles and gargles, which in this fight are deployed for ridicule by Sir Finley. It's institutional racism: Sir Finley is an "educated" Murloc fighting against the "savages" of his race, willing to kill those "inferior" to him to get what he wants. This is made completely clear after we dispatch the boss. "A shame," Sir Finley says. "With a better upbringing he could have been a decent sort." So far in *Hearthstone* we have encountered the issues of repatriation, colonialism, and racism, all of which are themes of nineteenth- and (many would argue) twentieth-century archaeology. Archaeology can (and has) been used to forward political goals, and here in *Hearthstone* we see it again. It is fun to play of course, to collect those cards. But there is not a little darkness at the heart of the theme.

At the end of the game, I fight a protracted battle with Rafaam, the "Supreme Archaeologist." Rafaam is an archaeologist reclaiming artifacts from those who had taken them. During the fight, Rafaam begins to sack the explorers' Hall for its artifacts. Rafaam states that he will reclaim "just the good things." He continues the nineteenth- and early twentieth-century trope of archaeologist-as-collector, which is in line with the behavior of the other characters in the game. Not unlike other cultural heritage professionals acting to protect their institutions under siege in the real world now, however, the League's members begin to secure the artifacts.

Winning earlier parts of the fight rewards players with two of the Hall's artifacts to keep. This is an example of the earlier real-world practice of "partage," when archaeologists and governments come to an agreement where each party gets to keep a portion of the finds discovered on an excavation. Again we have another example of a hundred-year-old practice from early archaeological culture.

As the final showdown continues, Rafaam brags that he has "collected artifacts from hundreds of worlds," continuing his race's (Ethereal) predisposition for appropriating cultural heritage, but without context. The behavior harkens back to the Nazis of *Raiders of the Lost*

Ark who were tasked to find artifacts of occult use to aid the Third Reich's war effort.

The corruption of Rafaam from archaeologist to thief mirrors those archaeologists who succumb to various pressures to loot their own sites or sell off artifacts (see the next section). While rare, the behavior exists, and it is reflected in this card game. Although there are tropes aplenty throughout *Hearthstone,* the darker aspects of archaeology do appear, largely from the discipline's distant past. Whether these whispers and themes were intended by Blizzard is unknown, but they are eerily prescient when considering the reception of archaeology and of archaeologists past and present.

Looting

It all goes back to *Dungeons and Dragons.* In 1979, Gary Gygax published the first edition of the *Dungeonmaster's Guide,* instructions for people running their friends through modules containing monsters, mayhem, and, of course, treasure. Kill an enemy? Loot the corpse. Someone in the party dies? Loot the corpse. The noun, "loot," and the verb, "to loot," are no strangers to real-world battlefields and warfare, and the lingo carried over easily into fantasy books and then games, both analog and digital.

Although the earliest video games (including 1980's *Adventure* by Atari) had a loot mechanic (walk over an object to add it to inventory) as well as a drop mechanic (a slain enemy drops something of value), the game documentation does not specifically mention looting by name. Even the manuals for 1982's and 1983's *Advanced Dungeons and Dragons* games licensed from TSR by Intellivision are mute on identifying player actions as "looting." This is true even into the early 1990s with *AD&D*-licensed titles such as *Eye of the Beholder.* Even a loot-intensive title such as the original *Diablo* by Blizzard Entertainment (1996) does not use the word "loot" as either a noun or a verb in its official documentation. But the concept of looting—of taking treasure or other forms of portable wealth or of lifting weapons, armor, and magic/practical items—was well into the gaming vernacular by then. So how does this translate into gameplay, and are there real ethical issues at work when considering that some loot is actually classed as an artifact and even has in-game archaeological context?[6]

When I am personally in-game, I am a bad archaeologist. Indiana Jones bad (especially when I am playing him as my Lego alter ego). I do not take notes. I do not measure. I do not photograph. I do not document. Truth be told, I am just into archaeology for the loot. Dig in, dig out. Loot whatever is there, and leave a hole that in many games just fills itself in after a few minutes as if nothing ever happened. But I know what I did. I am guilty in other games, too. I took that piece of Dwemer machinery from an underground city in *Skyrim*. I took that Night Elf artifact from a corpse in *World of Warcraft*. I set those ancient wheels in motion in the dungeon in order to get to that end goal, to finish that quest, to get that experience. And whatever artifacts I cannot use, I sell them at the auction house or even online for either virtual or occasionally real currency. I might as well be starring on a televised episode of *Kalmidor Digger*. As Iggy Pop once wrote, I am using technology, and I am using it to search and destroy, which is a bit like what proper archaeologists do, but at least they keep good notes.

Perhaps treating in-game artifacts as loot helps desensitize gamers to real-world finds and what to do with them ethically. In games, we are often taught to collect and/or sell out of self-interest, or to add to the guild bank. This is not excavation out of enlightened self-interest either. It is plain greed. It is extremely satisfying to be rewarded for a job well done in a game such as *Skyrim* with a Daedric artifact. Who does not want the Mace of Molag Bal that not only drains both the stamina and magicka of the enemy you are fighting but also steals its soul (if you kill it fast enough)? Given the choice, do I equip it (or give it to my minion to carry), drop it on the ground, or stash it in one of my houses in Tamriel? Those are my choices. There is no museum I can go to if I suddenly find myself with a conscience and realize that I have just found a sacred relic of incredible power that also bears huge spiritual meaning for the race or family to which it once belonged. There is no place to turn it in for an equally fabulous, not-looted weapon, piece of armor (or cloth), buff, or the like. Finders keepers. Or I can drop it and watch it fade away.

"It is only a game. There are no ethics in the archaeology of the gaming world." That statement used to be true, but some scholars— most notably L. Meghan Dennis at the University of York's Centre for Digital Heritage—are now actively engaged in understanding issues of cultural heritage in-game and how looting and trade manifest in a game-space. What if there were ethics in the archaeology of the game being played? Dennis writes that "working within a game world is not that different from more traditional archaeological fieldwork. . . . The same issues of ethical practice arise. Those the archaeologist interacts with . . . still have to be considered as a community and treated as actors with agency and rights" (Dennis 2016: 30). This is true when interacting with cultures created in-game, but it is especially resonant when working within a game-space that features other human players and groups. In single-player games, the archaeologist must consider "how she behaves within the narrative and world presented by the game's designers" (Dennis 2016: 30).

What if a player incites a mob of creatures that they have positive reputation (rep) with because they detected you trying to pry loose a sacred gemstone in their hometown? That might make players think twice about trying it. What if by looting, players lose rep with factions? What if players are no longer able to enter towns safely? What if players are forced to pay higher prices for things in the marketplace? Or in the most severe cases, what if players were banned from the auction houses all because they stole an artifact that is too hot to do anything with, or nobody wants to buy it from the player because they don't want that stain on them? So much thought is put into aggro mechanics (player proximity that draws enemies out to attack) and in-game reputation with factions (doing good deeds makes other races friendly to you) that it should not be too difficult to include this kind of quid pro quo for bad archaeology in-world. People might stop digging altogether. They might choose not to level up an archaeology skill. Many players would probably attempt to sneak in and steal these objects, behavior that amoral realms such as those in the *Elder Scrolls* series or in *World of Warcraft* support, just as they support leaving things alone. It is up to the player to decide. But there should be consequences. And not all of those consequences should be bad for the player.

What if the player recovered a stolen artifact and returned it to the race or village from whom/where it was stolen? What if the player found something of great importance to the lore of the world and turned it in to a museum curator (much like the find-and-return-lost-books-to-the-library repeatable quests at the College of Winterhold in *Skyrim*)? What if players did this for things they found that were completely unrelated to quests in their diaries/logs? Would players do it? What would the rewards be? Skill points maybe. Improved rep perhaps. An unlocked quest chain.

In some online games (mostly combat games, but even *No Man's Sky* with its grenades and terrain manipulator tool), real-time physics can destroy buildings and landscapes. Imagine what would happen if a *Call of Duty* title pits a squad against Taliban fighters where a museum or UNESCO World Heritage Site is in the line of fire. Do players protect it? Does it become collateral damage? And what are the repercussions in the game if this is part of the story, or do players earn an achievement/trophy by preserving a cultural heritage site, monument, or museum?

In a game, especially one within a massive environment, players are always trapped in an endless cycle of rewards (or punishments). It is black and white. This applies to archaeology in these games, too. Using archaeology in a game to solve a puzzle leads to a prize, or poisoning, or something else. But how many players will "do archaeology" in a game just because? Who will pay sixty dollars on a game just to catalog ruins, collect books, and look for artifacts to draw (or take screengrabs of) and record? I would argue that whenever archaeology is explicitly included in a game, it is there to (1) give players loot (or the ability to trade loot in for something else of equal value), and (2) to advance the story. To AAA game developers and players, this model is a universal. Archaeology equates to either treasure or knowledge.

I would argue, too, though, that players can opt to ignore both of those predefined archaeological outcomes and instead explore and document worlds and their lore just because it can be fun. It is certainly interesting. Players not only are exploring whatever happened to a vanished race but they also are paying attention to how the game architects approached that culture, lore, and material remains. In a way, players are asking questions of the gods of the game, those on the outside looking in, asking those universal "why" questions and, more often than not, receiving no answers. Chapter 4 explores these concepts in more detail.

The next time a player logs on to an MMO they love (or when they play *Elder Scrolls Online* for the first time), they should stop treating archaeology as something that has an objective and instead take a fresh look at those ruins and think about why they are there, who put them there, for what purpose, and what informed their design. Are they ruined just to be ruined, or did a great dragon arise from below the surface to fracture the world? And if no reasons manifest themselves from these observations, question the invisible makers then and wonder what kind of gods would build an imperfect world. Shake that HD fist and begin to doubt that in some games there is no such thing as intelligent design.[7]

Looting and Ethics: *Elder Scrolls Online*

I put in-game looting ethics to the test in *Elder Scrolls Online*. The storied and vast *Elder Scrolls* universe continues to delight and surprise the archaeologist in me, and one day's adventuring led me to the Ayleid ruins of Rulanyil's Fall, a public dungeon in Greenshade offering two heritage-themed quests, both of which seemed to be ripped from the headlines. The Ayleids (wild elves) are a Daedra-worshipping ancient race in the world of Tamriel, and in *Elder Scrolls Online* (*ESO*), these ruins, a prime example of Ayleid architecture, have been repurposed as "Endarwe's Museum of Wonder and Antiquities."

Endarwe, the museum's director, has a problem: the Worm Cult. Think of the cult as ISIS/ISIL/Daesh, but with the power to raise and enslave the dead. Much like what happened in the real world at Palmyra in August 2015, the Worm Cult has engaged in a campaign of looting, destruction, and death.

As the conversation with Endarwe proceeded, I learned the Worm Cult's true purpose, as well as the main attraction of the museum: Warlord Ceyran. The museum serves as a reliquary, preserving the remains of the feared warlord as a revenue maker (think Lenin). If the Worm Cult gets its way, it will raise and enslave the warlord for its own ends.

I also learned a little bit more about Endarwe. He is not just a keeper of the museum but also a collector, historian, and the leader of the Merethic Society. The Merethic Society aggressively collects antiquities, presumably for preservation and display. The note about government intervention with collection resonates with real-world laws such as various memoranda of understanding between governments regarding the trade in antiquities, as well as the 1970 UNESCO Convention outlining rules governments should follow when dealing with antiquities collection and sale. To the Merethic Society, all is fair in collecting, and what is collected goes on display for the public, perhaps not before being laundered first.

The Museum of Wonder and Antiquities was the first official museum I found in *ESO,* and this comes after leveling my character to fifty and punching out every item on every map prior to arriving in Stonefalls. This means that for the citizens (and players) in Tamriel in *ESO*, there is only one public museum to share, and only one focused on Ayleid culture to the exclusion of other races in the game. I found myself wondering if there are other public collections within the world, and I will continue to look for them.

The museum is windowless, lit with ambient light and candles and glowing crystals. There is no signage to be seen and nothing to explain the antiquities on display, not even a QR code. There is a historic sword in a historic fountain. Who owned the sword? What was the fountain's function before this place became a museum? There is no didactic text. There is a horse-art reliquary, but again, it is fun to look at and adds to the feel of the space in the game, but there is nothing more.

Halfway through the museum I stumbled upon a Khajit (race of cat people) named Dulini, one of the few things alive (or undead) in the museum not trying to kill me. He had a quest-giver icon over his head, so we spoke. He thought I was a cultist, which is reasonable seeing as the space is currently overrun with them. Dulini asked me to find four items of historic importance that she hid in advance of the Worm Cult's arrival. One can easily draw a parallel with the occupation of Timbuktu by Ansar Dine and the partial destruction of manuscripts in the archives, partial because of the efforts to secure thousands of other manuscripts by Abdel Kader Haïdara and others. Another parallel is the hiding of antiquities in Palmyra and their defense by senior archaeologist Khaled al-Asaad.

I agreed to help, and the hiding spots were revealed on my map. Dulini dedicated his life to save these artifacts, and I agreed to do the same. Note that this is an optional quest, and also note that the player does not have to turn in the antiquities once recovered, although Dulini is putting his faith in the player to do the right thing.

I set off, still looking for the remains of the warlord Ceyron for my original quest. I quickly came upon the first hiding spot, a vase. Searching the vase revealed an artifact: Compass of the Lost Fleet. I collected it and continued. Around the corner, I approached some suspicious rubble. Digging revealed the Crown of Mansel Sesnit. I collected that artifact, too. Getting closer to the holy of holies, I noticed a loose tile and pried it up. Underneath was the Sword of Aiden Direnni. I took it. Lastly I found the Horn of Borgas stuffed in a bookcase, and placed it in my rucksack. The four artifacts secured, I continued to the chamber holding the body of Ceyron.

The warlord rested face-up on a stone dais with lit candles and two tall candlesticks nearby. He wore a chestplate and "shoulders" as well as a spiky crown. His hands met over his heart. Nothing but bones remained. Further examination awakened a spirit, but not of the Warlord Ceyron. Instead, it was the spirit of a dead archaeologist, Nanwen. Were the bones of Ceyron switched? Stolen?

Nanwen was a hired hand, killed in a cave-in. As with most of the archaeology-themed quests in *ESO*, safety issues are a priority, but they are often absent from excavations. I told him what his body was being used for. As it happens, the museum's keeper was looking for the warlord, but any set of bones would do. This meshes nicely with the trade and promotion of fake relics in the Middle Ages, drawing in crowds while making piles of cash for the owners.

I decided to complete the quest, turning the items in. I received 265 gold for my trouble, about average for this kind of quest in this kind of environment for characters normally leveled to between twenty-five and thirty. I also got the opportunity to learn about the recovered items. Finally there is some history to be had. The Merethic Society follows the bent of nineteenth-century antiquarianism, finding extraordinary pieces for an exquisite collection. "We leave the archaeologists and the Mage Guild to fawn over potshards and jewelry" (see Figure 2.3). The society buys and sells on any market, black or otherwise, but these artifacts recovered for the quest will not be sold, and will be publicly displayed.

I asked about each of the relics. I learn about Borgas and his horn, about Aiden Direnni, Manel Sesnit, and the Lost Fleet. All of this is Elder Scrolls canon, the series of six games being incredibly rich in lore. Finishing this conversation, I made my way back to Endarwe with the ghost of Nanwen in tow. Endarwe, surprised to see us, dressed himself as a Worm Cult member, admitted to his fraud of switching the bones of the warlord with those of his dead archaeologist colleague.

I was used to protect the ruse. Killing the members of the Worm Cult was not done for ideological reasons but a strictly pragmatic one: money. If the hoax was made public, the money would stop coming in. This final reveal in the quest was, for me, breathtaking in its cynicism.

As with the completion of all quests, I was given a cash award as well as a prize. I am offered this as hush money, and Nanwen's Sword is a decent weapon, which I could choose to use, sell, or deconstruct for my blacksmithing skill. I have to complete the quest in order to complete the dungeon on my map, get the achievement, and earn experience. It is a trade-off easily done in the synthetic world. Why? Because in MMOs, the relics always repopulate in their original spaces after a certain period of time has passed.

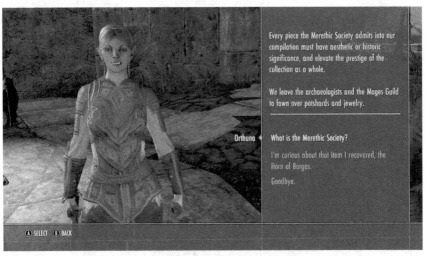

Figure 2.3. Archaeological dialogue in *Elder Scrolls Online* (Zenimax Online). Screen capture by author.

How many adventurers choose not to complete the quest, or choose not to hand in the four artifacts, taking the moral high road even though the Worm Cult was defeated within the walls of a museum it sought to rob and destroy? And what other meaning do players take away from this surprisingly complex duo of quests? For most players, it is grab-and-go, cash-and-carry, quickly on to the next adventure. If we are to consider games such as *ESO* as places to educate players about looting and about conflict antiquities, the space is correct, but player habits often mean that these nuggets of wisdom, these in-game morality plays, get glossed over and dismissed with the press of the "A" or "B" button. Getting players to pause and let something like this sink in is a tall order, but at least *ESO* makes the effort to at least try, more than most of its contemporaries.

Conclusion

Video games, as other media before them, afford the public the chance to play at archaeology as archaeologists. It also offers archaeologists the chance to critique how they themselves are portrayed, and potentially to get involved in the game-making process in order to apply ethics to games and to add more realism to what archaeology is and what archaeologists do. Unlike books, television, and film, however, games allow consumers to actively engage with characters and situations within an imagined archaeological or historical setting, which should require critical thinking from developers and players about what appears onscreen. Archaeologists have the power to address and update media stereotypes, but this will require entertainment companies to meet them halfway in order to begin changing public perception.

The next chapter describes how actual archaeologists can conduct real fieldwork within the games themselves, something that might also help change public perception of what archaeology is and what archaeologists do while encouraging them to help.

Notes

1. Two long lists are available both at the Archaeogaming and Gaming Archaeo websites: https://archaeogaming.com/2014/11/08/you-play-an-archaeolog ist/ and https://docs.google.com/spreadsheets/d/1xf-J_Ao9ZPS__S30TvBS r1v4eOtgOgkJ_zxMpJlxlPQ/edit#gid=0 (retrieved December 8, 2016).
2. Play *Buried* here: http://taracopplestone.co.uk/buried.html.
3. http://www.valueproject.nl/.

4. Read the full article and see the complete results in Mol et al. 2016.

5. C. Morgan, "Stop Saying 'Archaeology Is Actually Boring,'" https://mid dlesavagery.wordpress.com/2014/03/05/stop-saying-archaeology-is-actua lly-boring/ (retrieved December 7, 2016).

6. Archaeologist and ethicist L. Meghan Dennis (University of York) focuses on archaeogaming ethics with an emphasis on archaeological representation and looting. A growing list of her work can be found here: http://york .academia.edu/LMeghanDennis.

7. For a thorough analysis of pre-ruined ruins in video games, see Lowe 2013.

Further Reading

Holtorf, C. 2007a. *Archaeology Is a Brand! The Meaning of Archaeology in Contemporary Popular Culture.* Oxford: Archaeopress.

———. 2007b. "An Archaeological Fashion Show: How Archaeologists Dress and How They Are Portrayed in the Media." In *Archaeology and the Media,* edited by T. Clack and M. Brittain, 69–88. Walnut Creek, CA: Left Coast Press.

———. 2012. "Popular Culture, Portrayal of Archaeology: Archaeology on Screen." In *The Oxford Companion to Archaeology,* 650–51. Oxford: Oxford University Press.

Meyers-Emery, K. and A. Reinhard. "Trading Shovels for Controllers: A Brief Exploration of the Portrayal of Archaeology in Video Games." *Public Archaeology* 14(2): 137–49.

Chapter 3

Video Games as Archaeological Sites

How Is a Video Game an Archaeological Site?

Video games are both artifacts and sites. It is perhaps clear to see how a video game can be an artifact; one needs only to recall the 2014 excavation of the Atari Burial Ground in Alamogordo, New Mexico, where more than thirteen hundred Atari cartridges from the early 1980s were removed from a landfill containing an assemblage of over eight hundred thousand games (see chapter 1). Understanding video games as sites is a bit more complicated. A video game is a built environment (albeit digital), something made by people for other people to use—and in some cases "inhabit" if the game is complex enough to hold one's attention for months or even years.

A video game is also an archaeological site. At the superficial level of any game set within an imagined landscape, one can observe the art and architecture placed there by a team of developers and artists. In games such as *World of Warcraft* (*WoW*), there are actual sites and examples of invented "ancient" heritage within the game: runes and ruins, ready-made material culture, and ancient artifacts to find. When one ceases to be amazed by the attention to the visual (and audio) detail in games, one can perceive the game, all of its content (material culture), and its community of players as being appropriate for archaeological study, regardless of whether or not a game contains depictions of architecture in it.

In order to better understand how a video game is an archaeological site, we first need to learn what defines a site in the real world. In meatspace an archaeological site is a place in which evidence of past activity is preserved, which may be investigated using the methods of archaeology, and represents part of the archaeological record (the body of physical evidence about the past).

When dealing with the concept of sites, one needs to address the more general concept of the archaeological record, which can generally be defined as "the entirety of past cultural materials that have survived into the present day, but which are no longer actively engaged in a living behavioral system" (LaMotta 2012: 70). The archaeological record is formed over time and can change based on human (or another agent's) interaction with the material in the record.[1]

Vince LaMotta outlines four basic ways in which the archaeological record can become inscribed by traces of a particular activity: (1) conjoined elements of an activity are abandoned; (2) conjoined elements could be removed from one place and entered into the archaeological record someplace else; (3) waste, byproducts, and breakage; (4) modifications (LaMotta 2012: 75, 79). Several conjoined elements compose an archaeological assemblage, which can either comprise all or part of a site. The archaeological record is written in a number of ways: when the site is abandoned, moved from one place to the next, destroyed, or changed in some way, caused by any number of internal and external factors. The causation can happen via mechanical/natural changes wrought upon materials that ultimately provide us with recoverable residues (i.e., artifacts), leaving archaeologists with these artifacts to explain why people once acted to create different material realities (Barrett 2012: 146). The things we make are made for a reason, and they are also changed for a reason (although those reasons can be difficult to tease out; we cannot know for sure what was in the minds of makers and users). Archaeological sites are populated by material remains, which can be grouped together into data sets and interpreted.

LaMotta's definition of the archaeological record is a limited one, however, because (1) it restricts archaeology to sites that are no longer used, and (2) it does not account for the fluidity of time or of potential identification and uses of archaeological sites by contemporary archaeologists. Cornelius Holtorf's more liberal interpretation acknowledges that the meanings of archaeological sites and artifacts always change and cannot be fixed to a particular locus in time or space. Archaeological sites mean very different things to different people, and these meanings are equally important (Holtorf 2005). These meanings also include those emerging from the sociocultural and political baggage within the archaeologist conducting research, or of the many voices (multi-vocality) of the site's occupants past and present, something Ian Hodder defines as "reflexive methodology" (Hodder 2005). This anti-prescriptivist approach allows us to treat the recent past and even the present as archaeological, that the past and present constantly commingle, voiced by thousands of people past and present. The library I use now was built twenty years ago, and while its primary function has remained unchanged (to provide free access to people to use its resources), the resources have changed (internet access, borrowing digital media, an entire section dedicated to Japanese comic books [manga]). The space is older, but it is also revitalized. The same can be said of video games as they are patched and modified (modded) over time to meet the needs of both old and new audiences. Archaeologists should be able to recognize and describe the modes of existence of various objects and account for the numerous connections that flow out of these streams of experience, investigating the making of objects in contemporary societies (Yaneva 2013: 131).

When we deal with the digital, the conceptual approaches and concerns involved are the same as when dealing with real-world sites. Everything tends toward a state of entropy, which is why the archaeological record is both incomplete and difficult to define. While natural/mechanical processes constantly work to erase/change the archaeological past, similar processes occur within digital media, which are by their nature degenerative, forgetful, and erasable (Chun 2011: 192). Digital media are stored (or have storage), not unlike the Earth itself (planet-sized storage). Archaeological data are locked in structures and in assemblages both underground and aboveground, just as digital data are stored. In both cases, data are gradually lost, the methods of storage imperfect. But there is also memory (an intangible archaeology), something to be interpreted when the real or virtual site is explored. Storage is finite; memory is boundless (Chun 2011: 195). There is no difference between the archaeology of the digital and the non-digital. The concepts of formation processes of the archaeological record and the methodological approaches to them are the same. Sites, like artifacts, have a history of use that continues from their origin into the present day. Sites are never not used, although they may exist in stasis until (re)discovery.

The above definitions of what makes up an archaeological site—which is part of the archaeological record and is affected by formation processes—apply to video games. I propose the following points in an attempt to further define and defend video games as archaeological sites:

1. A video game is a discrete entity where the place can be defined as the space in which the game is installed (not necessarily its installation media). The past activity is the coding that created the game. Its elements can be directly observed and manipulated, part of the record of the game.
2. Video game installation media (e.g., a tape, cartridge, or disk) is not only an artifact but also an archaeological site. Just as with real-

world sites, installation media is bounded within the confines of the physical space containing smaller entities that comprise the media, adding a level of cohesiveness to all of the digital parts that make up the overarching game. These directories, files, structures/hierarchies are all themselves discrete entities, but they combine to create a unified whole, just as a site is defined by its boundaries and the sum of its parts. The game media were created by one or more people for others to inhabit, generating a culture around those players who choose to inhabit the space of the game (e.g., the community of players in the original *MUD* in 1978). The game media become part of the archaeological record upon production and leave behind evidence in the form of material remains as well as a documented history of occupation by both developers and players.

3. The game-as-played, which is accessed via installed digital media, is also an archaeological site. The game-as-played is its own world in which one or more players interact, and which contains its own digital artifacts, either created via errors in code or created as artificial constructs to be perceived by players as actual representations of real-world things that can be manipulated in game-space. Past activity includes, at the extra-game level, updates, patches, bug fixes, mods, and expansions. At the in-game level, past activity includes the actions of one or more avatars and their effects on the game-space, whether it be moving in-game items from one place to another or the destruction or construction of something semi-permanent in the virtual world.

Archaeologists can explore these game-sites on the surface (analyzing the game media), from within (via file systems and structures), and through play (by interacting with the game-space as created by the developers). The games preserve evidence of past activity, from production to use to disposal, from installation to use to deletion, from beginning to gameplay to the final boss. The amount and nature of preserved evidence varies from game to game, as it does with real-world sites. Sometimes what remains is data rich, and other times one is left with only a trace of fleeting occupation.

One of my criteria to define a traditional archaeological site is that it can be assigned GPS coordinates. A site is a physical space of occupation, however temporary, for some purpose: a camp, a settlement, a building's footprint. But can archaeological sites exist without a specific, immutable location? In the real world, there are a handful of examples. There are sites, which have been recorded in literature (e.g., Herodotus) that might have existed at one point in time but have yet to be found. One example of moving sites with relative locations (one must identify features in relation to the moving site's boundaries) include those that are trapped in glaciers or icebergs and sites such as the so-called "Great Pacific Garbage Patch"[2] that are big enough to see and document yet have no fixed position.

With synthetic worlds, there are a number of ways to document the locations of archaeological sites on both levels: the in-game and the extra-game. In-game, some games contain their own location systems (e.g., *Tomb Raider: Definitive Edition* 2014) where players can record X-Y coordinates on a Cartesian grid. With games featuring maps, depending on the hardware used to play the game, one can take a screenshot and then apply a regular grid over the top of it as a layer using image software (e.g., Photoshop). Other mapless games still allow for the assignment of in-game locations via textual descriptors (e.g., level name and a description of the player's surroundings); these lack pinpoint exactness, reading more like an explorer's journal entry. The usefulness of these qualitative notes becomes less clear when dealing with games comprised of vast regions to explore. But if Heinrich Schliemann could find the ancient city of Troy by way of reading the *Iliad,* then perhaps there is hope than an intrepid player could do the same based on observation, reading literature provided in-game and online, and a little luck.

Considering the loci of the physical sites of the games themselves, this could be an IP address of a game server, server farm, or local client hardware. These boxes or arrays occupy physical space and could be considered as "meta sites," the plastic-and-metal wrappers containing the game-site. Games might also be located by knowing the whereabouts of the development computer(s) or possibly the master media onto which the game's design was saved. With these game-sites come a stratigraphy of build numbers and versions, sometimes stacking on top of each other, other times replacing the code that came before—not unlike the levels of the ancient city of Troy—or using *spolia* to create new monuments and cities from the old.[3]

Just as light is both a particle and a wave, digital games are both archaeological sites and artifacts too, through no great leap in logic. A game is a place. It is also a thing. One could consider a copy of Atari's *Indiana Jones* (1982) to be a portable antiquity: a physical example of material culture that can be (and in this case intended to be) moved from place to place by people. Coins, statuettes, pots, tools are all examples of portable antiquities. As was shown in chapter 1, cartridges (and other media) are now portable antiquities, too.

The game-artifact as it existed in the past (and still does, but to a lesser extent with direct downloads taking over the market[4]) was created by at least one person, but with the help of machines, resulting in a distributed thing, sometimes with market value, that contains within its production a history of creation, possible inscription, and has a find-spot (or more than one findspot as its biography grows). The artifact of the game provides the heart (sometimes still beating) of the game-space as well as metadata, its developer-created information, a mobile inscription, a container of text-and-image. The cartridge or disk is a vessel with the wine, the stone upon which the writing was carved containing the deeper meaning born of words and syntax. It is the physical manifestation of code wrapped in layers of instructions that created the portable package, a world in itself containing a world within. Games that exist independent of physical media, accessible only through hardware connected to a network or to the internet, are digital artifacts lacking in materiality, yet they behave in the same way as their physical counterparts: the copy of *Uncharted 4* I downloaded plays exactly the same as the copy purchased at a brick-and-mortar retailer.

The final question to consider is, "When may we call what we are looking at a site?" In the real world, the archaeologist can determine the boundaries of a site through investigation of the material remains, whether a fixed border of a wall, for example, or the petering out of a distribution of flakes left behind from tool production. The archaeological record gradually transitions from site to other like the layers of the atmosphere transitioning from the Earth to space. As archaeological sites are composed of the remains of human occupation, the archaeologist must consider those things left behind to create a provisional history of the site, or at the very least a definition of the site itself.

When dealing with digital media, archaeologists such as Gabe Moshenska (Moshenska 2014), Colleen Morgan, and Sara Perry (Perry and Morgan 2015) have explored USB sticks and hard drives as archaeological sites. These containers hold a file structure composed of directories, subdirectories, and files that when taken separately are themselves artifacts. Taken together, they compose an archaeological site.

Games are no different. For older PC games, one could browse the installation directory and gradually tease out the files and contents of those files that when used together generated the game-space onscreen. As installation media has grown in sophistication, those files and their contents have become obfuscated, but all of the elements used to create the game for the player remain. These games are sites composed of artifacts working together, an electrified society of automatons.

But each game is also an artifact composed of digitally moving parts. An artifact such as the Antikythera mechanism, the world's oldest known computer dating to around the second century BCE, contains gears, springs, rods.[5] When found in the machine, they are not themselves artifacts but are part of the artifact. When found apart from the context of the machine, these gears and springs are individual artifacts that might one day be reunited with other pieces to recreate a larger object. So it is with games: they are made from files that are not separate from the game itself (when the game is studied) but are taken as part of the game-artifact, a part of the whole. Other archaeogaming investigations might, however, focus on legacy files and snippets of code from an abandoned game, perhaps ultimately finding a way to determine the nature of what had been (or what was being) designed prior to abandonment.

In traditional archaeology, one cannot pick up a site and move it. For the game archaeologist, all sites are portable, as are the artifacts they contain. Both have multiple moving parts that all contribute to the meaning of the site they comprise. The artifacts form a network created by culture. In the case of a video game's history, its creation originates from pop culture, industry trends, and the design spec (Therrien 2012: 21). The game-site is constructed, then reconstructed, always in a state of modification. The networked pieces contribute to an emergence of a broader meaning and the creation of an interactive environment. As with any archaeological site, real or virtual, the site is a system, a network, that the archaeologist can attempt to break down into its constituent interacting agents, from whose behaviors and interactions various systems-level properties may emerge (Kohler 2012: 108). This is the definition of agent-based modeling. Pieces of the whole work together to create an interactive environment, be it the city of Athens or a digital simulation of it.

An archaeological site communicates many things and can be used in several different ways at once. Holtorf describes the uses and appeals of archaeological sites as having monumentality (big/visible = important); factual detail (conformity with educational values); commerce (commercial exploitation of sites); social order (reception that mirrors the present); identities (personal relation to the past); aesthetics (romance and scenery of ruins); reflection; aura; nostalgia; ideology; adventures; magical places; and progress (Holtorf 2005: 92–111). Take a game such as *Assassin's Creed: Unity* as a site, and you will find that all of the above uses apply equally to the synthetic as they do to the natural. In the case of open worlds—games that allow for free movement/play—video games behave even more like their real-world counterparts. In *Eve Online* there are no developer-ordained goals or a traditional endgame. Instead, players band together to create their own goals, annex their own little corner of the universe, form alliances, foster animosities with other groups (Stanton 2015: 300–301), and create their own in-game lore (Stanton 2015: 298–300). There is no difference between the archaeological understanding of a real-world place and a video game. These sites are formed in the same way, grow and change through mechanical, natural, and human intervention, contain the same data, which lends itself to the same questions archaeologists have asked for over a century.

Perhaps most simply put, as stated in the introduction, is that video games are built environments (which can also be classed as archaeological sites). Archaeologists understand built environments to be constructed by people for people, creating a manufactured space for everyday living, working, and recreation. For many people (including myself), that includes video games—digital built environments—especially in the case of MMOs and open worlds. I give these digital spaces hundreds (sometimes thousands) of hours of my time, spend my real-world money to inhabit these environments, and build my own social networks within them (e.g., my "Carpe Praedam" *World of Warcraft* guild).[6] Some people even make a real-world living through their in-game interactions and activities (professional community managers and professional eSports players come immediately to mind). These games have become the sites for a new archaeology, one that simultaneously embraces the real with the virtual.

Landscape Archaeology in Video Games

During a spectacular flyover above the southern tip of Greenland, I looked down and instantly saw small ice floes, rocky beaches, extinct volcanoes, blue-green lakes, and glaciers. There was no evidence of humanity, at least in that small part I could see of the country (population approximately fifty-six thousand). I wondered where people might live, where they might fish, hunt, build a place to live. I also thought about where they might shop, where they might work, and scanned for clues far below.

I feel similarly when I play *No Man's Sky* or other games where I can cruise over the landscape in a ship or on a mount, watching it unfold as I make decisions on where to land based on the quests/missions that I have. It's landscape archaeology even though it's in a synthetic world, and to conduct a project within a synthetic world one must follow an established method (before ground-truthing requires on-the fly modifications). Any landscape archaeologist must create a research plan, must then select an appropriate site in which to do the work, and then conduct a variety of activities ranging from aerial reconnaissance to remote sensing, shovel tests, field-walking, finds analysis, and more.

In order to better understand how landscape archaeology works in synthetic worlds (largely digital games, but this can be applied to all digital built environments), we need to understand the definition of a landscape and the varieties of landscape archaeologies, all of which shift neatly between the natural and the synthetic. Synthetic worlds are designed, the creators and their blueprints/code known. For the digital landscape archaeologist then, we can explore these spaces asking exactly the same questions as our natural-world counterparts. I'm willing to bet that what we find will not be that dissimilar.

In the preface to 2008's *Handbook of Landscape Archaeology*, editors Bruno David and Julian Thomas identify three broad themes of landscape archaeology (David and Thomas 2008a: 20):

1. Landscapes are *fields of human engagement* as in Heidegger's notion of dwelling. These include both explorations on conceptual *ways of approaching* and experiences of landscapes as fields of engagement, as the "in" of "being-in-the-world";
2. Landscapes are *physical environmental contexts* of human behavior (such as investigations of the tree cover or topography of the environments);
3. *Representations* of landscapes, such as in landscape art, or the identification of colonial tropes in landscape analysis of textual preconceptions, should be reflected upon.

Both natural and synthetic landscapes share these three themes: (1) for synthetic worlds, players are very much "in-the-world," completely engaged with their surroundings as they explore and play; (2) synthetic worlds do provide physical environmental contexts, which can include understanding vegetation and topography that can (and often do) dictate player behavior; and (3) synthetic worlds very much provide representations of landscapes, typically created by one or more designers based on how they conceive of landscapes, as well as how landscapes advance narrative or drive player behavior.

When we engage with synthetic worlds, we occupy a place within a place within a place, inhabiting multiple landscapes at the same time. We sit in the natural world before engaging with the synthetic. And once inside the synthetic landscape, we visit multitudes of places dotting our field of vision and beyond. The landscape beckons us in and affords us new frontiers.

Landscape archaeology seems to be preoccupied with human presence and engagement within the spaces they occupy over time (David and Thomas 2008b: 38). It doesn't matter if that space is natural or synthetic. Synthetic worlds have nearly infinite space with which players can engage, creating lived-in environments where players can spend more time than in the natural world. Players inhabit these spaces, invest time, money, and resources, and create their own culture side by side with any synthetic culture pre-built by developers and/or algorithms. Some synthetic worlds (e.g., *Minecraft* and *No Man's Sky*) offer players the chance to manipulate the landscape themselves for whatever reason, be it for entertainment or for something more practical. Create a real or synthetic garden. Dig a hole to see where it goes and what resources might lie beneath your feet.

Every landscape (natural or synthetic) can contain material remains and networks connecting agents, materials, and places. A goal of the landscape archaeologist is to connect the two (Heilen, Schiffer, and Reid 2008: 605). While this can be easy in designed games (synthetic worlds where everything has been crafted by the software developer), it becomes increasingly more difficult (and arguably more "real") in worlds where everything is procedurally generated. This is especially true when algorithms are entrusted with the task of building a world and populating it with things for the archaeologist to discover. This placement is almost random, but it bears some logic based on the landscapes discoverable within the synthetic world. The landscape shows the archaeologist where to look.

A landscape, either natural or synthetic, can be interpreted in any number of ways. A synthetic world's designers interpret their digital built environments from the perspective of narrative, player engagement, and aesthetics. From the player's perspective, the landscape exists as something to explore, as something to be traversed, and as a provider of materials for quests and recipes. In the natural world, one must also consider the landscape from the indigenous perspective(s), understanding how the landscape is a permanent resident, a host of memories, and perhaps a space of spiritual resonance (Strong 2008: 54). How do nonhuman denizens of synthetic worlds "perceive" their landscapes? For now, automatons unquestioningly operate within the constraints of a world's rules. They "see" the landscape through software instructions. They engage with that space based on parameters, acting when acted upon. It's little different than a human commuter in a rut.

Inhabiting synthetic landscapes can, over time, create a material record of that occupation through in-world crafting and building, through rubbish, but also through documentation of what came before. Players record and photograph their creations, share them, save them. It's a rich record of space and time that the natural world will never see. It is perhaps easier to illustrate synthetic landscapes because they can be recorded during exploration and can even "instanced" for exploration by others on their own hardware; this is helpful if one wishes to have results independently confirmed by others, something not normally possible in field archaeology, which can be a destructive process leaving only data but not the primary source(s) of that data (i.e., strata).

Speaking of visualization, how does the player-archaeologist map the landscape of a given synthetic world? Some games come with built-in maps, while others tease out their mapping only through a player's progress. Other synthetic worlds have no maps at all, so players may either hand-draw their explorations or rely on memory, the latter of which most nonhuman entities do. In many games, players rarely see their world from above, but frequently at eye level. We remember how to get from one part of the forest to another through experience, or from following something, curious to see where it goes. We create a mental map, which is visual, at times aural, occasionally punctuated with memories of events that happen along the trail or traverse (see Hill 2008: 99 for research on primates and how they map their environment). We learn the game's rules for wayfinding in the synthetic wilderness and then lead others to what we've seen, or we write about it so others can follow in our footsteps. Some of these writings are literally called "walkthroughs." With an active player community (or a preserved collective memory), we also have what can equate to "tavern archaeology" in the natural world. Yannis Lolos wrote about this in *Land of Sikyon,* about approaching local Greeks in taverns and other gathering spots to share a drink and listen to stories (Lolos 2011: 6). At times these stories would provide clues to where to look for previously undocumented archaeological sites, which were then compiled into a gazetteer for future archaeologists to use as they continue to understand the history of Sikyonia. Video game archaeologists should do well to spend time with player communities on reddit and elsewhere for the same reasons as Lolos. We can learn from indigenous populations, can work together with them, and can share what we find with them.

When an archaeologist explores the landscapes within a synthetic world, they notice both presence and absence in the archaeological record (Darvill 2008: 69). The archaeologist applies filters, scanning for vegetation, animal life, water, and other topographical features, as well as evidence of current or past use and occupation. One landscape flows into the next, synthetic biomes bleeding into each other. The archaeologist looks for boundaries, for patterns, whether confronting the landscape head-on or floating above it in a flying vehicle or in a dis-embodied "photo mode" provided by the game. The archaeologist can ask why some spaces are neglected and others used, and if used, how frequently and why. It is a search for an underlying algorithm or a set of landscape behaviors as designed. In most synthetic worlds, landscapes are very much characters and have their own rules on how to act, which include weather-making and resource-production. Landscapes in synthetic worlds have personalities, or at least that is how players perceive the spaces in which they occupy.

There is a haptic necessity to understanding landscapes. In order to write about landscape in an archaeological way, it must be experienced firsthand by the archaeologist.[7] What applies in the natural world is also applicable in the synthetic. Christopher Tilley articulates this in "Phenomenological Approaches to Landscape Archaeology" (Tilley 2008: 274). The more we experience a landscape in person, the more we understand its rules, which include formation processes and use by both human and nonhuman actors.

In "Object Fragmentation and Past Landscapes," John Chapman writes that "landscapes consist of a network of places, some natural, some culturally constituted, some created by human manipulation of the landscape. It is this network of places that gives human lives their meaning, through an identification of past activities and present embodiment" (Chapman 2008: 188). This also describes synthetic landscapes and the networks that run atop them: some created by human manipulation (players create networks through their own agency in a synthetic world), some culturally constituted (these networks are created in advance and by design prior to player arrival), and some natural (emergent behavior independent of player or designer agency).

So what's in a landscape then that immediately grabs the archaeologist's eye? Architecture is a start, and is one of the things most easily recognizable in synthetic worlds (McFadyen 2008: 307). Players expect architecture, and most games deliver. As part of the synthetic landscape, architecture behaves in the same way as its natural counterpart: it is recognizable, is used/reused, assists in wayfinding, and contributes to the understanding of a place's present and past. This raises an interesting point regarding determining the age of something in a synthetic world. How do we do this?

Dating landscapes in synthetic worlds varies greatly from those that are natural. This is perhaps the greatest difference between the two. In synthetic worlds, there is no real stratigraphy, and no real superposition of layers of earth, and therefore no way to assign a numerical (quantitative) date based on evidence found within the game-space (Roberts and Jacobs 2008: 347). For most synthetic worlds, there is no geologic time. The spaces just sit there not eroding, unless you count "bit rot," the slow decay of underlying data. The archaeologist is left with software version and build numbers, which are tied to absolute dates in the natural world. But inside the game, landscapes can be made to look old (or to imply age), even though the game itself has only been playable for a few days. Even playing older games results in landscapes that look exactly the same now as they did in 1983. Little, if anything, changes.

Regardless of when they were created/accessed, these synthetic landscapes in games can provide insight into how people (and their things) move from place to place, offering glimpses into what players (or nonhuman agents) carry with them, use, sell, or discard (Summerhayes 2008: 530). In observing in-game habits of players as well as coded entities, especially in games where the landscape can vary (or can be varied), the archaeologist can begin to experiment with agent-based modeling (ABM), making modest (or radical) changes in order to run experiments to see what happens. In some cases, landscapes could be modeled after those in the natural world to assist in answering archaeological questions about earthbound places and the people who used them.

How does an archaeologist conduct landscape archaeology within a synthetic world? It's not terribly different from working in the natural world, as articulated by Thomas Richards in his article "Survey Strategies in Landscape Archaeology": first develop a research question (Richards 2008: 552). Once a research question is developed, a suitable landscape must be selected. Research problems often require a landscape to be representative of a larger area, so the distributional patterns of the surface record and associated human behavioral interpretations can be widely extrapolated. Following the selection of a regional landscape study area, the formation of its present surface characteristics needs to be considered in developing a survey strategy: geomorphology and vegetation (which affect visibility of the ground surface). Try to determine human land-use history, particularly large-scale ground disturbance activities. Determine the intensity and coverage of your initial survey. Decide on the scale of the survey and what (and how much) to sample. Decide on whether or not to conduct remote sensing or invasive subsurface testing. How will you record this data? Will there be follow-up surveys allowing for more detailed collection and analysis? At the survey's conclusion, can you develop any kind of predictive model for where one might find other artifacts or settlements?

The survey and research plan points are applicable to the archaeological investigation of synthetic worlds. Any archeological fieldwork much be driven by research questions and a plan on how to answer those questions. For my online archaeological survey, I needed to find a site that extensively used procedural content generation, which would perhaps exhibit evidence of "machine-created culture," material remains created and organized by algorithms that would populate a synthetic landscape. *No Man's Sky* seemed to be the best fit for this need. I wanted to check distribution of sites and artifacts, to see how buildings and landscapes interacted, to look at animals and vegetation and their relationship to the landscape and these structures, and to see how these manifested in the nearly infinite worlds that could be explored. Barring a multiplayer option (which would materialize in a basic way one year after the game's initial release), I had to conduct my surveys as a lone fieldwalker and as a lone pilot. I used different levels of granularity in my surveys, less detail when flying (counting structures and times between them), and more detail when on the ground (noting artifacts, brush density). Future surveys can be undertaken in synthetic worlds that actively encourage guilds (groups of players) to survey together in the same landscape on the same server. This will also allow for specialization. Depending on the synthetic world, we can sample and "shovel test."

I mentioned noninvasive survey techniques above. Paul Cheetham covers this for natural worlds in "Noninvasive Subsurface Mapping Techniques, Satellite and Aerial Imagery in Landscape Archaeology" (Cheetham 2008: 564). Prior to starting a noninvasive survey, consider survey objectives, archaeological questions, previously remotely sensed evidence and results, current land use, former land use, underlying solid and drift geology, other local geomorphological and topographic factors, degree of access to the land, time, money, personnel, and equipment available for the survey.

Depending on how the synthetic world is constructed and what it allows players to do, it can be possible to conduct a variety of remote sensing tasks. For example, in *No Man's Sky* it is possible to orbit planets like a satellite prior to penetrating atmospheric cover for high-altitude overflight, followed by high- or low-speed travel a few meters above the deck, giving the surveyor different kinds of information about what's on the surface of the landscape and if there are any patterns to be observed. Once on the ground with the proper tool equipped, one can conduct a rudimentary form of remote sensing, which produces icons showing players where to dig and occasionally revealing underground caverns and other geologic formations. Each synthetic world has its own rules of engagement, which must be followed by players in order to successfully survey these landscapes. Depending on the hardware and platform used to host these worlds, however, it may be possible to create modifications (mods) of tools and other equipment, which allows for bending the rules of a world in order to conduct aerial imagery or remote sensing. This raises ethical questions about whether modifying a world affects how archaeologists see the world, and how nonhuman agents operate within that world once it has been changed from its original state. Mods inject an additional level of complexity into a synthetic world, which might have unexpected/unintended results. At the same time, however, the archaeologist might be able to create a more useful digital toolkit for exploring these digital built environments instead of relying on more traditional methods that might not be the best suited for the task. To mod or not to mod recalls the decision to dig or not to dig, to use an invasive approach on the landscape in order to retrieve information about it.

When one thinks about landscapes in games, one typically considers those that contain mountains, trees, lakes, and similar things anyone would consider to be part of a natural landscape such as the ones featured in *Elder Scrolls, Dragon Age, World of Warcraft.* I propose, though, that in order to have a landscape archaeology of digital games and other synthetic worlds, the archaeologist must apply definitions and methods to any game or world, not just those that are facsimiles of recognizable natural environments.

Every game is a landscape. There is an architecture of space on the plateau of the screen, which can be measured and engaged with, that utilizes time and location in order to function. Every definition, every principle of landscape archaeology applies to games specifically, and more generally to software—anything with a graphical user interface (GUI). We are working on a micro scale, but it is easy to tell when an application's GUI nudges users down a path of activity, reacts to user agency, offers up artifacts (glitches/bugs), and is the subject of communities and cultures (e.g., Apple v. Microsoft). Most of us belong to at least one digital tribe, and we interact with that software as an indigenous population, as developers, or as users who made their pilgrimage late.

One final thought: all of the above about conducting landscape archaeology (or archaeology of any kind) within a synthetic world might sound daft, especially when we know that these are all designed environments. Think of these, however, as a proving ground for ideas on method and theory, testing on software we know that is well documented in anticipation of digital spaces that create new environments on their own. I predict that by 2020 we will finally see video games set in completely procedurally generated worlds where the cultures that players encounter have never been considered by the game's designer(s), instead created from a complex set of rules that, when mixed together, create emergent cultures distinct from one another. We are already getting glimpses of these "machine-created cultures" (MCCs) in games such as Mark Johnson's *Ultima Ratio Regum,* and more are coming. One day we will have a Turing test for cultures to determine what is real. How will we determine that level of reality, and if a new, born-digital culture thrives, what obligations do we have to interacting with it and, ultimately, to preserving it?

Dwelling in Synthetic Worlds and Landscapes

Most of us do not live in isolation but instead reside in towns and cities, which we expect to last forever—or at least as long as we live. We expect our needs to be met through city infrastructure, that there is clean water when we need it, public safety, maintained roads, groomed parks, open space. We pay taxes and bills to keep the towns running, to keep the (street)lights on.

Most of us live in apartments, houses, duplexes, condos, dormitories, flats. These are personal spaces for us, and we expect them to give shelter (if not comfort) for as long as we need it. Because we look after our own needs and the needs of our families first, our residences must be permanent, but only so far as we need them. If I live in a house for ten years and then get offered a job in a different city, my house need only be permanent for me until the day I depart. Afterward, I don't care what happens to it. It has served my needs for the time when I was there.

We need cities to be permanent for us, too, or to at least provide the illusion of permanence during the course of our residence. We need to assume that everything will be the same each day when we rise and go to work or school and, if something needs to be repaired, that the city will maintain or improve upon things to continue the illusion of permanence. The status quo is comforting to the stable population.

To borrow from the work of Martin Heidegger, we build and dwell in the landscape. "Building" to Heidegger meant interacting with a landscape, interacting with structures, using natural resources. Building creates landscape by defining locations and spaces within it relative to human interaction.

As Heidegger wrote in 1978, "dwelling" represents how we occupy and experience a landscape. Building creates the landscape around us through our dwelling; and in turn the experience of this landscape modulates the form of our dwelling within it. Our dwelling determines the form our building takes and by extension how the landscape is created. James Robinson wrote in his archaeology MA dissertation for the University of York, *Being and the Past,* "Dwelling (the created ideological construct of consciousness) is encoded throughout the past manifestations of Building: the material record. Therefore the ideological constructs driving and created by Building are accessible through its study." We ask the question of the past: "*Who* or what is it that Builds and Dwells?"

When we think about towns and cities and the spaces there in which we live, we bias our thoughts about permanence, the people and things that are always there. We often fail to perceive how these permanent spaces appear to the temporary visitor just passing through, maybe stopping for a time, but ultimately moving on to another destination. We fail to consider fully how a migratory population builds and dwells for a short time within a permanent space. For this group of "transhumans," nothing is permanent, and these spaces and locations become commodities to use and leave behind. Hotels are a perfect example of this, buildings with a temporary population that always changes, supported by permanent staff who keep the building in working order to support the infinite migration of families and businesspeople. This shared environment is built to serve two populations who build and dwell within it differently. For one population, the hotel is a source of employment and income. For the other, it is a place to sleep, bathe, eat, and recreate. People know about the general idea—the phenomenon—of "hotel" and what that space means. For most of the population, we visit, we use, we leave. Over time, the hotel might be sold. The building might be converted into another kind of space, or it might be destroyed so that the land underneath it can be reused. The building is semipermanent, constructed over a permanent landscape.

How then can the concepts of Building and Dwelling be applied to built digital environments, specifically video games? I have proposed that video games are archaeological sites and that landscape archaeology can be used to explore and understand them. I propose now that all video games are created as semipermanent "dreamscapes."

With notably few exceptions, any video game is an imagined space produced to be accessed by a user via hardware, which includes a screen. Through the development process, that game becomes a functional space stored in a box, bounded by rules of engagement, which the user may either follow or manipulate. The ideas from the developer(s) transmit to the mind of the user who can then react to the stimuli of the game. The interactions exist in the mind through the mediation of hardware, technologically enabled dreamscapes where users can dream lucidly through the act of performing operations within a game.

I also propose that all video games from the 1970s until today have always been envisioned as semipermanent. Arcade games were played by the quarter and competed for floor space in malls and on boardwalks. To the user, the game was only as permanent as the bankroll permitted. To the developer, a game was only as permanent as its popularity. With the pace of technology and commercial competition, new games replaced the old, with the exceptions of games that became classics, expected in the spaces of arcades. Games such as *Joust* became permanent monuments within a changing landscape. When we visit Washington, DC, we expect to see the Washington Monument. When we go to the arcade, we expect to see *Pac-Man*.

The same could be said of cartridge/cassette/disk-based games. In the 1970s and early 1980s, these games were designed for relatively quick play based on player skill. It was rare to be able to save your progress. The game existed as a place to inhabit for a few minutes or hours, and then we would change the locality of play by replacing one game with another, or we would place the game on the shelf with the others to await our return, a site or monument to be revisited and engaged with. Games exist to be played. That is their grand purpose, but a purpose driven by human need: to be entertained, challenged. Cities exist to be inhabited, meeting the human need to create and to have shelter and community.

With contemporary games, their complexity and size (size not just from the perspective of landscapes but also for those games that contain infinite levels) lend themselves to a lengthy visit during each encounter. They encourage us to stay. The developers are human, and the better games do an excellent job of winning our discretionary time and money. This is by design, human-to-human. We build what satisfies us, and that which satisfies us will likely satisfy others. Game developers build spaces, which they hope will invite people in and encourage them to stay. To revisit a term from earlier, we are invited by games (and their builders) to "dwell" in these spaces for as long as they exist in their semipermanent state until the next game comes along, encouraging migration.

There are no permanent residents of games. Sooner or later players move from one game to another. At times they return to old favorites, motivated perhaps by nostalgia or through the release of a major update or new content, much like we return to places we love to remember them as they were or to visit new features recently added to the landscape. We dwell within games always with the underlying understanding that we will leave. It is the commercial nature of game development to always make something new. As good as a game might be, all players will leave it to engage with something new. With video games, we are all transhuman, and we experience these places as things we are just passing through. Sometimes we have a brief stay, an overnight in a hotel. Other games encourage an extended stay. But we see new cities built, appearing every Friday, beckoning us to relocate.

With video games, we rarely see mass migration away from them (unless they are universally reviled and players abandon these places at more or less the same time). Instead, we see mass migrations to new games, drawing on the player-populations of old playscapes. The new game is the city on the hill, a shining beacon of promise and opportunity, and players leave whatever it is that they are currently engaged with, where they currently dwell, in order to have a new experience in a new place until they tire and the next new city springs up in a landscape littered with abandoned towns of dwindling populations. It's similar perhaps to people leaving their farms to work in the nearby metropolis. But then these cities get drained of their populations as other cities arise. But unlike brick-and-mortar urban centers, games are designed to be abandoned. We always quit the games we play. That functionality is built in, and we as members of a transient population expect that. We have places we love, but we cannot escape our need for a new narrative and a new place to explore and inhabit.

We very much dwell in synthetic worlds. It is a conscious act for us as players to engage with games like we do with cities. There are things to see and do, based on underlying infrastructure of mechanics and rules. We pay (most of the time) to access these spaces, a kind of engagement tax to continue to play for as long as we like, or for as long as our money lasts. Developers update the infrastructure and hope that players will stay. The more players, the healthier the economy, and the longer the game-city remains vibrant and viable. When people leave, the infrastructure of the digital built environment remains, becoming a shell of what was. Compare this to what happened with Detroit, at one time the destination for culture and industry, now overwhelmed with abandoned buildings and entire neighborhoods.

All things tend toward entropy, and entropy occurs over time driven by casual absence or conscious neglect. While cities manifest entropy in a visual way, we don't necessarily recognize the effects of abandonment on video games. For MMOs that were purpose built to house thousands (or more) players at a time, many of those that have been abandoned can still be revisited. *EverQuest* was launched by Sony Online in 1999, and all development of that MMO ceased in 2010. Players can still access the game, however, returning to see what's changed and to indulge in some nostalgia.[8] These games are ghost towns, but their contents remain buffed, shiny, and welcoming, ignorant of the decline of their own civilizations, waiting for players until modern hardware can no longer run them or until the developer decides to pull the plug on the last public server hosting the game.

Because video games are archaeological sites, they grow and change over real-time. For example, the still-popular MMO *World of Warcraft* continues to evolve with new updates and expansions and is currently in its "Hellenistic" era, perhaps having peaked in its "Classical" period of the "Cataclysm" expansion, which in effect broke the world, forcing players to rediscover familiar landscapes changed by the cataclysmic return of the dragon Deathwing. It is not possible for players to go back in time to revisit previous iterations of the game-world through Blizzard Entertainment's servers, but some players have formed archival teams for preservation and conservation of those earlier times. The most notable of these is the seven-year-old Elysium Project,[9] which maintains a server containing the "vanilla" version of *WoW* from 2004. Anyone can visit this maintained "Archaic" version of the game to actually experience what it was like to navigate the landscape before the creation of mods (modifications), flying mounts, and even entire regions in the world of Azeroth. It is the closest thing we have to time travel, and it allows us to bridge the temporal gap between past and present as we study this game.

We experience time (as Heidegger understood it) within the context of the present as well as in the past (even though we occupy the present). We can experience things as they were even though we exist thirteen years after the birth of *WoW*. We can dwell in that space now just as we could then, a conscious occupation of place. Upon its initial release, players dwelled within *WoW* as explorer-adventurers, not only interacting with the game, but also building because of it. The earliest players created guides for other players to use, built communities both within (and outside of) the game, and began the *WoW* tradition of creating "mods," free, downloadable tools for making the game easier to play.

Revisiting the vanilla version of the game today, players dwell within that landscape for additional reasons besides play: nostalgia is a driving factor for those players who started their adventures in 2004; curiosity brings other players who arrived in *WoW* later, who want to see what their beloved game used to be. Still, apart from the team of volunteer archivists who maintain this Archaic version, those who dwell there do so temporarily before leaving again for other worlds.

We are just passing through, staying long enough to form memories, continuing our migration to other places either new or familiar to us.

As players we are constant tourists in the games we inhabit. Occasionally a rare game occupies our attention, and we turn it into a kind of summer cottage, a long-term retreat until it is time for us to rejoin the real world. But for a time we dwell within the semipermanent dreamscape and explore our humanity through the grace of play.

Archaeogaming Tools and Method

What does it mean to "dig" within a game? Is there a dirt archaeology equivalent? This section outlines tools and methods as it raises issues that make archaeogaming different from more traditional fieldwork.

Tools

Meatspace field archaeologists use some (or all) of the following tools in their day-to-day on-site: shovel, trowel, screen, brush/dustpan, dental pick, pick-axe, tape measure, line level, plumb-bob, camera, computer, notebook, transit/total station, drone, as well as remote-sensing equipment and other specialized tools. Most of these tools are useless when in-world, unless a game uses these as part of its archaeology game mechanic where players can pretend to excavate and recover artifacts via their computers or consoles.

What about tools used for archaeogaming? For now it is a computer or console (likely both), a pointing device, and software for capturing screens, audio, and video. Services such as Twitch and YouTube Gaming allow the archaeogamer to live-broadcast an expedition to the public,[10] and these sites also host edited videos. Public engagement is a key to the survival of archaeology anywhere, so having a public channel for excavating in synthetic spaces is helpful.

One of the most useful tools for both traditional and synthetic archaeology? Drones. For the archaeogamer, these drones are mainly in-game flying mounts or air/spacecraft that allow one to hover over something or fly by it while taking images and video from any altitude. The benefit of in-game drones when compared to their real-world counterparts is the ability for the archaeologist to be actively in the cockpit (or saddle) as opposed to fiddling with drone controls from the ground, or relying on third-party images taken from aircraft not piloted by archaeologists.

As of 2018, the archaeogaming toolkit is not as big or as useful as it needs to be, although this is slowly changing. Archaeogaming can adopt and adapt most of the tools from its real-world contemporaries, but it needs archaeogaming-specific software, too. Following the lead of Open-Context.org, GitHub, and other repositories, new apps/mods should be shared as open source. One benefit of doing game archaeology is that many video games are available on the Steam platform, which already has a robust modding community that creates everything from skins to tools. It is possible that these mods can be created in Steam and then mimicked for PC/Mac. Archaeologists can create these mods, or better yet they can partner with members of the modding community who can create mods based on specs provided by archaeologists. At this writing, however, one cannot mod for closed platforms such as Xbox and Play-Station. Here are a few possibilities of things that could be developed by the modding community, which could include archaeology students who are also becoming digitally literate and learning how to code:

Overlay: Traditional archaeologists apply a grid over the sites they investigate to assist with mapping and organization. The proposed digital overlay will place a grid over the screen to assist with documenting where things are on any given screenshot. Having a standardized grid can help archaeologists worldwide studying the same game to remain consistent with locations, distance, and measure, with a "smart" version of the overlay able to be tuned for scale. Even though some games do contain coordinates and complex global and local maps, many games do not. A standardized grid overlay will help.

Smart-Measure: In-world distances vary from game to game and are occasionally not to scale. Physicist and philosopher Karen Barad wonders, "What can measurements tell us or how are they useful outside of classical physics?" (Barad 2007: 342). Why measure something that is not "real" or is affected by game-created physics? I think that distance is still important: it helps provide context, regardless of the weirdness of a synthetic world's map. This app would allow you to assign a unit for a distance of measure, converting it to English/metric units for perspective. The tool can be configured to record "as-the-crow-flies" distances as well as real distances over in-world topography, much like what is available in Google Earth. Other parameters can include volume and area for a user-defined space, or guides can identify and snap to borders for a room or region.

Smart-Clock: Time works differently from game to game, and often does not reflect the passage of time in metaspace. The clock app, after parameters have been set, will keep track of both real-world time and its passage in the virtual world, displaying both side by side. Screen- and video-captures can include this data for record-keeping purposes, much like one sees on DVD "screeners" of films. Some games offer a "speed run" option where players can time themselves completing levels or an entire game. This option provides a timer that could be repurposed for recording time/distance in a game, but having a dedicated mod will give the archaeologist more flexibility in when and how to tell time and measure it.

Probes: Much like those in the Ridley Scott film *Prometheus* (which featured archaeologists as lead characters), probes could be used to map areas of a game not yet visited by the archaeologist, reporting locations of finds or structures, possibly recording geotagged images of them as well as a video of the trip. This is no different than launching probes to other worlds not easily reached by people or sending robot-mounted cameras into tight spaces inside ancient buildings here on Earth. Game developer Hello Games sent probes into the universe it created for *No Man's Sky* to discover planets created by algorithms.[11] Mapping a game ahead of time (or borrowing maps from other players) can allow the archaeologist to make decisions on how to spend time and other resources within the synthetic world, knowing in advance where to go and what to look for.

While the above is a brief list of software to be created for archaeologists to use in synthetic spaces, some software already exists and can be adopted by video game archaeologists. For the *No Man's Sky* Archaeological Survey (NMSAS), special software was created to handle the in-game collection of survey data for an entire virtual universe (see below for a detailed case study). The NMSAS team used a version of the Federated Archaeological Information Management System (FAIMS), created by an Australia-based team at Macquarie University that makes software apps for mobile devices for archaeologists to use in the field. Other open-source software continues to evolve for data collection/recording (such as CollectiveAccess), data publication/sharing (such as OpenContext.org) as well as digital imaging and reconstruction in 3D, augmented and virtual reality (e.g., Blender and SketchFab). It is also possible to create maps in GIS software (e.g., QGIS, ArcGIS) based on game maps.[12]

Methods

As archaeologists begin to turn their attention to digital built environments, I continue to consider how to conduct archaeological survey and excavation based on methods already proven in the natural world for traditional sites.[13] My Ur-text is Martin Carver's *Archaeological Investigation* (2009), a well-regarded how-to guide for designing, implementing, and publishing archaeological projects. I supplemented Carver's book with Steve Roskams's *Excavation* (2001) to see if I could apply his methods to "excavating" digitally. The danger of course is in trying to put techniques from the natural world to work in the digital, that this might cause me to overlook other ways for doing digital work digitally based on my research questions and the digital environment in which those questions would be asked and hopefully answered. There are many similarities shared between the natural and synthetic worlds and how to conduct archaeological investigation in them. The difference between the two is that synthetic worlds are created digitally by people (or by algorithms created by people). Both the natural and synthetic worlds are real. There is no "virtual" here.

Why Survey/Excavate Digital Built Environments?

Carver begins with an explanation of why we should conduct archaeological investigation at all. It starts with "pieces of the past, life's *disjecta membra,* the stuff. This is what we study. . . . Our first task is to appreciate why we have what we have. All these cultural remains belong to people who deserve a history, but they do not equally leave us one" (Carver 2009: 7).

Digital history, however, is even more elusive, because outside of the hardware (most of which gets deposited in dumps or recycling facilities or ultimately African "disposal" sites), the software engaged with, and the history of use by communities is completely invisible, a kind of intangible heritage. We have what we have now because users have documented what they do, but this is done informally, often on ephemeral community message boards, groups, and chatrooms, with no guarantee of preservation.

When we consider surveying or excavating a site, those sites are often either forgotten or deserted, either buried some distance under the earth or hidden in/incorporated into the modern landscape. Carver writes that "even when archaeological sites are deserted, they do not entirely die. They have a long and varied afterlife . . ." (Carver 2009: 7).

This statement is equally true with video games. Players can certainly return to old games, abandoned games, and also synthetic, shared worlds that are now devoid of players. The sites largely remain in the digital world, much like they do in the natural. When dealing with sites in the natural world, one must consider the pre-deposition of a site (subsoil, topography, culture) and post-deposition (natural and human attrition). Human activity after the abandonment of a site can include curate behavior, vandalism, stone-robbing, cultivation, digging; natural activity includes bacterial, chemical, vegetation, burrowing animals, frost, flood (Carver 2009: 8).

We don't really see these in abandoned digital spaces, but post-deposition activities do occur. These can include bitrot (degradation of interior code) and/or degradation of physical materials exposed to the elements (or just to time). Games are reliant on hardware on which to run, and older games also relied on physical media, which served as a catalyst between the player and what is played. Just as with any other material artifact, these materials change over time. Post-deposition, the digital is just as susceptible to the whims of the environment as the natural.

Carver identifies (Carver 2009: 9, fig. 1.6) five stages for what happens to a human settlement in the natural world, each with its own factors and properties: before deposition, during occupation, at abandonment, the site gets buried, after burial. It is easy to see how these apply to traditional sites of human occupation, but how can they be mapped to the digital?

Use depends on landscape and environmental factors. A place has to be able to be occupied (or to communicate the ability that it can be occupied prior to people arriving and making use of that space). For games (and other software), one could consider this to be either the marketplace (demand creates supply, e.g., people want to play online with their friends, so companies such as Blizzard Entertainment create MMOs) or people (or companies, which are groups of people) who feel the need to carve out a niche for themselves, creating their own space(s) to inhabit. Once the space is occupied and developed, culture follows. Consider the popular MMO *World of Warcraft,* which has millions of players (four million active accounts according to Blizzard's February 2017 figures), has its own annual convention (BlizzCon), has fostered books and a feature film adaptation, and has licensed its in-game material culture to real-world companies to produce for players to buy in order to signal their love of the game to other kindred spirits.

The game is the structure inhabited by the players online, their activities preserved in massive databases hosted by the game's producers. Over time, most games are abandoned in favor of newer titles, or players find other ways to use their discretionary time and income. Populations dwindle until the game is but a shell of what it used to be. Unlike sites of human settlement in the natural world, these game-spaces do not erode, are not "robbed" of resources, and do not weather. They remain in a kind of stasis, abandoned yet timeless, ready to be enlivened at any moment by hordes of returning players who never arrive. Following a game's abandonment, the game can be buried. As explained in chapter 1, this happened literally with the case of *E.T.: The Extraterrestrial* (Atari 1982), where unsold/returned copies of the game were trucked to a landfill in Alamogordo, New Mexico, to be dumped to make room for new merchandise. In other instances, companies retire the games they produce. They no longer sell the games and, after a period of years, cease technical and community support. The games disappear, maintained in players' memories or archived by game developers or player communities. After a game gets abandoned and then buried, it can suffer a few fates: bitrot (see above definition); disappearance, where the game and its code are lost for all time; and archaeological excavation, where recovered games are studied through either play or deconstruction.

Designing an Archaeological Project Plan for a Synthetic World

Once a game is identified as a candidate for archaeological investigation, the researcher(s) must follow protocol in creating a publicly proposed project design. "The project design must be published before work starts, and not just because this results in a better managed programme, but for ethical reasons. . . . The *project design* itself must contain a programme of long- and short-term conservation as well as programme of research" (Carver 2009: 33).

This statement is as true for synthetic sites as it is for natural ones. The project plan should be shared online publicly, especially with those user groups who actively play (or played) the game to be studied because they are that game's indigenous community. This opens it up to community critique, in effect becoming public archaeology and engaging the game's "local" population, many of which will spot mistakes and pitfalls or who might be willing to help in the research as volunteers. The plan should also identify conservation and preservation efforts for the game-site as well as for the research both pre- and post-publication. When I was organizing the *No Man's Sky* Archaeological Survey (NMSAS) in 2016, I publicly broadcast the team's reasons for investigating a synthetic universe and how we proposed to do it. Within days of posting the research plan, I was contacted by several community groups interested in conducting citizen science within the gameplay and sharing our data. We were able to work with these groups and follow their own discoveries on various community bulletin boards online and through social media. These communities also helped the NMSAS team revise its project methods during our survey period, correcting serious misconceptions about measuring distance on synthetic worlds. As Carver says, "Archaeological project design is mandatory. . . . Researchers are bound by a contract with society" (Carver 2009: 33). In the case of games, the project design is a contract with society as well as with the player community.

Carver breaks down a field archaeologist's research agenda into three parts (Carver 2009: 47, fig 3.8): fieldwork, objective, and outcome. What are we trying to accomplish with whatever it is we're doing on-site? This is universal for both natural and synthetic sites. We excavate to see a sequence of use in order to confirm or change what we know about the site and its occupants. We survey in the site area to create a map of settlement and other features in order to determine where to dig (if we need to dig at all). We survey the area surrounding a site to map and identify other settlements in order to note changing land use or to recognize settlement/cultural patterns. We study other areas in order to compare and contrast them with what was found on-site. We can follow these same procedures in any digital built environment. Software can be mapped and even excavated, compared to earlier or later versions of itself, and compared to similar software designed to match the needs of the same user community.

At the start of any archaeological project planning, preliminary reconnaissance is key. In the natural landscape, one must visit that space to experience it firsthand, to identify its challenges, and to begin to inform yourself of how to proceed based on operating in that environment. For the video game archaeologist, this necessitates ample gameplay. Playing a game (or using any kind of software) familiarizes you with the landscape. You play where others played, and the more time spent in that synthetic environment, the better prepared you will be to conduct an archaeological survey and/or excavation of it.

Surveying the Synthetic

Before any kind of excavation can occur, a survey must be conducted, either landscape or site (or both). There are three techniques of landscape survey: cartography, surface inspection, aerial photography (Carver 2009: 65). In synthetic worlds, cartography can be done either with in-game maps, by mods (see above), or by hand-mapping during exploration. Surface inspection can be done by the player on foot in much the same way as field-walking across natural landscapes. As stated earlier, many games feature flying drones, ships, or "mounts," which allow players to see the landscape from above and even to hover at various altitudes over the surface, using the computer or console's native screen-grab features for aerial photography. Anything digital shown on a display (computer monitor, flat-screen, television, etc.) can also be considered as a frame for a map or plan, a top-down view that can be captured and measured.

The European Landscape Convention defines a landscape as an "area as perceived by people, whose character is the result of the action and intersection of natural and/or human factors."[14] By this definition, games are landscapes. Players have agency in games, and their actions mark the intersection of their decisions upon the game-world and upon other players in a shared space. See my section on landscape archaeology in synthetic worlds for a more in-depth look at how games are landscapes that can be studied archaeologically.

Landscape survey combines geography, environment, and archaeology to explore the unknown world in deep time (Carver 2009: 86). The same is largely true in digital built environments, but the question of time (specifically deep time) is tricky. In games, deep time can perhaps be measured by version numbers, but it will not appear graphically in a visual layer on a screen. Time in games is strange, with people playing in real-time, even though that game features the rapid passing of days and seasons while no one (or thing) ages, erodes, grows, decays.

Following landscape survey comes site survey. To Carver, a site is "an area of ground in need of investigation" (Carver 2009: 89). Games also fit this definition. To Carver (Carver 2009: 89), a site survey is simply a landscape survey on a smaller scale: the area is smaller, but the focus is finer. Surveyors sense archaeological features but do not damage them. A site survey can be invasive in its exploration (e.g., shovel-testing), but these surveys attempt to leave everything intact. The objective of a site survey is to know as much about a site as possible before deciding what to do about it. The same works in digital spaces: observe, focus, and then decide next steps.

Site survey techniques in the natural world include using maps and documents, topographical mapping, surface collection, geophysical survey, and sample excavation (Carver 2009: 89). In a digital space, all games will allow for surface surveys and mapping, and some will allow for surface collection. Some might even allow traditional excavation. It all depends on the game's mechanics, or what a game allows players to do. If actual digging in a game is not possible, the video game archaeologist must consider other ways of conducting synthetic shovel tests should those be considered necessary. This is especially true when documenting material culture created by nonhuman actors/ agents within synthetic worlds, placed there by algorithms. What can be determined through observation alone, and later through interaction (if ethics permit)? What do we as archaeologists introduce into a game-world through physically interacting with that space? How might that affect future experiences in that world and with its digital residents?

Part of a site survey might include a sample excavation, which can reveal strata and other data. While some games might exhibit stratigraphy during play, this is exceedingly rare if not unique. Strata instead can be visualized between different versions of the same game, changes mapped in a software matrix, a variant of the Harris matrix. If possible, the site survey should conduct some kind of remote sensing (which some games allow as part of their mechanic). It may become apparent that digging is not necessary based on the survey/sensing results and what they say about the overarching research questions decided upon at the beginning of the project. What is appropriate in the natural world might need to be adapted for use in the synthetic world. These methods will grow and change over time, but it is imperative for all video game archaeologists to document what they did and why and what the results were. This will enable the discipline to advance and grow.

"Excavating" the Synthetic

If excavation is indeed necessary, Carver cautions that "excavation is not an unvarying ritual, but a creative study, carefully redesigned every time it's done. The methods used depend on what you want to know, the site and the social context in which you work. These are always different, everywhere" (Carver 2009: 123). So once spade is put to soil, what happens?

We can turn to Roskams's *Excavation* (2001) for details on how to conduct a successful excavation. I have flagged several details with an asterisk (*) that can be applied to excavation in a synthetic world. Pre-excavation strategies include aerial photography,* field-walking,* shovel-testing,* reading documentary material,* studying previous excavations of the same site,* performing ground-based remote sensing,* chemical mapping, coring and auguring, evaluation trenches.*

Background preparation for an excavation includes defining finance/administration,* identifying staff/support facilities,* and planning for a safe excavation.*

Site preparation includes site clearance,* site grid,* spoil removal,* shoring, de-watering, finds retrieval.*

Recording includes defining the stratigraphic unit, creating and using numbering systems,* creating a recording process and related sheets.*

The photographic record includes determining the reasons to photograph something,* photographic preparation,* and technique.*

The spatial record includes techniques,* equipment,* and drawing conventions*; types of plan*; techniques of measurement*; types of section*; piece-plotting finds.*

The stratigraphic record includes types of stratigraphic relationships,* representing these relationships,* calculating stratigraphic relationships.*

Deposit descriptions include who records and when,* computer storage of records,* deposit descriptions in relation to sedimentology and pedology, deposit color, soil particle size, compaction or consistency of deposits, inclusions within deposits, thickness and surface characteristics.

Non-deposit descriptions include masonry and brick features, timbers, inhumations, cuts, finds groups.

Excavating the stratigraphic unit includes sampling strategies for finds,* methods of collection,* troweling methods, making stratigraphic distinctions, completing the record,* checking the record.*

Stratigraphic analysis includes tidying the record*; on-site interpretations*; correlating between units,* stratigraphic nodes, and critical paths.

Prior to excavation, we need to determine what to do with the things we find. Carver stresses that a site's recovery levels are always variable, changing from site to site (Carver 2009: 124, fig. 6.10). The table is organized from general to specific, from large to small, defined in advance by how they might be discovered and how they will be collected and described. Surface finds (not collected) are followed by large finds (examples recorded and kept), visible finds (all recorded, examples kept), then sieving of samples (kept), total samples (all visible finds), and micro-sieving (done in the lab). For synthetic worlds, sieving is likely not an option (nor necessary), but in many instances examples can be documented, the smaller artifacts kept in player (or team) inventory for later analysis, everything from architecture to small finds, whatever those might be.

Regardless of the environment in which excavation occurs, stratigraphic excavation records multi-concepts: Component (grain of sand) among which are Finds (anything kept), and these belong to the following: a Context (any defined set of components—a layer, a surface—recorded with a Context card, plan, section; a Feature—any defined set of Contexts recorded with a Feature card, plan, section, photographs; a Structure defined as a set of features recorded with a Structure card, plan, photographs; a Horizon is a defined interface between truncated contexts recorded with a survey, plan, photographs (Carver 2009: 139).

These terms can be defined on a game-by-game basis. The terms are scalable.

A major component of both survey and excavation is recording the work done and what the work recovers. Each project in a synthetic world needs to determine in advance what will be recorded in writing, what will be drawn, and what will be photographed. For games and other synthetic worlds, it may also be possible/advisable to record video. All should be done before, during, and after survey and excavation to create a complete visual record. The record must include notable elements on sites.

For Carver (Carver 2009: 198, fig. 8.2), notable elements on sites are both reassessed and managed. Assemblages (artifacts and biota), chronology (stratification and dating), and spatial (contexts to features, features to structures, and structures to site) are reassessed. Management includes records (digital, context/feature cards, maps/plans/sections, photographs, and program of analysis), objects (conservation, packing/ storing, program of analysis), and samples (storage and program of analysis). These elements exist equally (reassessment and management) for the archaeology of synthetic worlds but differ in their execution. For management of archaeological content from a synthetic world, any digital assets/artifacts recovered will likely include digital records (i.e., database entries), short- and long-term storage of other digital media (photos and captured video). It is unclear at this writing what digital conservation might entail for items recovered in a digital space.

Documentation, Chronology, and Location

Depending on the nature of the archaeological investigation to be completed within a synthetic world, archaeologists can follow the example Carver sets out in table 8.1 (Carver 2009: 199). Different kinds of investigations require different levels of documentation, some requiring a fine grain. For example, if one is performing a reconnaissance of a possible site, the archaeologist will keep a notebook of observations, draw a map, create digital maps from GIS points, photograph the area generally, and note surface finds. A landscape survey differs slightly, as it includes artifact photos. Excavation, however, requires a written notebook as well as context sheets and notes on features, drawn plans/ maps/sections/3D plots, digital context records, coordinates, and photographs that are overviews and portraits, with assemblages noted. As above, this same methodology, this same way of organizing what to do depending on what you are doing, is scalable to digital built environments. The location of these sites is different, but the method is the same.

The purposes of documentation fall into two categories: (1) preservation of the archaeological record, and (2) analyses of recovered data. Documentation can help establish a site's chronology (absolute dating as well as a site's sequence of strata and events). For games/software, stratification is easier to read because it is identified by version and build numbers. Version 1.0 appears earlier in the record than version 2.0. The documentation allows the archaeologist to produce synthetic text on assemblage, space, and chronology—what happened, where, when. These all interrelate. So what gets collected from a site and why?

As stated above, site chronology can be divided into absolute and relative dating. Absolute dates are arrived at through scientific testing. Relative dating comes from the ordering of artifacts as well as their context. Dating is extremely difficult to accomplish within synthetic worlds when considering artifacts found within, especially when one knows the year in which the world was created (in real-time). Something might appear to be ancient yet is only (really) a few years old. Relative chronology is perhaps more important to the video game archaeologist rather than anything absolute. Or perhaps one can create a chronology based on absolute dates of discovery. In a procedurally generated game, it might be interesting to compare what is found in one site one day against another site found a few days later. Age would seem to be immaterial.

To get to any kind of dating, one needs sample artifacts/features/materials. Carver identifies five purposes for collecting samples from a site (Carver 2009: 223, fig. 9.7), and where these samples ultimately go (e.g., geologist, botanist, lab/other specialist): identification, dating, plant use, ambient conditions, chemical mapping. Depending on the nature of the synthetic world and the research question(s) being asked of it, these purposes might change. Identification remains a constant, however, asking the universal questions of "What is this?" and "To what purpose what this used?"

In both the natural and synthetic worlds, a variety of materials from sites are present. For Carver (Carver 2009: 224, fig. 9.8), each material (e.g., stone, pottery, metal, etc.) has an identifiable fabric (the kind of stone, pottery, etc.), a specific form/type/style, and a history of use (function/symbolism/discard). In a digital built environment, it is up to the archaeologist to determine the general kinds of material available for collection and to assign types, forms, and styles to them, either based on personal observation and experience within the space or in adopting the vernacular of the player community for that specific game. Contemporary games have shown seriation within types and also diversity in style between cultures within a game. Identifying in-world artifacts through context and then through type/style can assist in dating them or creating a biography for a particular digital artifact. It is likely, with examples of machine-created culture, that new materials, fabrics, forms, styles, and history will manifest, alien to the human experience. The archaeologist can then create a typology, updating as future discoveries yield new data.

Artifacts typically comprise assemblages, a collection of objects—either objects of the same kind spread across the site or, more typically, objects of different kinds of materials found in the same place. Assemblages are common within games. In fact, an individual game might itself be considered an assemblage of code, the sum of its parts. But most games collect disparate items together in a single space to be discovered by a player, whether it is the remains of a fallen warrior or an abandoned building. The assemblage gives the player-archaeologist context and understanding, just as it does in the natural world. When artifacts/assemblages are found, they must be documented and then (if possible/permitted) removed for conservation and additional analysis.

The care of finds from a digital space is perhaps the single major difference between conducting fieldwork in a synthetic world versus the natural one. For a traditional site with traditional artifacts, one must be mindful of foreign substances attached to an item; how to clean the object (if at all); potential risks when handling, packing, or conserving the object; how to apply "first aid"; how to pack; and where to deliver (Carver 2009: 226, fig. 9.9). For digital artifacts, the archaeologist is reliant upon photography and videography, plus inventory management both within the game and also within an external database. Any conservation or transportation occurs with cleaning and sharing the digital media that documented the artifacts found within the synthetic world. One additional option, which is finally available at a very low barrier to entry, is to create 3D scans of items found in-game, exporting the data to an open-source platform such as SketchFab, allowing these scans to proliferate online following the Jeffersonian principle of "lots of copies keep stuff safe." These 3D scans can also be sent to 3D printers for real-world visualization at various sizes, allowing the archaeologist to manipulate real-world manifestations of something only previously available (and created) in a digital environment.

Prior to their removal, all artifacts in the real world can be tagged with a specific location with X-Y-Z coordinates tied into GIS for the purposes of plotting and mapping. We know the Earth, and we have established a universal way to give everything a number, which designates a precise location to anything. At first glance, this is not the case with synthetic worlds. Modern role-playing or adventure games might contain a relative GIS or map, which allows for occasionally specific markers for locations, objects, and players. Most games do not. One workaround to establish at least relative positions for an individual site is to take a screenshot of the site. The siting of artifacts (including structures, environmental objects, etc.) can then be mapped on a grid based on the size and shape of the display on which the screenshot was taken. The screen has an aspect ratio, and also X and Y axes. Most hardware will also tell the user the absolute pixel dimensions of the screen. Knowing these hardware basics, one can then assign basic Cartesian points to things of interest in the screen capture.

The drawback to this is that there is no Z axis for height/depth. For most games, this will not be an issue, mostly because 3D is an optical illusion for games played on a flat screen. However, with the advances in virtual reality, a more complex system of documentation must be invented in order to place the locations of objects in a truly 3D space. One possible workaround is to note the orientation of the player's eyes through the use of a compass rose, and the position of the head-tilt, then take a 2D screenshot and annotate it with regard to how the player was oriented in the real world. I think this method is both complicated and inexact, but one hopes there is a way to extract that data from the middleware that connects the VR headset to the player and also to the game.

In continuing his consideration of the space occupied by sites, Carver distills these neatly into types of field records, which are then defined by tasks, outcomes, and significance (Carver 2009: 252, fig. 10.7). For example, records of the locations of monuments can be mapped by monument type to create a plot of dated monuments, which can then show the location of monuments through time. An artifact survey creates a map by type to illustrate dated occupation areas and a sequence of occupation. The data visualization of different kinds of records for different aspects of a site provides the "why" for the survey or excavation, potentially answering the original research questions.

Carver does the same for landscape survey data (Carver 2009: 255, fig. 10.10), noting the possibility of creating a linguistic map based on placenames, or the possible location of other sites based on the mapping of artifacts gathered during surface-collection. Both the visualizations of data from site and landscape survey can apply to synthetic worlds, specifically those that use a natural-looking landscape in which players can operate. One might also be able to visualize data via maps in games that have nothing to do with adventurous navigation through perilous lands. One can still draw meaningful conclusions about landscapes and the sites they contain even when recording a digital card game or the elements of a word processor's graphical user interface (GUI). It all boils down to the fact that we are looking for social relations in the space; function; chronological development (all re: building distribution in a settlement) (Carver 2009: 255).

In order to make the most of the artifacts found either on survey or in excavation, their pinpointed locations can help define patterns that can then be interpreted by the archaeologist, pattern-seeking through computation. Analytical routines developed by geographers have helped archaeologists to squeeze more meaning out of their patterns (Carver 2009: 258). Pattern recognition should actually be easier when applied to synthetic worlds. The natural world is messy but fractally ordered. Most games are directly designed by one or more people who apply a logic into their coding of a game-space. The algorithms within the code organize the placement of elements in a digital built environment. It seems to be a necessity to apply GIS software to any virtual world in order to view various maps of data, but it will likely be impossible to standardize such a resource because of the plethora and diversity of synthetic worlds. Perhaps the geographers' "analytical routines" can be applied to the data of any synthetic world, if their formulae are universal and not written for a specific location or even planet.

Patterns retrieved through running locations through geographer's mathematical routines could then be used to create additional visualizations of that data. Carver suggests, for example, the use of Thiessen polygons (Carver 2009: 260), which are polygons whose boundaries define the area that is closest to each point relative to all other points. They are mathematically defined by the perpendicular bisectors of the lines between all points. Carver also suggests that archaeologists can utilize Local Density Analysis and Presence Absence Analysis in order to identify patterns of settlement or of artifact creation and use (Carver 2009: 261).

For Presence Absence Analysis, archaeologists can take a page from ecologists who are mapping presence or absence of species within a particular environment, creating models for predicting the distribution of organisms from environmental data. Perhaps there are similar models for archaeology that can use the mathematics of ecological distribution, which can be applied to both the natural and synthetic worlds.

For Local Density Analysis, this looks at things such as concentrations of bones or flakes to identify sites of use or production. We could possibly use this within synthetic worlds, too, based on what we find. The mathematics/statistics should be scalable, and I will test this in my video game case studies.

One other source of pattern recognition can take a look at how human and nonhuman agents in synthetic worlds move. Carver notes that exploring the way that centers of population interacted with each other assumes that there will be preferred pathways rather than random connections and that these pathways will themselves promote the establishment of new settlements on the route (Carver 2009: 262). This is true in the real world, but is it true in synthetic ones? In a game such as *Fallout 4*, settlements are found on roads, but also in the wilderness. In many role-playing games (RPGs), wandering monsters are more frequent off the road, but major settlements are on the routes. It depends on the game and its design, but by and large things of interest happen on pre-established routes. These routes can be created by the game's developers or, in the case of *No Man's Sky*, through procedural generation (ProcGen) where the software determines (a) if there will be creatures present, and (b) if there are, what paths they should follow based on the parameters of movement assigned to the creature depending on the kind of animal that it is and on the landscape in which that creature is situated.

During analysis of site data, there are always two analytical programs working in parallel: one working on objects, the other on contexts (Carver 2009: 272, fig. 11.4).

In the natural world, one might find a timbered house built a hundred years ago, yet made from wood hundreds of years old. There are two timelines at work: materials and the objects made from those materials. In games, sometimes this will be the same date. In ProcGen games, the material and the object made from the material are exactly the same, created mere seconds ago (even if they have the appearance of being old). In other cases, one might record when a material was mined and when it was later used to craft an object. One could also consider that a material or artifact was made on the date the game was released, or when a game was played by a player. One can argue if these dates are even important. In most cases, probably not. But in some cases, dates might be necessary if only to form a relative chronology from which to order items and to sequence elements within a game.

Sequencing of a site includes stratigraphy. This is often done through the creation of a Harris matrix. The matrix includes all the contexts, so it constitutes a total account of every stratigraphic event that occurred, or rather, those that could be observed and recorded (Carver 2009: 278). As an experiment I created a Harris-style software matrix to record the stratigraphic sequence of the game *No Man's Sky*, which treated each version of the game as a stratigraphic layer to see how one version of the game related to the next regarding functionality and bug fixes.[15] While stratigraphy is practically impossible to determine within a synthetic world, it is quite easy (if laborious) to identify and document when looking at the software from the outside in.

Seriation (the arrangement of a collection of artifacts into a chrono-logical sequence based on characteristics such as shape, color, material, etc.), however, can (and should) be conducted within digital built environments. Sir Flinders Petrie was able to use seriation to determine that graves with the most similar pots were nearest to each other in date (Carver 2009: 280). Seriation may or may not be as Petrie described when dealing with synthetic worlds. It is dependent on the game's logic. For games that contain objects to find, one might find artifacts in many locations, which might make sense in the game but would make no sense at all in the natural world.

Continuing considerations on how to order sites, Carver shows in fig. 11.11 that different types of sites (e.g., deep urban, rural settlement) have varying levels of stratification and ways to order context (Carver 2009: 281). Most games will have none of this within the space of play. There is no need for it. Almost everything is superficial in the game-space.

Synthesis and Publication

Once the survey and excavation is complete and the features have been analyzed, it is time to synthesize the material in order to draw conclusions from the data and to create a site model. For this synthesis, Carver starts with the outcome of primary analysis, followed by a literature search, looking for ethno-parallels, then experimentation in order to create models (Carver 2009: 311, fig. 12.12). For the identity of features, for example, he recommends searching the literature about features identified on other sites, looking for features used by comparable cultures, constructing/using/disuse of replica features in experiments, in order to model the activities of the site being synthesized. Synthetic worlds perhaps provide an easier way of synthesizing data as conditions can be recreated (much of the time) and reproduced by others who also have access to copies of the same synthetic worlds. It is possible in some games to tweak a variable or condition in order to experiment, and to rerun those experiments to test a hypothesis, which falls under the rubric of agent-based modeling (ABM).

Following synthesis, it is time to publish the results. Publication is key to any archaeological project, and it is especially so for new, possibly provocative research into nontraditional areas such as the archaeology of synthetic worlds, video games, digital built environments. Carver lists eight kinds of publications, how they are presented, and for whom: field reports, lab reports, client reports, research reports, popular books, media (magazines, site guides, television), displays, and presentations (Carver 2009: 316, fig. 13.1). The latter half of these publications is intended for the public, those who visit sites/museums, and those who have an interest in popular historical nonfiction. The other reports fulfill the responsibility of writing up the data for other researchers and for the project's sponsors. The bottom line is that the ethical project must produce similar work for distribution to colleagues and to the public as a conclusion to the original, public research plan.

The publication plan for an archaeological project set in a synthetic world would include a research report describing the investigation, findings, interpretation, and context, authored by all of the principal participants in that project. The report should be published as Open Access for maximum discoverability and use, and should be published digitally in order for the report to link to published data sets and to related digital media, including photos and video, and, if possible, a digital copy (or links to accessing) the digital site that was investigated. This will allow other archaeologists and researchers to return to the site for additional research or to test hypotheses and results as provided by the report's authors. A preliminary report should precede the final report of research to outline methods, findings, and interpretations, published immediately online.

Popular books and other public media should come second, but these should not be ignored by the archaeological team. In the case of synthetic worlds, many of these are popular spaces, and conducting archaeology within them generates enormous public interest. Public reports, interviews, etc., can draw archaeologists closer to the communities who occupy game-worlds or who actively use software, which can lead to additional support, be it financial or, perhaps more importantly, for networking purposes. The public can also raise questions overlooked by the researchers, and can critique the work, allowing the archaeologists to revise theories and reconsider results.

Carver states that "without a pre-released project design, a field archaeology project must be judged to be inept, at worst unethical. . . . A project design is therefore a consultation document that is prepared and circulated widely before serious fieldwork begins" (Carver 2009: 335). This sentiment is shared in both the natural and synthetic worlds. Both professional and community input are important prior to the start of the actual project. For synthetic worlds, archaeologists who are not directly involved in the project can critique its archaeological plan of attack, while the community can assist by providing expert/native-level intelligence on what to expect within the digital environment to be studied.

In the natural world, archaeology can appear as an inconvenience when it comes to land use. One must speak with property owners and government representatives to acquire permission and permits, and one must also address the public. Blocking off a section of land for an excavation can cost others money and opportunity, and the archaeologist must be sensitive to those people affected by the project. In synthetic spaces, the issues are perhaps less sensitive but must still be considered, especially if work is being done in a game-space populated by other human players. Consideration of their gameplay and use of the site must be respected. Some games also have nonhuman actors/agents that should also be considered prior to embarking upon a project. How will the archaeological work interfere with their operation in the shared digital space, and are such interruptions ethical?

Carver takes a very commonsense approach to creating a project plan, taking time to consider what needs to be done and why as based on the research questions being asked (Carver 2009: 337, fig. 14.1). We need to know how big we want our survey to be prior to conducting site reconnaissance; we need to know the location, problem, and project scoping before evaluating the site; we need to evaluate what these early stages have told us prior to designing the project; we need to continually update the project design during fieldwork to adapt to the site and its environment; we need to assess the data collected prior to creating a formal analysis; we need to understand the results of that analysis prior to publication. This should be applied to any archaeological project regardless of where it takes place.

Carver offers a few "starter" questions for archaeological research projects, and these can be applied to those synthetic worlds that contain ready-made (or algorithmically generated) cultures that are alien to all prior human experience (Carver 2009: 342). How are communities and territories defined, and how are societies organized? What are the "people" like, and how are they organized? What are the gender roles (if gender is present)? What do the people in this new culture think, and what is their worldview? What do they eat; how do they make and use tools; what contacts do they have? What is their environment like? Why (or how) did things change? These are universal questions that can be put to any culture on Earth, but they can also be used on Mars or within a synthetic world. These are questions for which archaeologists seek answers, deriving those answers by following archaeological method as determined by their research plans.

Carver lays out the contents of a project design in table 14.1, breaking it down into an introduction, evaluation, research options, conservation options, and recommended integrated program (Carver 2009: 353). Completing each of these sections is essential and once done must be shared publicly for comment/critique. The original research plan should also be included as part of the final report as a way to document if things changed during the project, and how and why.

Video Game Ethnoarchaeology

Many video games from all time periods have situated their characters and action in imaginary worlds—which Mark Wolf calls "diegetic"—where part of the game's objectives is to explore and learn about the game-space (Wolf 2014: 125). These game-worlds have space, time, and causality (Wolf 2014: 125–26). Things happen to players, and things happen because of player action.

One of archaeogaming's great potential areas of scholarship is in conducting ethnography and ethnoarchaeology within synthetic worlds. Standard ethnography is the scientific description of the customs of individual peoples and cultures. This can also be done in video games on two levels: in-game, where the ethnographer studies a particular culture as designed by the developer; and extra-game, where the ethnographer reports on a culture of players who not only play a specific game but who choose to play as a certain faction, race, and/or class. In both the real and virtual worlds, players interact with cultural systems, and archaeologists need to abide by a code of ethics regardless of which world it is that they choose to explore (Dennis 2016). For the gaming ethnoarchaeologist, the following applies to studying the entangled cultures of both worlds:

1. Cultures are the way they are because they are adapted to an external environment;
2. elements of culture are observable;
3. one can compare systems from culture to culture;
4. elements of cultural systems are interdependent;
5. different elements of cultural systems are linked to one another and explained by function;
6. we can examine links between subsystems in terms of correlation rather than simple causes. (Johnson 2010: 72–74)

Ethnoarchaeology goes one step beyond ethnography in studying people/cultures through their material remains, and it is specifically applied to modern and contemporary "living" societies. Because it is less than fifty years old, gaming culture qualifies for ethnoarchaeological study, archaeogaming being driven by that mission. As with ethnography, ethnoarchaeology requires two levels of analysis: material culture of real-world players and the games they play (including software, hardware, as well as everything from game-related fan-created art and fiction to official documentation) and the culture created within the synthetic world itself, independent of outside forces.

Within procedural games, the ethnoarchaeologist analyzes the resulting material culture of whatever the algorithms produce. Taken liberally, this could mean that everything created in a procedural universe is an artifact, be it a planet or a pixel manipulated to create that planet. Both the pixel and the perceived world (which is really just pixels organized to convince the player of its "world-ness") appear by the grace of code. The pixels align, inherit color, position, and function, and link up to create the manifestation of a planet, or a weapon, or some kind of imagined onscreen life-form. The ethnoarchaeogamer must determine the level of granularity of study framed by research questions. What is to be studied and why?

Regardless of the answers, the material culture to be researched has been machine-created. A game's Ur-code was created by one or more people, or in the newest cases of artificial intelligence, people make the tools that are then used by machines to create the code that creates a world to explore. With procedural generation, especially in newer games, the player is an extra step removed from the developer, engaging first with whatever the algorithm creates as interpreted by the hardware running the code instead of engaging directly with the manifestation of the code itself. If you play *Uncharted: Drake's Fortune*, you can memorize what you need to do and where you need to go. The environment is always the same. In a procedural game, higher-order thinking is required both on the part of the player and whatever is being played. Depending on the hardware used, the software version, and the player, the same game will produce different outcomes, even if the end goal of the game (or a quest within a game) remains unchanged. But even now those rules are changing, with games (e.g., *Undertale*) moving the goalpost depending on player behavior at earlier points in the adventure.

What remains in these games and in-game situations is the universal issue of agency. People do things, and the game reacts, and vice versa. Without the player, in most instances, the game remains in a static state. It "waits" to be interacted with. This is no different than any real-world artifact discarded only to enter deep time until a future disturbance, sometimes at the hands of archaeologists. Archaeogaming therefore includes human behavioral ecology, which is concerned with exploring the socio-ecology of individual agents and the dynamic context that define the cost and benefits that they encounter. Bird and O'Connell write that "the individual is the nexus of human relations and is concerned with complex behavioral strategies that underlie artifact patterns; it has much in common with agent-based approaches in archaeology" (Bird and O'Connell 2012: 54).

"Agent-based" focuses on the individual and its actions, studying how those actions combine with the other actions of individuals to create interesting, group-based behavior. In archaeology, agent-based models help archaeologists reconstruct the processes responsible for the patterns observed in the archaeological record (Kohler 2012: 111). In traditional archaeology as well as in video games, agent-based modeling deconstructs the rules down to a very fine grain, where the small combines with other individual entities to create simple actions that grow to become complex, resulting in emergent behavior. With games, the in-world mechanics operate through coded procedures, but they acquire additional meaning through player interaction. The player then actively engages as a creative agent, helping things happen. Players realize that their actions have effects not only on themselves but also in the game-space. This is not unlike what happens in the real world. As theorist Karen Barad mentions in *Meeting the Universe Halfway: Quantum Physics and the Entanglement of Matter and Meaning,* "Learning how to intra-act responsibly as part of the world means understanding that 'we' are not the only active beings" (Barad 2007: 391). Everything is entangled with everything else.

Archaeology takes the concepts of human agency and entanglement and includes the inanimate as well, calling it "actor-network theory" (ANT). ANT includes nature and things (anything nonhuman, such as machines and other technology) as active agents in the past, present, and future (Latour 2005). Devices are nonhuman social forces (Schut 2014: 327). Contemporary human life is completely defined by our nonhuman technology, and it is easy for humans to blame that which humans created for faults that affect the lives of those same humans. Sometimes we play the game, and sometimes the game plays us.

With video games then, ethnoarchaeology takes us further into what might be as the lines between the real and virtual blur. Anthropologist Penny Harvey says that this "new curiosity concerning other ways of relating to non-human worlds is central to the survival of our species" (Harvey 2013: 61). We must understand our interactions with things or ignore them at our peril. That study must delve into media archaeography, modes of writing that are not human textual products but rather expressions of the machines themselves, functions of their very mediatic logic (Ernst 2011: 242). Archaeogaming is central in identifying and understanding the inner dialogues of machines by virtue of the games we play on them, transferring that knowledge to the real world.

But where to begin? I attempted to tackle these issues in the *No Man's Sky* Archaeological Survey.

Archaeogaming Case Study: The *No Man's Sky* Archaeological Survey

No Man's Sky (Hello Games 2016) is not the first procedural game; it is an heir to much earlier examples such as *Elite* (Acornsoft 1984). *No Man's Sky,* however, has elevated procedural games to the next level where algorithms are used to create everything in a universe-sized universe, including photorealistic planets, plants and animals, weather, sounds, and even language. Because of the scale of the game and the fact that it would contain procedurally generated material culture, I thought this would be the first earnest candidate for in-world archaeology where archaeologists could document never-before-seen, machine-created cultures.[16] I wanted to explore emergent behavior that evolved from the complexity of such a large game; I wanted to see firsthand how material culture was created on the fly through procedural algorithms; I wanted to conduct ethnoarchaeology on beings and their habitats that were created by the software to have the illusion of having history.

To explore these ideas formally, I created the *No Man's Sky* Archaeological Survey (NMSAS) in 2016 to explore and document examples of built environments and material culture, all made from the "interpretation" of lines of code (see Figure 3.1). The NMSAS took a heuristic

Figure 3.1. Ruins in *No Man's Sky* (Hello Games). Screen capture by author.

approach to the archaeology of a virtual space, both practical and experimental, to do and to discover.

In anticipation of conducting a proper archaeological survey, which included transects (orbital and suborbital) and field-walking, I researched current survey methods used on Greece and in Cyprus, most notably the Eastern Korinthia Archaeological Survey and the Pyla-Koutsopetria Archaeological Survey. Team member Catherine Flick with L. Meghan Dennis composed a code of in-game archaeological ethics with me, which appends this book. I also partnered with the Australian archaeologists behind the Federated Archaeological Information Management System (FAIMS) to create customized survey forms for team members to use via smartphones and tablets while they played. I created several spaces for work, storage, and internal and external communication.

For anyone who wanted to follow the project online I set up a Twitter account, @nmsarchaeology, where news, images, and recorded video of our travels would post. I also set up a public Twitch channel, nmsarchaeology, so that subscribers could ride along with the archaeologists as we explored new worlds. For internal communication, I created a Slack team and included channels for general, finds, procedures, and ethics where we could have real-time discussions. Images, video, and field reports, along with procedures and other team documentation, lived on a shared Google Drive.

But all of that preparation did not account for the new universe we were about to experience. After one month of exploring *No Man's Sky,* it was clear that the game we expected was not the game the team was prepared to study, although like any good archaeologists, we improvised. The game did not ship with any maps or navigational features at the planetary or local level, and because there were no poles on any of the worlds we discovered, it was impossible to determine cardinal directions. Perhaps most damning was the lack of any kind of Cartesian coordinate system for assigning X and Y (and possibly Z) coordinates to points of interest, features, wrecks, buildings, and the like. We were unable to be exact regarding locations of things, and even if we could have been, the waypoints we discovered and logged via the *NMS* game interface were forgotten by the system itself two weeks following discovery. The only data maintained on a permanent basis by the game are galaxies, systems, planets, and moons. That changed, however, with the November 2016 release of the "Foundation Update" v1.1, which allowed for custom, permanent waypoints, along with UTM-like coordinates to record anything of archaeological interest.

At this writing, there are no active civilizations in the game. There are no surface finds other than crashed spacecraft containing discoverable technology, and occasional "jettison pods" that dot the landscape. The only pottery to be found are static "amphoras" in ruins, and these artifacts are always the same shape and even the same disposition in the buildings in which they are found. There are no bones and no graves (other than the player's if killed by animals, ships, or the environment, and even the marker is temporary). There are animals, but no sentient life. There is nothing to interact with other than static cutscenes with four races: Korvax, Gek, Vy'keen, and Travellers. One can push buttons and solve simple math puzzles to gain locations of spacecraft wrecks, trading posts, monoliths. But the worlds are empty except for the buildings left behind by "ancients" or the ones currently in use by colonizers. In space there are space stations and trade ships.

In this game, there is nothing one could traditionally call "archaeological," things one would expect to find on a survey or excavation. But that is the point in studying games and game-spaces archaeologically. Games can be simulations, but everything within is the creation of the developer and the algorithms deployed by the developer to, in this case, populate a universe. Although the game fails to deliver on traditional archaeology, it does present the archaeologist with a number of interesting things to consider.

First, there are monoliths (different from ruins, which are explained below). These structures can be interacted with in order to teach players race-specific words as well as Atlas vocabulary (the Atlas is mysterious, almost divine technology) based on how a player answers a culturally significant question. Players learn about the history of the Korvax, Gek, and Vy'keen through these structures, and they learn a bit of the language. It is as yet unknown what happens if you answer all the questions about each race, or if answering a question correctly unlocks something else in the universe to discover. The monoliths themselves have a typology from simple rectangular prisms to cubes to spheres, and as one progresses toward the center of the galaxy, these shapes become more complex to include inverted pyramids, Atlas prisms, and more, some of which have visible mechanical parts inside. The monoliths are tied to the race of the system visited; there are no Gek monoliths on a Vy'keen world. There is robust typology in the presentation of monoliths, but their general purpose remains unknown even after "finishing" the game, and their appearance in the landscape (or underwater) remains apparently arbitrary.

Next are the shipwrecks that dot the landscape and can be found either at random or via distress beacon. When the game begins, players are at their own shipwrecks. It is possible that these wrecks also indicate other potential player starting points, but that is speculation. Each shipwreck is marked by a banner. These banners are of different colors, have different borders, and contain a logo in the middle, also different from one banner to the next. The colors and logos signify factions, sometimes matching the dominant race of a particular star system and at other times signifying exploration on these worlds by others.

Buildings of various types dot nearly every planet visited. These buildings include trading posts, shelters, observatories, pods, factories, beacons, all of which are waypoints, which allow the player to save progress and discoveries. Every race has the same types of buildings, although they differ slightly in their design based on whether or not this is a Gek, Korvax, or Vy'keen world. Buildings are occasionally painted and occasionally have writing on them, sometimes identifiable as Arabic numerals, although whether or not they can be read as such is a mystery. What does the writing mean, if anything? When on a planet, players are rarely more than three minutes' walk from another structure or waypoint no matter where one is on a planet. The coverage is almost gridlike, and in many cases it follows a spiral design for the placement of structures to discover.

Ruins are perhaps the most archaeologically interesting, namely because they hint at age and prior civilization. Ruins can be discovered by accident, but they can always be found by solving puzzles at observatories. Solving several puzzles and several observatories does not yield a succession of more advanced ruins. Types of puzzles (three or four numbers in a four-digit puzzle or two numbers in a four-digit puzzle) seem to determine the type of ruin to be found, either a standalone structure or a two- or three-building complex.

The ruins themselves can be grouped as either "stone" or "adobe," although some ruins use both materials. Some are painted green and others red. All ruins appear to be landmarks or "plaques" or are commemorative, but they are not dedicated to a historical figure or to a deity or specific event that happened at that location. No ruins are habitations. Ruins follow a typology based on footprint, roof-covering, number of staircases, shape of the object one can interact with to learn vocabulary. Some ruins have monumental sculpture, although it is always the same: a lizard-like head on its side. Some ruins have gold spheres incised with circles and lines, and plinths for these. Players can move these spheres, and they can also be moved by strong winds.

Many ruins also have one or two flagpoles topped with flags of different sizes and shapes. The tops of the flagpoles show one of three shapes: hexagon, triangle, or spiral. In earlier versions of the game, by traveling in the direction of a flagpole (using it like a reticle), one can discover "portals," tall structures with an arch at the bottom. These portals are exceedingly rare and allow "attuned" players to fast-travel to other worlds after entering a complex sequence of glyphs.

It remains unclear how or why ruins and portals appear where they do. Some appear on flat ground, and some appear on slopes or even underwater. Most appear in isolation, but at least one ruin has been documented mere meters away from a modern structure.

The ruins are the same throughout the galaxy and exist independently of the three factions with their own unified architecture. Ruins appear to have been built and then ruined at the same time, and they all have the same kind of pottery arranged in the same way. After seeing dozens of ruins, the arches are all identically broken (when there are arches). It is bizarre to see this kind of behavior of buildings as an archaeologist in a game, but this kind of repetition along with a kind of uniqueness to each structure makes for interesting, non-Earth, non-"real" archaeology. We can see how the algorithms decide to place the ruins and how they build the structures, and we can attempt to derive some rules based on environment, landscape, even purpose. In the real world, ruins are not placed to be ruins or are created as ruins. They were not built to teach the future anything but were instead built as practical structures for use by people at the time, with no thought given to their afterlife. In *No Man's Sky*, the ruins were built as ruins for the modern explorer with no thought given to their initial intent, to their builders, and to their first users. We are the first users of these pre-ruined ruins, and that, too, is interesting archaeologically.

After the first month of the survey the NMSAS team decided to continue exploring and documenting a flawed virtual universe. With a universe as large as *No Man's Sky* with quintillions of worlds, there may yet be planets with sentient life or Easter egg worlds with who-knows-what on them. This is very much like humanity's real-world current hunt for life elsewhere in the universe. But there is still plenty to do on every world the team explores:

1. See if the landscape affects how and where structures are placed, as well as if it determines the types of structures positioned by the game.
2. Continue to learn the languages of the Atlas and of the three races. Because language is delivered by ruins and by monoliths, does the language learned here differ from the language learned by modern speakers at space stations and in the buildings you visit?
3. Is the writing pure fantasy, or can meaning be found in it? Is it comprehensible language? If not, it is still interesting to try to determine why the game chose to decorate buildings and space stations with writing that never seems to repeat.

4. Continue to collect and keep a record of the context of banners and flags, their colors, shapes, and emblems.

5. Do a bit of "train-spotting" but with ships that come and go at a space station. Are the ships always different? Do any ships return? Can you follow a ship to see where it goes? Do all ships belong to a single faction? Do all ships contain the same cargo?

6. Study the trade market. Is there rhyme or reason to supply and demand? Is this behavior consistent from system to system and faction to faction?

7. Is there rhyme or reason to how waypoints are situated in the landscape? Is there a rule that a shelter is always a few minutes "east" of a beacon and a few minutes "south" of an observatory?

All of the above discussion focuses around conducting archaeology as archaeologists within the game environment while occasionally stepping back to determine how the algorithms are working. I also encouraged the team to be mindful of glitches as well as anomalies. There is a difference.[17]

As will be described in detail below, glitches are clearly program errors that disrupt play. Players of the unpatched, original version of *NMS* will recall the constant crashes during warps, which were fixed in later patches. On my first day of play, I got my ship stuck in a pillar of ore and had to die in order to reset the game, this time with my ship balanced atop the pillar and just enough jetpack fuel to make it to the door of the ship.

Anomalies are weird things that happen in the game that behave differently than how players might expect based on previous play. For example, I found a spinning gold sphere embedded in the pavement of a ruin. This might be a glitch, or it might not be. But it was unique to my experience. I also found ruins set on slopes that had levitating knowledge stones and stairs I could walk under. I originally thought this was a glitch, but this is actually an anomaly. The algorithms are working as intended; they just positioned the ruin in a strange place.

Glitches and anomalies are archaeologically significant when documenting the game, but they could be considered to be the "shinies" when compared with the coarseware of everything else in the universe. These common structures and material culture are just as important and yield just as much information about how the universe was built, even if it is not what we had been expecting. For this reason, *No Man's Sky* remains worthy of archaeological attention. Although it was not the game we expected, it is the game archaeologists needed at this stage of doing fieldwork in virtual worlds.

More robust, procedurally generated worlds are coming, and *NMS* is preparing us for what's ahead. With these publicly shared, massive universes to explore, the data collected by the games and their developers can provide rich insight into player and game behavior. How many ruins were discovered by players in *No Man's Sky*, and is there a distribution pattern? Are the words learned in that game all procedurally generated, meaning there are infinite lexica for the three races and for the Atlas (universal repository)? Will developers such as Hello Games release non-sensitive data (i.e., discoveries and their locations in the game) or data-mining tools to the public, or to researchers? The ethics of this kind of data collection and sharing must be considered, but I hope to see at least some information about what is out there in these virtual universes.

Conducting a Transect of a Moon in No Man's Sky

As part of NMSAS, I wanted to complete a transect of a moon in order to see what I could find as I traversed the landscape on foot, to see if field-walking was possible in a game, and if it could provide any useful information. The moon I selected, Aobandan Elemen, is one of two orbiting Gapacazuso LR474, the sole planet in the O-class system Etenqintasy, about 140,000 light years from the center of the Euclid Galaxy (the home to all *No Man's Sky* players when they begin the game). With warm weather, average Sentinel (flying robot guardians of the environment) presence, common flora, and bountiful fauna, plus its relatively small size, this moon seemed the best place to test archaeological survey/transect methods in version 1.1x, the so-called "Foundation Update" released by Hello Games in November 2016.

Methods

With version 1.1x, players could finally place their own permanent beacons as well as "signal boosters," which contain exact coordinates, allowing for proper recordkeeping. I wanted to do a long transect of a small moon to see what non-natural discoveries I could find along the route. Having played the game for a few months, I knew that it is rare that things align exactly, so I allowed myself the chance to zig and zag a little, deviating from the line by a maximum of one minute's walk from my current position in order to reach an area flagged on my head-up display (HUD). These areas appear in the game as question marks, and hovering one's pointer over them indicates travel time at one's current speed.

Prior to starting the survey, it was important to mark a start- and end-point. I scanned the surface of the moon from space, and a "habitable base" and "abandoned building" were flagged as discoveries awaiting my arrival. These two structures mark fixed positions on the surface, and they were roughly poles apart on the equator. Because planets and moons have no poles in that version of the game (which was fixed in v1.3, August 2017), it was impossible to determine cardinal directions, so I let these structures serve as the poles of the moon's prime meridian, creating the transect to walk along. In order to mark the poles, I landed my ship at an Abandoned Building and planted a beacon and a signal booster, recording the coordinates prior to leaving. I then flew to a Habitable Base and planted another beacon and signal booster. By doing so, these two fixed points would appear on my display and allow me to see my distance traveled (in minutes and seconds) as well as the distance yet to cover (also in minutes and seconds).

Start (Habitable Base): VAER:05B9:007C:02C6:0118
End (Abandoned Building): ABST:05B9:007C:02C6:0118

To calculate distance, I used both a stopwatch and my "distance traveled" Journey entry. The game records the total distance traveled by a player on foot, measuring by "u" for "units." One unit = approximately one foot. I deduced this figure by checking my distance traveled before and after traveling for sixty seconds across a flat area on the moon. I traversed 276 units in one minute of walking. This equates to 16,560 units per hour. Assuming one travels three miles per hour, this would equal 5,520 units per mile (a mile on Earth is 5,280 feet). Unfortunately, I figured this out about two-thirds through the transect, so I was unable to record absolute distance between sites. I did, however, time my travel between sites, and one can multiply time traveled by units to arrive at distance (D = rt).

I resolved to plant a signal booster only at any sites I found along the way. Planting a permanent beacon would have confused my north-south direction, cluttering up my viewfinder with other points of interest. Planting a signal booster would give me coordinates, however, permanently tied to a structure. I opted not to plant a signal booster next to deposits of trash, feeling it would add even more clutter to the landscape. I did, however, note whenever I came upon more discarded boxes and jettison pods. For the next transect, I think I will plant a signal booster next to everything I find, not just permanent structures.

Whenever I reached a site (a non-natural feature in the environment), I took a screengrab that included the name of the moon as well as the coordinates provided by the signal booster. I occasionally shot video of glitches and of unique (to me) animal behavior.

Research Questions

- How many built environments would I find on the transect, and of what type would they be?
- Would these structures be tied to one of the game's three races, or would there be buildings placed by different races?
- How much trash would I find along the transect, and of what type would it be?
- What kind of landscapes support different kinds of non-natural intrusions (trash, buildings, ruins, monoliths, etc.)? Can any conclusions be drawn?
- Are non-natural finds (artifacts/sites) evenly spaced apart by time, distance, or both, or is placement more or less random?
- Would there be any glitches, and if so, how would they manifest?

Environment

The climate of Aobandan Element is classed as "warm," but daytime highs were in the mid-40s C (115° F), and overnight lows in the high teens C (60s F), with frequent dust storms propelled by excessive heat (70s C, 160° F) and wind. There was zero precipitation during the seven moon-days that it took to complete the transect. The day-night cycle is twenty minutes in Earth real-time, cycling between ten-minute days and ten-minute nights bookended by very fast dawns and dusks.

The moon is hilly but not mountainous, with occasional flats that morph into modest canyonlands and simple rock arches. There is no running or standing water (or other liquid) anywhere, above- or underground. The geology is largely iron ore trapped in five kinds of rocks, with occasional crystal deposits of plutonium and quite rare chrysonite and titanium (these latter two typically found together). Plant life is limited to tall, isolated bi-leafed stalks or stalks topped with balls of vegetation. Scrub dots the landscape. Occasional plants bearing platinum or thamium9 signatures appear, typically in spaces of transition between the flats and sloping walls of red rock. Animal life varies between three types of megafauna (all peaceful), mid-sized quadrupeds (one type is carnivorous), several types of rodents (which the carnivore eats), and a human-sized "land-crab" with eight legs.

Navigating the transect was not too difficult, but occasionally I had to choose a route around steep hills or to avoid the carnivore. The most challenging environmental aspect was the excessive heat and storms, which required constant maintenance of my suit to keep me from burning up. Fortunately, overnight travel did not require any mad scrambles to find iron or platinum for immediate suit repairs.

The Transect

The following notes are organized by total time to each discovery. Whenever I stopped at a structure or rubbish site, I would stop the clock in order to make notes, restarting it only when resuming my journey. The total time to walk halfway around the moon was 140 minutes, although I spent about twice that long taking photos, video, and making notes. Time is presented in this report as hh:mm:ss. In order not to aversely affect the time between points, I walked the entire way, never engaging the "run" function and only occasionally activating the jetpack to soften landings when I had to step off of cliffs along the straight transect route.

00:00:00: Start at the Habitable Base.

00:00:39: Cargo drop (four containers requiring Atlas Pass v1 to open, health box, green cargo box)

00:04:04: two damaged machinery pods

00:10:10: "The Okpod" waypoint (EWIX prefix). This waypoint contained one shelter building with a banner featuring an orange field topped by a black square from which dropped two black vertical lines, and three black horizontal lines at the bottom. The shelter contained a multitool tech station, restore shield station, and an encyclopedia station that displayed the Gek word for "beam." The waypoint also had two "Atlas cans," one damaged machinery pod, and one health pod.

00:19:23: one damaged machinery pod

00:23:00: "Mexiguerr Crossing" waypoint (ULDI prefix). This waypoint contained one shelter with an orange-and-black banner as described above. The shelter housed a multitool tech station only. Next to the shelter was a "Quonset"-style hut, two jettison pods, and one crate.

00:25:57: "Ebuey Moor" waypoint (no permanent structures, so no coordinates recorded). This antenna was flanked by a cargo box and one suit upgrade pod.

00:28:05: one damaged machinery pod

00:33:56: one "Atlas can"

00:35:23: one jettison pod and one crate

00:42:02: "Naglet Desert" waypoint (CODIV prefix). This waypoint featured a platinum resource depot (a five-cylinder building), as well as an orange-and-black banner as described above. The structure was surrounded by three crates, two jettison pods, and three "Atlas cans."

00:43:52: two health pods

00:49:19: one Knowledge Stone with the Gek word for "permanently"

00:49:58: one jettison pod and one "Atlas can"

00:50:11: one damaged machinery pod

00:55:20: one jettison pod

00:56:46: one damaged machinery pod

00:57:28: "Luysia Plains" waypoint (BUDUL prefix). One shelter containing a multitool tech station. Another orange-and-black banner hung outside. There was a Quonset hut and a short tower.

00:60:00: cargo drop

01:02:00: "Ruzanna Crater" waypoint (LOTE prefix). Gek observatory, the "Ticssold Reflector." There was also a Gek Knowledge Stone with the word for "idiot." Solving the observatory's puzzle yielded the location of ruins approximately thirty minutes away and off-transect. I opted to ignore the ruins during the transect, returning to them after completing the survey.

01:24:00: "H-CF5 Interface" trading post (LUBB prefix). The trading post also marked the spot of one of three glitches I found, this one being three suspended spacecraft, unmoving in the sky. Other elements moved as normal, but these ships were stuck in the air, the first time I have seen this in the game.

01:32:24: "Mepare Desert" waypoint (ENJA prefix). This waypoint contained a single shelter with a multitool tech station, outside of which stood another orange-and-black banner. A small tower and a Quonset hut stood nearby.

01:38:03: one damaged machinery pod

01:42:32: "Nodaya Plain" waypoint. No structures or crates to report, so no coordinates taken. There was an orange-and-black banner next to the antenna, however.

01:47:21: one damaged machinery pod

01:48:40: "Yevio Dale" waypoint. No structures or crates to report, so no coordinates taken. There was an orange-and-black banner next to the antenna, however.

01:55:39: "Lovars Moor" waypoint (MUPDO prefix). Two shelters and one Quonset hut. No banner. One shelter had a research specimen station and a health station. The other shelter housed a multitool station and a shield station.

02:01:55: one damaged machinery pod

02:04:43: "Effit Moor" waypoint (ORBU prefix). Two shelters and one Quonset hut. The banner outside the shelters was NOT orange and black, but rather a black chevron on a purple field. This was the only odd banner found along the transect. One shelter contained a multitool station and a shield station. The other shelter contained a research station.

02:07:34: "Indhaudley" waypoint (PAYEM prefix). Platinum resource depot next to an orange-and-black banner as described above.

02:13:00: Drop pod. This area was glitched, as attempting to move forward caused me to spin rapidly instead of advancing. Logging out and logging in resolved the issue, and I was able to proceed along the transect route.

02:14:59: one damaged machinery pod

02:16:02: Gek plaque, "Donetuswe Landmark" (OKTI prefix). Activating the landmark revealed the Gek word for "devastation."

02:20:00: Endpoint of the transect reached.

Post-Transect
I realized dumbly that after finishing the transect I would have to walk back to my ship, or at least to a building that would allow me to summon my ship to my location. I decided to walk to the ruins I'd located via the observatory, about an hour's walk away. As I walked (about thirty degrees off-transect), I stumbled upon a few things:

"Oennyidu Tower" (Korvax transmission tower). This was the only non-Gek site/artifact/feature I discovered on this moon. Activating the tower broadcast a distress signal from a crashed ship. An empty Quonset hut stood next to the tower. No coordinates taken.

"Iwaiduc Station" waypoint (RUVA) prefix. This was a massive area featuring a Gek landing pad and Gek observatory. The landing pad connected to a commercial office crewed by "Trade Envoy Hilau." The office contained a stock transfer station, a multitool tech station, a sales terminal ("K-C-IXO"), and a weapon terminal featuring the gun "Shaodw of Yakodawaj." After speaking with Hilau, I discovered the NPC was a "SynthetiGek," a Korvax representative wearing a Gek disguise. I opted not to interfere, thus increasing my reputation with the Korvax. Solving the neighboring observatory's puzzle pointed me to the same set of ruins I was heading toward. I summoned my ship and flew to the ruins.

"Ruins" (ULKI prefix). As with all ruins in the game, this set featured three Knowledge Stones. Words learned were all Gek, for "rare," "dampening," and "slug." The ruins themselves were a complex elevated on lofty pillars of carved rock atop which sat a Gek monumental sculpture head, a gold sphere knocked off its plinth, a flagpole topped by a triangle, and a spherical Gek plaque, "Remnants of Maviande-Aiam." Activating the plaque yielded the Gek word for "ammunition." Note that none of the above features of this ruin are unique to it (other than its name). I have seen these features in various combinations in other types of ruins.

"Koriguchi S31" abandoned Gek ship (LUPBA prefix), as identified by the Korvax radio antenna discovered earlier. The ship's banner was yellow on a blue field.

As I prepared to leave the moon, I accidentally flew over a monolith, so I landed to record it:

"Urtetuus-Foss Landmark," Gek monolith (UUJJ prefix). As with other monoliths, three Knowledge Stones were present, these offering up the Gek words for "speech," "emergency," and "balarian." Correctly solving the monolith's challenge yielded the Atlas word for "leave." This monolith was of the "sphere" type, with a blue eye open to the horizon.

Improving Methods

Future transects should plant a signal booster (containing coordinates) at every non-natural feature/artifact/site.

Record not only time between points, but also distance in units by way of the Journey feature in the menu.

Upon finishing the north-south transect, fly to the midpoint and then plant beacons to mark east-west termini for a second transect.

Immediately upon finding a banner, research it on the game's reddit pages to see if similar examples have been found, and in what context.

Record letter-forms and sigils that mark some buildings, and compare these against what others have found and have placed online.

Determine how to read the coordinate prefixes given by the signal boosters. Learn how to map these on the world's surface to look for placement patterns.

Preliminary Conclusions

Completing this short transect allowed me to do some "slow archaeology," and I was able to learn much more about this moon and its features than I otherwise would have through just a flyover. One cannot see the small crates and canisters from the air or appreciate the landscape and how it affects where things are. By far the most common non-natural find were the damaged machinery pods, followed by dump-sites of crates and boxes. A handful of building types also occurred along the transect, but not all building types were discovered (when compared to others I have seen on other worlds). There seems to be no pattern of placement or of how far things are from other things, although I was never more than ten minutes' walk from something of archaeological interest.

The most intriguing things to me when playing *No Man's Sky* as a game are the subtle differences in the procedurally generated shapes of buildings, in the words discovered, and in the names given to sites. Are these truly random, or are they tied to specific races in the game? How does the morphology and phonology work? I am also keen to learn more about the intersection of the game's three races; seeing the Korvax banner on a Gek moon was striking.

The fact that I found this much stuff over about seven Earth miles of actual walking was also surprising, and it reflects the artifact/site/feature-density I have seen on other worlds (but have not measured with as much precision) in v1.1x of the game. The density of structures was much higher in v1.0x. After visiting nearly a hundred worlds, I have found that only a handful have been devoid of non-natural intrusions/structures. Everything, however, appears to be about the same age, appears not to age, and appears to be largely unaffected by the various climates/environments on different worlds. The ruins are certainly different, appear to be older, and are actually ruined. It remains unclear who put them across the galaxy. These, too, share architectural morphology, perhaps seeded by an earlier spacefaring race.

When viewing *No Man's Sky* as its own built environment, there are still "holes in the roof," or glitches (aberrant behaviors). Observing these, one is immediately taken out of the space of the game; the illusion of immersion breaks. Seeing ships frozen in flight, seeing animals scrambling over the ground while getting nowhere, and being personally able to walk forward without spinning made an interesting walk more so. My presence on the landscape allowed me to observe these behaviors, and likely caused them just by being where I was at a certain point in time. I did nothing out of the ordinary to trigger this odd behavior, yet there it was, the residue of the complex construct of the gaming environment.

The No Man's Sky *Archaeological Survey, One Year Later*

NMSAS stalled after the first few months of play, but the release of the "Atlas Rises" update (v1.3) in August 2017 resolved most of the game's issues for archaeologists. The survey procedure remained largely unchanged: The first step for a survey team was to choose a system in the nearly infinite galactic map into which we could warp. There are four types of stars, each with variations in the nature of the worlds orbiting them. We remained curious if the types of systems affected what we would find in an archaeological context. Following the warp, we would select a planet and then conduct a series of orbital surveys, much like what "space archaeologist" Sarah Parcak does with reviewing satellite imagery of culturally sensitive areas on Earth.[18] Following the orbital survey, we would drop our spacecraft down into the landscape to conduct a series of low-altitude transects to identify and count features, both natural and not. Then we would conduct a series of field-walking surveys in sites or over swaths of territory to look for settlement patterns, construction, waste, etc. We would also identify sites and features, marking them for a second team who would return for thorough documentation and possible excavation. For each level of the survey, we would take screen grabs and video capture to tie to custom software context sheets coded by the FAIMS project at Macquarie University (see below). At least that was the intent.

In-Game Problems at Launch (with Game Mechanics)

The archaeological sites archaeologists find are not necessarily the ones we want, and we must do our best to document the methods and results of our investigations. The game that we (and others) had hoped for had not been realized, and it was nearly impossible to do anything archaeologically meaningful in the initial versions of *NMS*:

- There was no Cartesian coordinate system (or any other kind of coordinate system) to allow us to pin a thing or place to a map.
- There was no way to determine which way is north.
- There was no way to dig/excavate or set markers or lay out a grid.
- There was no way to communicate with or see other players even if they were on the same planet.

- High-altitude orbits yielded nothing of note on the surface below, as what was found on the surface was not reflected from what we saw from orbit.
- Every two weeks, all discoveries were wiped from the game, preventing any kind of backtracking or revisiting sites of interest.

Things We Got Out of NMSAS

Because of the above issues with the game-site over the first year of play, the NMSAS team saw a 99 percent attrition rate, and it appeared at first review as if the project had been a failure. We weren't able to accomplish our goals in the digital universe, and what we found was largely contextually meaningless. We did, however, find some benefits that can now be applied to future projects in digital built environments:

1. Prior to launching NMSAS, Catherine Flick (DeMontfort University) and L. Meghan Dennis (University of York) recommended that the team and project follow a code of ethics on how to conduct ourselves and our work within the confines of an unknown universe among unknown "life forms." Our agency in the game might affect future investigation. Once the code of ethics was written by the three of us, we posted it publicly online and also emailed it to the other team members.

2. When NMSAS was announced, I was approached by Brian Ballsun-Stanton and Georgia Burnett of the FAIMS project at Macquarie University. They had created an Android app that would allow for data collection in the field via smartphone and tablet. I provided the workflow and data definitions, and FAIMS provided bespoke digital context sheets for the team to use that would update a central database in real-time. Because *NMS* lacked any kind of coordinates system or way to measure distance, we were unable to make much use of the software (which was quite good and easy to use). With the release of v1.3 of *NMS,* we should be able to renew efforts to use the software to document what we find on the survey. The software could also be changed to accommodate data from other synthetic worlds that are explored in a similar fashion to NMSAS.

3. It is likely a mixed blessing that *NMS* was released without expected functionality, as the team was able to test and modify its methods on the ground. Working in a "failed" environment also allowed me to streamline processes and reconsider when to create and launch digital field projects. We could also determine what tools we were lacking in the synthetic universe and could observe and adopt those that were created as mods in the player community.

4. Stepping outside of *NMS,* I was able to create an experimental Harris-style software matrix to track changes in the game between versions, treating each version as a stratum in order to read game stratigraphy. The methods of creating a software matrix can be applied to any digital built environment, game or not.

Lessons Learned

After one year of playing *NMS* and attempting to conduct an archaeological investigation within that space, I have taken away a handful of lessons about managing a team-based digital project set in a synthetic world:

1. Video game communities for games such as *NMS* contain thousands of citizen scientists and offer access to thousands and thousands of wiki pages, reddit threads, etc. Archaeologists must take advantage of this, involve the community in large projects, and treat this as a kind of public archaeology. The community will collect much more data than a team of archaeologists would. They will also create more mods more quickly in order to facilitate the navigation and use of a digital built environment.
2. Archaeology is social, and surveys are social events. In the natural world, no one works alone during a field season. It is a team effort. This should also be the case with digital projects. Working alone is no fun, is often thankless, and leads to abandonment of a project. Other reasons for attrition include professional and personal obligations, as well as leaving something boring for something new. Not having clear end goals or a timeline also contributes to poor morale.
3. Learn the landscape (play the game) before launching a project plan/ project. No archaeologist ever showed up while a new culture was beginning. Granted, with games we work on an accelerated timeline, but we should take time to play a game in order to fully understand its mechanics and what is possible to do within that environment, developing an archaeological project plan around that instead of discovering everything we cannot do in that space.
4. Manage expectations. Don't overhype and overcommit. *NMS* failed in the beginning because too much hype led to unrealistic (and unattainable) expectations by players and the media. Later patches rolled out quietly, and over the past year have made the game quite close to what it promised to deliver in 2016. Managing team expectations is also key to project success, letting members know what is expected of them, and what the goals are, both in the short and long term.

5. Publish successes/failures (and data, media, etc.) as Open Access so that others can easily discover and use your work to advance their own. Blog/tweet regularly about the project's progress, and encourage archaeology "ride-alongs" via streaming services such as Twitch. Not doing more of this was a serious failure of NMSAS.

The (Unexpected) Future of NMSAS

I was ready to end the NMSAS project after delivering a post-mortem at the 2017 EAA meeting in Maastrict, but Hello Games released v1.3 ("Atlas Rises"), which contained much of what players (and the team) had been expecting at the game's initial release:

- Portals exist for fast travel between worlds across the universe by use of a combination of sixteen glyphs (which took me about twenty hours to find).
- Archaeologists can excavate trenches with the new Terrain Manipulator function for the multitool.
- Up to sixteen people can group up for synchronous play in the same world, which is crucial for field-walking with a team.
- We now can see where north is, and we can see units as well as time to calculate distances across the landscape (and across space).

There are also three major archaeological things to do now that v1.3 has been released:

1. With the Terrain Manipulator, all players can create their own objects and art, which can be discovered by others. This follows on the v1.2 "Pathfinder" update earlier in 2017, which allowed for base-building (and sharing) and the ability to build beacons and communication terminals that could be discovered by other players. NMSAS can now document these player-made artifacts throughout the universe.
2. With the advent of cheap and largely accessible 3D printing, players (and archaeologists) can print what they find. Thanks also to open-source tools, it is easier than ever to do photogrammetry in-world and to export to VR, granting access to spaces to people who do not play or own instances of synthetic worlds.
3. The most exciting new project stems from the fact that v1.3 was for some players a catastrophic event leading to a mass migration from one space to another. The "Galactic Hub" was a planet shared by five thousand plus players. They built bases, shared gardens, and created

a Utopian society of scientists who used that world to explore the surrounding systems and record what they found on a communal wiki. When v1.3 launched, it changed the nature of all of the planets in the universe and turned the Galactic Hub into an uninhabitable wasteland of ice. The population is migrating to a new world, leaving behind the "Legacy Hub," on which are the remains of that human society's material culture.[19] This is the first time a mass migration has occurred in a video game, and therefore it demands archaeological attention. I arrived in the Legacy Hub on September 15, 2017, set up my excavation house, and conducted a preliminary survey prior to beginning the Legacy Hub Archaeological Project (L-HAP) in October, in which the team will document and catalogue the material culture left behind by the evacuated human population.

Glitches as Artifacts

One aspect of archaeogaming is looking for "artifacts" within a gaming environment. Think of it as a bug hunt. The last thing players want to experience when exploring a virtual world is a bug or a glitch. These technical aberrations interfere with (or even halt) gameplay, and they are unwelcome intrusions into the illusion of reality. Bugs and glitches in games are common, especially in more current titles that can be overburdened by the complexity of code, of poor quality assurance testing, or a combination of both. Bainbridge recalls glitching in *World of Warcraft* as the virtual world being held hostage by real-world storms, server emergency maintenance, and even hitting the "Windows" key by accident (Bainbridge 2010: 214).

One can draw an analogue to pottery found on excavation. A lot of artifacts are grotty and common, occasionally beautiful, but all convey data to the archaeologist and form what becomes the archaeological record. "Gamifacts" are rare finds among the common environment in which they are discovered in synthetic worlds. While odd and at times entertaining, glitches taken together with their digital environments create a game history, a snapshot in time.

Take *Elder Scrolls V: Skyrim* for example. Bethesda Softworks released the game in 2011 just ahead of the holiday season (we've seen this happen before to disastrous effect with Atari's *E.T.* in 1982). Almost immediately players began complaining about some spectacular glitches/bugs, including things such as mammoths falling from the sky and dragons flying backward (see Figure 3.2). Bethesda patched the major bugs in early December: no more reverse-flying dragons, non-player

Figure 3.2. Glitch of a falling mammoth from *Elder Scrolls V: Skyrim* (Bethesda Softworks). Screen capture by author.

characters without heads, or suspended laws of physics. These massive (and massively entertaining) glitches disappeared from the game and became the stuff of game lore with evidence remaining online in images and gameplay video. These bugs are real artifacts, and the photographic, video, and anecdotal evidence are all that remains of the archaeological/archaeogaming record.

Finding a Gamifact in Elder Scrolls Online

As an archaeologist and as a player, I am always on the lookout for something out of the ordinary, something weird, something that clearly should not be part of the game. I've put in dozens of hours on Xbox One playing *Elder Scrolls Online: Tamriel Unlimited.* My level 44 avatar had been visiting eastern Coldharbour doing what one does: exploration, completing quests, farming materials, and killing enemies. I was supposed to meet a friend that evening to punch out some mini-bosses in a few delves, so I waited in the Shining Star Tavern in the Hollow City. I was early, so I had a drink and talked to the NPC clientele at the bar, a few of whom I'd seen before, but elsewhere. And then I saw Holgunn, an NPC, drinking an ale in what appeared to be "bullet time" from *The Matrix*. I stood there for a couple of minutes watching Holgunn stand still while at the same time chugging ale, almost as if his still, silent self was wishing he was drinking the place dry (see Figure 3.3).

Figure 3.3. Glitch of the NPC Holgunn from *Elder Scrolls Online* (Zenimax Online). Screen capture by author.

It was a glitch. It was also an artifact. In archaeogaming parlance, it's a "gamifact." As an archaeologist, what did I do? I took several pictures. I took video. I noted the date (September 1, 2015) and the time of discovery (10:12 pm). I noted the location (Shining Star Tavern, the Hollow City, Coldharbour). I also noted the quest I was on (The Army of Meridia) because NPCs often wander off somewhere else in a game after the completion of one quest in anticipation of another. But then I wondered if this glitch could be reproduced by someone else on different hardware, PS4 and PC. Does this glitch occur only on this quest, or is it just there all the time? What code is behind this glitch?

After noting this gamifact, I visited several *ESO* discussion groups and forums, but I did not find this glitch reported anywhere. Either it is new or so subtle that no one's noticed it yet. Because the glitch is benign, it is likely that nobody cared enough to report it. As an archaeologist, I did. And when an upcoming patch is released that fixes the glitch, we will be reminded that archaeology is a destructive process.

Once we find an artifact, it is pulled from the earth, documented, filed away. Anyone who comes by later might not know that there was something special in place. So it is with glitches and patches.

The following day, I tried to reproduce the glitch. I returned to the tavern to look for Holgunn at exactly the same time as I did on the previous day, but he was absent. I forgot, however, that time is accelerated in *ESO*. The tavern in the daytime has an entirely different clientele than it does at night. It could be that Holgunn, like some, works during the day, and then relaxes with a few mugs of ale in the tavern after sundown. I checked a few times, but he was gone.

New games, just like newly discovered sites, will yield the most of these, growing more rare over time as patches fix things. These glitches are part of the game and its history, adding to the story surrounding the media, and should be recorded.

Glitches Defined Archaeologically

One of the chambers of the heart of archaeogaming lies with understanding glitch-artifacts. Some assumptions as they relate specifically to video games:

1. Video games are each their own discrete archaeological site.
2. Video games often have glitches upon their initial release.
3. Glitches, which can appear at an observable game-space and game-time, are artifacts within the game and therefore have archaeological context.
4. Glitches are artifacts created from the complexity of code.
5. Glitches are artifacts created from the entanglement of hardware, software, and platform.
6. Glitches are artifacts that temporarily exist in a quantum state.

To deconstruct:

1. As discussed earlier in this chapter, video games are each their own discrete archaeological sites. A video game is a discrete entity where the place can be defined as where the game is installed (not necessarily its installation medium, which is a whole other story). The past activity is the coding that created the game. Its elements can be directly observed and manipulated, part of the record of the game.
2. Video games often have glitches upon their initial release. A glitch can be defined as unintended functionality created by code. 1978's *Space Invaders* had one of the earliest glitches, which actually re-

mained in the game, speeding up the aliens as the player killed off rows of minions. 2015's *Rise of the Tomb Raider* has a glitch near the end of the game that "breaks" the game if a player tries to save progress prior to entering the Bathhouse Challenge Tomb.[21] Despite quality assurance (QA) testing, games ship with glitches, and those glitches remain until they are patched by the developer. If you want to see more examples of game-glitches, there are loads of websites focusing on these, but in a non-archaeological way. Search for "game glitch" and lose hours of your life to the topic.[22]

3. Glitches, which can appear at an observable game-space and game-time, are artifacts within the game and therefore have archaeological context. An artifact, such as a tool or a work of art, is something recovered by archaeological endeavor made or given shape by a person (or people), especially an object of archaeological, historical, or cultural interest. In meatspace, an artifact is often excavated. Prior to removal, its archaeological context is recorded: its relationship to its surrounding environment, its absolute location, and other metadata, including the date on which it was recovered. Following discovery and preliminary documentation (notes, measurements, in situ photography), it is removed and relocated to another place for additional study. In game-space, the glitch is the artifact (and perhaps the only class of artifact) to be observed and recorded. Everything else within the game is a deliberate creation of one or more game developers, which taken as a whole could be considered landscape archaeology as described above.[21] But glitches are true intrusions into game-space, and as such they can be classed as "significant finds."

4. Glitches are artifacts created from the complexity of code. As stated above, video games are the summation of conscious design and coding decisions, where each element a player interacts with is there for a reason. No developer deliberately creates glitches within a game s/he distributes (otherwise they would be classed as "Easter eggs").[23] A glitch is the unintended result of coding. This raises two questions: (1) is a glitch made by the code alone, (2) and if so, is it still classed as made by a person and therefore able to be called an "artifact" in the classical, archaeological sense? I propose that the answer to the second question is "yes," arguing first that the code was written by a person (or even machine-written code derived from initial human-created code) and also that by analogy people make mistakes, and the archaeological record is full of physical evidence of those mistakes (e.g., misfired pots). Complexity, when used in this context, can be considered in the mathematical sense, specifically

computational complexity, where processes having a large number of seemingly independent agents can spontaneously order themselves into a coherent system, but that the complex system contains an inherent level of chaos or noise as created by the entanglement mentioned in number 5 below. What makes glitches so interesting is that they are unpredictable attachments to nonhumans in processes of making and experiencing (Yaneva 2013: 132).

5. Glitches are artifacts created from the intersection of hardware, software, and platform. This is called "entanglement," something archaeologist Ian Hodder has written about in his book *Entangled: An Archaeology of the Relationships between Humans and Things* that explores the complexity of the human relationship with material things, demonstrating how humans and societies are entrapped into the maintenance and sustaining of material worlds (Hodder 2012). The same can be said of the maintenance of virtual worlds, where glitches are the product of the complex interrelationships between code, the code's platform,[24] and hardware used by players. It is not code alone that causes glitches (although there might be some instances where it does). Instead, it is the chaos introduced into the system by the variables of code, platform, and hardware that create these artifacts.

6. Glitches are artifacts that temporarily exist in a quantum state (i.e., they exist in a time and space that must ultimately be observed by a person, but that observation might be what actually triggers the appearance of the glitch). The classic example of a quantum state of being is the fact that light is both a particle and a wave. Things get weirder when we consider that we cannot know the state of a quark (a subatomic particle) without directly observing it but that the quark can exist in all number of states at once prior to observation. Quantum entanglement occurs when pairs or groups of particles are generated or interact in ways such that the quantum state of each particle cannot be described independently. Video games do not obey classical laws of physics when experienced as a player, even though the developer has spent time and effort to recreate a believable physics within the game-space. A glitch, then, is an aberration in which at least two states of being can be observed simultaneously: what is, and what is supposed to be. Going one level deeper, the actual game (code + platform + hardware) is subject to meatspace physics as well as quantum physics, which are operating within the twin theories of chaos and complexity, resulting in something unexpected by both player and developer alike.

These glitches, these artifacts, are destroyed (fixed) by patches and are then lost to time, living on only in the documentation of the archaeogamer as well as in the public record via media services. The memory of the glitch-artifact is preserved, but not the glitch itself, unless the archaeogamer retains an unpatched version of the archaeological site (the game). These glitches are part of the game's history and document a specific part of its development and life cycle, much like various stratigraphic levels of meatspace sites. The game's build and patch numbers equate to a time-based stratigraphy, and any glitch-artifact must be recorded not only with its game-time and game-place of observation but also with the build and/or patch number for proper contextual reference.

What can glitches tell us (if anything) about the space with which we interact? Michael J. Kramer teaches Digitizing Folk Music History, a seminar at Northwestern University. In it, he teaches the class how to hack JPEG images, turning photos of folk musicians into glitch art (Kramer 2016). By randomly deconstructing the images through a text editor, the images present new ideas of thinking about music, personality, fame, and more. Creating glitches allowed students to think about things differently. Video game glitches can do the same, offering the chance for players (and artists) to play with games in unintended ways, exploring the intersection of code and related visuals.

Artist Daniel Temkin specializes in glitch art, looking for visually interesting glitches within games and other software (Pangburn 2014). Temkin states that "the glitch aesthetic may be rooted in the look of malfunction, but when it comes to actual practice, there is often not much glitch in glitch art." Artists like Temkin tend to try to bend or break the rules inside the game-space to create glitches, using the environment in ways not intended by the developer.[25] I call this "gamejacking," which is also known as "counterplay."[26] Gamejacking is more akin to creating artifacts rather than discovering them as they are created by a game's natural errors, something that is likely disingenuous although unique at the same time.

In 2011, Temkin and his colleague Hugh S. Manon had a series of conversations about "glitch" (both a noun and a verb), fifty-six theses of which they published online (Manon and Temkin 2011), defining glitch theory and practice, defining the glitch as a real artifact in a virtual space, and exploring the formation process, which is often instant, unanticipated. The glitch-as-artifact differs from those artifacts found in the real world, which can be revealed slowly, and almost predictably, and can remain in situ until removed by the archaeologist. With glitches, they can disappear as soon as they are discovered, and it is up to the archaeogamer to be quick in documenting the happening. This documentation will need to include a typology, something Bainbridge hinted at when playing *World of Warcraft* from a cultural perspective: glitches (of which bugs are a subset), "bugged" quests (i.e., quests that are impossible to complete for reasons other than player incompetence), "bookkeeping" glitches (i.e., the developers forget to update part of the game), and "data corruption" (i.e., dropped internet packets) (Bainbridge 2010: 215).

Glitches are not the only artifacts created by complexity/entanglement, however. I believe that in procedural games (where code creates things in game-space in a more randomized but still logical way), the complexity of code leads not only to glitches but also to unexpected elements in built environments, a "happy glitch" (one that is intellectually interesting) instead of a "sad glitch" (one that crashes the game or otherwise disrupts play).

Garbology in Video Games

World of Warcraft entertains millions of players, and has for over ten years. The game-world of Azeroth revolves around things gained by collecting, looting, buying, selling, and earning. When you think about all of the monsters/mobs/bosses slain and all of the loot dropped, there is conceivably billions of metric tons of stuff, much of it unmemorable. This junk, informally called by the player community "vendor trash" or "grays" (because of the color of the item description text), ends up either sold by players to NPC vendors, left unlooted, or dropped on the ground. Because the game has a robust inventory infrastructure, players can purchase slots for their stuff in personal and guild banks (akin to safe-deposit boxes) and/or buy increasingly large bags/packs to hold as much mobile inventory as players care to carry.

Sometimes players run out of room and must discard something, making space for a more desirable item. I leave some leather scraps on the ground where they will remain for as long as I am logged in to the game. I can travel somewhere else and return to that drop spot, and my leather scraps will still be there, untouched and unseen by animals or other players. But as soon as I log out, my trash evaporates. If only that would happen in the real world. But if it did, much of the archaeological record would be forever lost instead of locked in a sandy matrix awaiting discovery and interpretation.

Traditional archaeologists often deal in rubbish. Much of what is recovered on excavation is fragmentary bits of pottery, of bone, stone flakes left over from the manufacture of tools and points. People break things and make mistakes, and once they come to the end of their period of intended use, their things get discarded, buried, thrown in a well, dropped down a privy hole, tossed out the back door. Pottery workshops and other areas dedicated to making consumer goods (including food) generate huge rubbish piles, which serve as literal data dumps for archaeologists interested in site economies, population, and trade. We learn much from sifting through people's trash. The field dedicated to that for modern and contemporary cultures is called garbology.

The Tucson Garbage Project was started in 1973 by William Rathje of the University of Arizona to study patterns of consumption by the city's residents. One of the insights of the project (which continues to operate years after Rathje's death) was that people lie about what they throw away. Comparing survey report data against what was actually tossed in the bin showed two different stories, one that was socially acceptable/expedient and another that demonstrated empirical actuality. Both the actual trash and the stories, however, are valuable to the archaeologist interested in how people deal with things, especially past the point of a thing's desirability. What was thrown away and why? The perceived end-of-life of an item is really just an interesting story of an object's journey into the future.

With video games, however, there is little physical evidence of anything ever having been used and discarded. In *WoW*, it is as if the Langoliers arrive to eat up the past, scrubbing it clean.[27] This is good news for the game's servers (shards), which would be overwhelmed with data, remembering where to place every discarded item from every player within the world. Over time, I imagine giant middens appearing, a Fresh Kills of Feralas or a virtual landfill in the desert of Tanaris (recalling that of Alamogordo, New Mexico).

Games with inventory systems (typically MMOs, first-person shooters, and role-playing games) must find a way to deal with player trash and unclaimed loot left by slain enemies and NPCs. In an earlier Blizzard game, *Diablo* (and its sequels), trash would gradually disappear over time. Players could leave loot on the ground, travel elsewhere, and then return to find a diminished pile. Logging out of the game would completely wipe the slate clean. Early adventure games (including Atari's *Adventure*) would leave loot on the floors of dungeons for the duration of play, but closing the game and removing the cartridge made the entire world blink out of existence. In *Dragon Age: Inquisition*, inventory that players wish to discard (instead of selling, trading, or banking) must be actively destroyed. The trash never hits the ground.

A similar trash-disposal mechanic exists in the MMO *Elder Scrolls Online*. Prior to the game's release, I had hoped that player rubbish would appear (and remain) in-game, virtual litter dropped singly or placed in piles. I wanted to see where other players had been. Because players can craft items, I wanted to look for dropped pieces made by others (identified by the character's name), drawing conclusions as to how that item came to rest at a given spot. Better yet, I wanted to see how players took items from one region of the game and transported them to others, leaving a trail of foreign trash throughout greater Tamriel. Alas, it was not to be. The questions I was asking of these open worlds are no different than those asked by archaeologists when considering how objects came to be frozen in time, prior to discovery and future movement as they continue their life cycles.

In most inventory-games (games that allow players to carry a lot of things), artifacts (and trash are artifacts) have been pre-placed by the developers (or their coded algorithms) for observation and collection. There is much for the taking, and the gaming archaeologist can decide to interpret this rubbish from within the cultural context of the game's lore or observe the higher-order thinking of the developer who made decisions of what artifacts to place, and where. How do game developers consider trash or collectibles? How do players interact with these? And how do these things impact gameplay and advancement of various narratives? Again, the questions much be asked on the in-game and extra-game levels.

But what of games that do allow players to discard inventory and that do record their placement so that players can see their own rubbish (and that left by other players) days, weeks, or months after items have been dropped? In the case of *ARK: Survival Evolved,* player rubbish (by way of abandoned, player-created structures), began occupying valuable game real estate, with some players actually becoming virtual demolition experts, blowing up the abandoned squalor to make way for new construction (Heaven 2015).

Disposing of something is a form of abandonment. We leave things behind, be they humble food scraps or broken automobiles. When considering video games and especially virtual worlds, these can be abandoned, too. The majority of video games created were done so for an audience as a form of interactive entertainment. As with other forms of entertainment media, these can be enjoyed/used and then either sold, traded, discarded, or kept unused, hibernating on a shelf or in a box.

In open worlds, these vast spaces largely remain accessible to those with the software (and sometimes hardware) to access them, long past the sell-by date when other players have found new worlds to occupy and explore. So what happens to these abandoned worlds still populated by never-aging NPCs who might wait years to assign quests that they used to assign thousands of times a day? The landscapes and structures remain unchanged. There is no visible decay, and no sign that any time at all has passed since the last time the world was entered like a cave of forgotten dreams. The notable thing about these abandoned spaces, just as we see in abandoned archaeological sites, is the lack of life in the form of people actively using the space. The kinetic energy is gone, as is the random element of play by the invisible operators of avatars.

Occasionally though, one finds signs of life in these ghost-worlds in the form of players or explorers, not unlike the perhaps apocryphal stories of finding a hermit in a cave who still thinks there's a war on, or to meeting a fellow adventurer visiting for curiosity, excitement, or both. One recent example includes the YouTuber vinesauce's 2016 delve into the 1995 MMO game, *Active Worlds*. In the abandoned game, vinesauce encountered "Hitomi Fujiko" whom he believed to be an NPC (Hernandez 2016). The dialogue, however, was real, and the explorer had discovered one of the last players alone in an abandoned game once inhabited by tens of thousands of avatars. Like most other video games set in virtual worlds, there is no decay, no environmental takeover, just a gradual absence of people until the server ultimately is brought offline. The players take their stories with them, and all that remains are the environments built as they were intended, ready to serve their narrative purpose, albeit for a new generation of archaeologists or tourists like those who visit Chernobyl or Pompeii.

Other In-Game Archaeologies

Any archaeologist will tell you that there is much more to archaeology than excavation. There are archaeological surveys, landscape archaeology, underwater archaeology, and space archaeology (to name a few), none of which require systematic digging while attempting to identify sites, answering questions about settlement and land use, and looking at material culture of things that are not landlocked, covered with overburden. Digging is one of the oldest manifestations of the discipline (later becoming systematic excavation), yielding itself easily to media tropes and popular perception, but archaeology goes beyond the spade and trowel.

Within a digital game, especially one set in a synthetic, open world, but also to some extent any game with a graphical, interactive interpretation of built or natural environments—from side-scrolling jumpers to roguelike dungeon-crawlers, procedural or fixed in their creation and layout—one has the option to conduct several kinds of archaeologies at once, both while actively playing the game as well as observing the game mechanics one level up. The fact that many games allow for any and all of the above archaeological variants again points to the fact that video games are archaeological sites and can be studied as such without a single grenade lobbed to remove ten cubic meters of digital soil.

Conclusion

This chapter attempted to demonstrate that synthetic worlds are landscapes and sites that can be studied archaeologically with gently modified methods and tools. Millions of people spend much of their discretionary time and income on video games, inhabiting these digital built environments while actively adding to game-based culture. Larger MMOs contain in-game populations that rival those of large cities, featuring constant personal and commercial interactions between players and their environments. The fact that these engagements are invisible in the natural world does not negate their importance to the archaeology of the Anthropocene. The fact that they are "immaterial" or "incorporeal" produces challenges to the video game archaeologist on how to document these spaces and the material culture they contain, which is the focus of the next chapter.

Notes

1. There are several ways of thinking about what makes a site a site, and archaeological theory continues to evolve that definition. For the purposes of this book and the material culture of the modern world, I have chosen to follow LaMotta's definitions, which appear on pp. 62–92 in the 2012 edition of *Archaeological Theory Today*, 2nd ed., edited by Ian Hodder. This book, as well as Matthew Johnson's *Archaeological Theory: An Introduction*, 2nd ed., published in 2010, are excellent overviews of the history archaeological theory.
2. *National Geographic* on the Great Pacific Garbage Patch: http://national geographic.org/encyclopedia/great-pacific-garbage-patch/ (retrieved December 11, 2016).
3. Ancient monuments and other buildings made use of *spolia*, taking stone from older buildings and incorporating them into new ones. For example, Rome's Arch of Constantine (CE 315) used reliefs from second-century buildings.

4. Andy Chalk, "Analyst says digital sales made up 92% of PC game market in 2013," *PC Gamer,* August 19, 2014, http://www.pcgamer.com/analyst-says-digital-sales-made-up-92-percent-of-pc-game-market-in-2013/ (retrieved December 13, 2016).

5. Visit the Antikythera Mechanism Research Project's homepage: http://www.antikythera-mechanism.gr/ (retrieved December 11, 2016).

6. See Ducheneaut et al. 2007 for a thorough breakdown of guilds in *World of Warcraft.*

7. Stu Eve finds this necessity to hold true especially for those archaeologists equipped with technology, using what he calls "embodied GIS." For an explanation on how technology merges with real-world exploration, see his 2012 article "Augmenting Phenomenology: Using Augmented Reality to Aid Archaeological Phenomenology in the Landscape." *Journal of Archaeological Method and Theory* 19(4): 582–600.

8. https://www.reddit.com/r/everquest/comments/3368fm/to_do_list_for_ret urning_player/ (retrieved September 17, 2017).

9. elysium-project.org (retrieved September 17, 2017).

10. The public-facing channel for the *No Man's Sky* Archaeological Survey is twitch.tv/nmsarchaeology.

11. https://www.polygon.com/2015/3/3/8140343/no-mans-sky-space-probes-gdc-quintillion-worlds (retrieved September 17, 2017).

12. For step-by-step instructions on how to create a GIS map from an image of a game map, see https://archaeogaming.com/2018/01/28/landscape-arc haeology-of-rorikstead-and-environs-in-skyrim-vr/ (retrieved February 20, 2018).

13. Prof. Bill Caraher recently published a list of archaeological project/field manuals from a variety of sites and institutions: https://mediterraneanworld.wo rdpress.com/2017/04/25/a-survey-of-archaeological-excavation-manuals/.

14. http://www.coe.int/en/web/landscape (retrieved September 17, 2017).

15. See Andrew Reinhard (2018), "Adapting the Harris Matrix for Software Stratigraphy," *Advances in Archaeological Practice* 6(2): 157–172.

16. Other, earlier games (such as those in the *Ultima* series) had begun to look at ethics, player action, and their effects on in-game cultures where these actions had scripted consequences (King and Borland 2004: 78). Games such as *No Man's Sky* offered the chance of facing brand new cultures with unscripted interactions based on ethical choices by the player that had completely unknown consequences.

17. Thanks to L. Meghan Dennis for pointing this out to me.

18. See Professor Parcak's TED Talk on how she uses satellites to conduct archaeology from orbit: https://www.ted.com/talks/sarah_parcak_archeolo gy_from_space (retrieved September 19, 2017).

19. See http://kotaku.com/no-mans-sky-players-who-colonized-a-galaxy-now-have-to-1798357453 (retrieved September 19, 2017).

20. For an explanation of the glitch's history and how to avoid it, see http://www.kotaku.co.uk/2015/11/27/how-to-avoid-rise-of-the-tomb-raiders-ga mebreaking-bug (retrieved February 20, 2018).

21. For twenty-five classic examples of video game glitches, watch: http://www.smosh.com/smosh-pit/photos/hilarious-video-game-glitches (retrieved December 11, 2016).

22. A comprehensive resource for understanding landscape archaeology is Bruno David and Julian Thomas, eds., *Handbook of Landscape Archaeology* (London: Routledge, 2010).

23. *Video Whizball* has the first Easter egg in a published video game, which in this case was played on the Channel F system. This predates by nearly a year the Easter egg placed in *Adventure* (1980). The egg in *Video Whizball* displays the programmer's name "Reid-Selth." It was discovered in 2004 by Sean Riddle.

24. For a definition of "platform" in this context, see the journal *Platform Studies.*

25. A good introduction to the art of glitch is by Mallika Roy, "Glitch It Good: Understanding the Glitch Art Movement," *Periphery,* December 2014, http://www.theperipherymag.com/on-the-arts-glitch-it-good/ (retrieved on December 11, 2016).

26. See Alan F. Meades, *Understanding Counterplay in Video Games* (2015).

27. Stephen King, "The Langoliers," in *Four Past Midnight* (New York: Viking, 1990).

Further Reading

Bradley, R. 2015. "Repeating the Unrepeatable Experiment." In *Material Evidence: Learning from Archaeological Practice,* edited by R. Chapman and A. Wylie, 23–41. New York: Routledge.

Castronova, E., et al. 2009. "Synthetic Worlds as Experimental Instruments." In *The Video Game Theory Reader 2,* edited by B. Perron and M. J. P. Wolf, 273–95. New York: Routledge.

David, B., and J. Thomas, eds. 2010. *Handbook of Landscape Archaeology.* New York: Routledge.

Fernández-Vara, C., et al. 2009. "Between Theory and Practice: The GAMBIT Experience." In *The Video Game Theory Reader 2,* edited by B. Perron and M. J. P. Wolf, 253–72. New York: Routledge.

Ingold, T. 1993. "The Temporality of the Landscape." *World Archaeology* 25(2): 152–74.

Nardi, B. A. 2010. *My Life as a Night Elf Priest: An Anthropological Account of World of Warcraft.* University of Michigan Press.

Rathje, W. and C. Murphy. 2003. *Rubbish! The Archaeology of Garbage.* Tucson: University of Arizona Press.

Schut, K. 2018. "*No Man's Sky.*" In *The Routledge Companion to Imaginary Worlds,* edited by M. J. P. Wolf, 425–32. New York: Routledge.

Chapter 4

Material Culture
of the Immaterial

Introduction

Archaeology traditionally deals with the artifact and its wider contexts as it relates to other artifacts found with/near it. The artifact's physicality makes it easy to comprehend as a "thing," something that was once created/manipulated by people, and upon discovery is manipulated again, this time by archaeologists. Even though the purpose of the artifact might not be readily apparent, its "thingness" is readily understood prior to further analysis to determine its true nature of creation, use, history, and ultimate deposition.

One can easily get lost in objects without considering maker-cultures. Karl Marx noted this danger of reification, summarized by Hodder: "Objects created by humans become so separate that they are perceived as having an external reality and an origin separate from themselves. . . . Objects have autonomy, deflecting societies' ability to be critically aware" (Hodder 2012: 32). Archaeology can fall (and at one point had fallen) into the trap of the fetish-artifact. We see this in modern media representations of archaeology where it is a treasure hunt, a quest for the shiny, elite goods. In these instances, material things are more important than ideas. Marx reappears, as noted by Johnson, defining history as growth of human productive power, and the modes of production as being the forces of production and social relations of production (Johnson 2010: 95). Therein lies a conflict of the formation of society dependent on the things it produces, separating production from humanity itself. There is more to archaeology than the object, and there is more to the object than the surface that can be seen and touched. Most artifacts have something to teach one level below the surface. This is especially true of video games.

To get to the software held within the media-artifact, we need to start with the artifact itself. As Buchli writes, "Engaging in immaterial practices almost always involves the manipulation of our understanding of our senses in relation to the material. The immaterial is often a radial effect of our manipulation of the sensorium—such as the rendering of sight separate from touch" (Buchli 2016: 5). Once discovered, the immaterial can also be interacted with. It has its own internal narrative of how it became created and embedded within the media like some genie imprisoned in a magic lamp.

The game-artifacts and the game-spaces held within them add to modern material culture of games and gaming. Johnson defines material culture as being like a text: (1) it can mean many things to many people who read it in different ways; (2) meanings can be actively manipulated (which is often unspoken); (3) there is no single right or wrong meaning of reading a text; (4) the meanings of a text are outside the control of the author (Johnson 2010: 109–10). This interrelation makes for interesting archaeology because of the countless ways people interact with the things they create/use. Hodder refers to these contextual relationships as social biographies (Hodder 2012: 33). These social biographies include the creation and use of objects, but they also introduce the intangibles of memory and meaning: We went to the arcade on a date. We played *Centipede* together. We remembered how to use the controls. But we also remember that the evening was not about the game or the gameplay; it was in the wider context of friendship. The game exists in its physical reality, but it is also a symbol. But as DeMarrais, Gosden, and Renfrew wrote, "The symbol cannot exist without the substance, and the material reality of the substance precedes the symbolic role" (DeMarrais, Gosden, and Renfrew 2004: 25).

Archaeologists know that things have multiple dependencies. In Hodder's book *Entangled: An Archaeology of the Relationships between Humans and Things,* he devotes the entire third chapter to the notion that "things depend on things." Objects are beholden to operational chains and sequences, and are dependent on materials, functions, and time. Things also depend on people in order to be useful, these human-made artifacts entrapping people in "long-term relationships of material investment, care, and maintenance" (Hodder 2012: 67). This is as true of taking care of one's computer or console as it is of taking care of one's character in an MMO. The avatar is as much a possession and investment (or arguably more so) than the hardware used to play it. As MMOs continue to update with expansion packs and later versions, the level caps increase, there is better loot, armor, and weapons, and also more lore to explore. Sometimes playing these kinds of games feels like a full-time job, even though one's avatar is an on-screen manifestation of player intent. The avatar is a dumb thing until interacted with, and it requires continual attention if it is to remain viable in-game.

This virtual interaction with a game is only possible (at least at this writing) through an object, in this case a computer, console, or hand-held device. Interaction is a process (Harvey 2013: 57). This process of interaction, of use, begins to add layers of meaning and history atop the original artifact. Objects and materials come to carry the weight of human history (Harvey 2013: 60). The constant risk, however, is losing that human history embedded in/on the artifact. Everything trends toward a state of entropy. Things fall apart. When the artifact is gone, does anything remain of use to the archaeologist? The archaeogamer can continue to interact with software on preserved media and machines, but there will come a time when both are gone and all that is left are quantifiable data and memories/emotions.

While we have the material to study, however, we should take advantage of it. The materiality of a thing embodies its own power (Cole 2013: 70), comprised of more than just objects and machines, but of the raw materials and waste that went into that object's manufacture (Parikka 2012). Without the material object, there is no interaction within the game-space. "The thesis that digital media are immaterial is premised on ignorance of how things work, carefully calculated in the guiltless consumerism of which digital media have become both vehicles and examples" (Cubitt 2013: 136). Cubitt adds that "the last great challenge to network archaeology will be the physical ephemerality of electronic media" (Cubitt 2013: 145).

The ultimate demise of hardware will not destroy the code left behind, which will exist so long as many copies are stored in many places both locally and online. We will be left with previously unthought-of questions regarding the games we study. Guins asks now, "When is *Space Invaders*?" and "Where is *Space Invaders*?" (Guins 2014: 12). Can we understand a game without a time or a place, or when that space-time is known but is no longer accessible? A video game can be studied on its own apart from the context of its original hardware and its original placement in time, but only when studying the game on its own internal workings in how it creates its own internal environment for human interaction. There is the material culture surrounding the game, but the code of the game creates its own, internal material culture, which has its own context and layers of meaning when actively played. The game-as-played is timeless.

The following sections will explore the material culture in games, paying special attention to the line between the natural and the synthetic and how things cross that line with regularity, reproducing the synthetic in the natural world, and introducing elements of the natural world into the synthetic game-space, a kind of transmigration of artifacts.

Material Memory in Video Games

"Material memory" can mean: (1) things (e.g., a pot, a building, etc.) provide a link to the past, an articulated/manufactured memory of what was that persists in the present, and (2) an actual memory triggered by interaction with a thing. When I visit my brother, I see the *Star Wars* toys I received for my sixth birthday, which his kids now play with. Holding the Luke Skywalker action figure triggers my memory of opening the present, taking the figure out of the box, activating the plastic lightsaber (and later learning how to remove it, promptly losing it). When I visited Athens for the first time in 1996, I walked among the ancient buildings atop the Acropolis. I had no real memory of these structures (aside from all of the data learned in school), but the buildings persist through time, a tactile memory of what was. So how does this work in video games?

Dunstan Lowe wrote about ancient architecture in games, "Always Already Ancient," where he notes that most games present Greek-y, Roman-y, Egypt-y buildings as weathered and time-worn (Lowe 2013). They rarely (if ever) appear as new. I see these buildings as representing a presumed past that never really was. It's a design choice, hinting at a lore to be written. In game design, the present writes the past. For simpler games (such as *Paper Mario* and *Mario Kart* and the Dry-Dry Ruins), the ancient is used as a backdrop created to evoke a sense of an older time while players negotiate the present.

The ruins-as-pictured are not from the ancient past (even though they reference an imagined past via design tropes). The ruins-as-pictured date to 2008, which in game-life is somewhat old. When I go back and play *Mario Kart Wii,* the ruins-as-pictured not only evoke an Egypt-y place that might have been (but never was), they also trigger a memory of the first time I raced this special course, and of the best run I ever had. *Mario Kart Wii* has become a material memory, the game itself a monument of the past that is played here in the present.

Let's look at another example: the Mace of Molag Bal from the *Elder Scrolls* universe. I acquired this weapon (a "Daedric artifact") by completing a quest chain (series of related missions), and I have enjoyed griefing my enemies with it. The material artifact of the mace contains robust lore of its initial forging and later use, a memory of the second and fourth eras of the *Elder Scrolls* canon. It is material memory of that bygone era. What I didn't know (at the time) was that the mace is available to players who complete other quests in earlier *Elder Scrolls* games (including *Daggerfall, Morrowind,* and *Oblivion*). In the game lore's terms, the mace is an ancient artifact. In terms of the absolute chronology of the series, the mace is evocative of CE 1996, 2002, and 2006 respectively, its initial creation courtesy of Bethesda Softworks in 1996. So the mace is the material memory of the second *Elder Scrolls* game.

Things get even more interesting/weird when you consider the fact that you can (as I did) play the *Elder Scrolls* games out of order, playing games made in 1996 but in the present, 2018. Material memory gets confused a bit, especially since I will remember playing the game in 2018 even though it was released in 1996, evocative of that time. I will remember the mace from one time period, but in a later version of the game (therefore a different time period). I am remembering something from the future, when considering the lore, yet I am experiencing the artifact in the present when I play the games out of order. There is then a web-of-material-memory instead of anything chronological, with the Mace of Molag Bal at the center of that web, its presence radiating out across all timelines and narratives, a kind of digital singularity. This is not unique to the experience of gameplay but is one of many examples of items found in video games that are tied to lore of manufactured antiquity, and also to present and future interaction through play. More strangeness: there is more than one of these maces; there are millions, one per player-character who ever experienced the game. This artifact is unique to me, but not unique to the player-community; yet we all have shared memories that this unique/not-unique artifact evokes.

Moving away from 100 percent–designed games, video games set in synthetic worlds, specifically those that are procedurally generated, exhibit a unique kind of material memory: there is none, at least not at first. As I travel over the brand new, procedurally generated landscape of a world I discovered in *No Man's Sky,* I note that the planet is perceived to be billions of years old but has in reality only existed for a few seconds upon my arrival. Walking the new landscape of this new-old world, I discover a building of indeterminate age. That building is also brand new. It has/exhibits no material memory. I actually create that material memory by observing the building for the first time. I can use the building for geolocation. The next time I see the building, I will remember it. I know its age because it appeared as soon as I saw it, which, when you think about it, is an utterly bizarre statement. Would it have appeared if I hadn't seen it? Probably not, based on the PCG algorithms in play that are tied to player agency. In a game such as *No Man's Sky,*

I make the landscape by observing the landscape. I make the building by observing the building. I remember the building because I made the building (with the unconscious help of an algorithm). I wonder then if this is what happens with new architecture, that material memory has as a starting point that can be traced back in time. The landscape remembers the footprint of a structure, of a site.

Concerning player-memory in MMOs, specifically *World of Warcraft,* do games such as *WoW* "remember" players? Likely not. As many years as players invest in that game-world and in their toons (avatars), those players leave not a material trace on their respective servers. Nothing they crafted remains in those worlds. They built no monuments. The world persists, but its occupants remain anonymous. They are small things, forgotten. For players who quit the game, their toons might have been scrubbed from the servers by Blizzard Entertainment based on their inactivity and cancellation of recurring billing. Unless a player has screenshots of their toons, it is possible that they will disappear without a trace either after quitting the game or after the game itself is retired by its developer.

When I played *WoW,* I remember when I hit the level cap of 80 I celebrated by returning to Bloodhoof Village where I began my adventures. I wanted to see the village Elders, to listen to the ambient sounds. The NPCs failed to recognize me as the prodigal son returned home. I was without place, not even remembered by ones I'd considered family so long ago, digitally homeless and alone in a world of millions. Just like everyone else.

Video Game Museums and Museums in Video Games

When talking about archaeology, one must consider the disposition of post-excavation artifacts. Where does the stuff go? On a modern, working excavation, excavated material can end up in a rubbish heap, in the lab, or in storage. Some excavations (like that of the Athenian Agora) have on-site public museums featuring the best (or most representative) items discovered. Unfortunately there is still the practice of looting and of clandestine excavations that bring illegally recovered artifacts to both private and public collections.

For those archaeological artifacts that do make their way into museums, what is their purpose for being collected and for potentially being displayed (no museum exhibits all of its collection)? And what is the purpose of the museum? Whom does it serve, and why? With video games, there are both real-world and digital museums offering their own interpretations of what is desirable to collect and display, and how the public in both the natural and synthetic worlds perceives not only the function of museums but also their role in interacting with, and even supplying artifacts to, these collections.

Terrestrial Video Game Museums

Video game museums (or video game exhibits in museums) have been slowly creeping into public view as the generations mature who grew up with the technology, have children of their own, and want to remember what the old games, consoles, and cabinets looked like and, in some cases, what it meant to play them. In another fifty to sixty years, those of us who recall playing the first arcade cabinets will be gone. These games and their related hardware comprise the material culture of people who grew up in the 1970s, the first to play in bars and arcades, and the first to own home gaming systems. For many people, a console became as essential as a VHS machine or a Walkman portable listening device, entertainment technology to be used on demand.

To understand material culture, one has to look at cultural meanings (Johnson 2010: 66). The museum exhibits and museums themselves attempt to do this, integrating didactic signage with "original" mass-produced gaming objects and prototype artifacts from pre-game development. Media technologies have, in differing ways, been elaborated as a condition of the modern mode of perception (Parikka 2012: 34). Museums can fall into the trap of nostalgia, treating game media and their design and even their promotion campaigns and package as practically quaint. We imagine what the 1980s were like (largely thanks to John Hughes movies and throwback television series such as *Stranger Things*), even those of us who lived through that decade. Tropes compete with actual recollection, and museums run the risk of almost taking a superior, colonial view of now vs. then, modern us vs. what we were thirty years ago, assuming that with age comes progress and refinement. As we see when considering the construction of the pyramids of Egypt, we cannot comprehend the technology and skill used to create such monuments. The same could be said of how the first video games were created, and of the creativity and ingenuity required to make something both new and lasting. Sometimes we perceive what we imagine instead of what is physically in front of us.

With video game history, container becomes content. Game ephemera, boxes, ads, and documentation are all collectible. They have value (Guins 2014: 173). Atari cabinets (furniture) sold in either 1984 or 1985 to collector Curt Allen contained, unbeknownst to the seller, design diagrams, graphics, and artwork. This ephemera was ultimately valued by Sotheby's at $150,000–250,000 in 2007, but did not sell (Guins 2014: 167). These materials give context to the games themselves and are part of the overall gaming experience of a certain era. They give an authenticity to the exhibit. Authenticity depends on the context of the observer (Holtorf 2005). It carries its own definition and baggage for every visitor as well as every museum that chooses to display items from video game history. History and museums play with the idea of memory, specifically cultural memory. As Holtorf proposed in his 2005 talk with Angela Piccini, "cultural memory . . . ought to be based on a notion of absence and not on some poorly preserved remote sites and rusty artefacts. Less preservation could be more memory" (Piccini and Holtorf 2011: 23). In this case, perhaps less is more, letting the objects stand on their own as artifacts without all of the nostalgic accoutrements. For those of us who can remember, we will note what is missing, which adds gravity to what has been preserved and presented.

When museums do decide to display video games, they should consider three things. The first is to follow the lead of the National Museum of Play's triangular model for curation: artifacts-interpretation-interactivity (Guins 2014: 43). Not only is it important to have the object but also to provide it (if possible) within a playable context. The game cannot be separated from the hardware on which it was played. *Jet Set Willy* by Matthew Smith has to be played on the Sinclair (Stanton 2015: 74). MAME emulators (software that ports arcade games to other platforms such as personal computers) can suffice to some extent, but there is no substitute for learning how to play a game using the original controllers. Players now experience the same learning curve as players back when the game was produced. Lastly, museums should forget about chronology and diffusion and think more about the processes involved (Johnson 2010: 33, paraphrasing Renfrew). How did these games come to be, not only in the act of creation but also in the act of play? Games are kinetic by design, their meanings made more clear when interacted with on a screen.

To begin with the natural world: In 2016 there are already a handful of museums featuring video games-as-artifacts (Detroit's Henry Ford Museum) or as art (MoMA in New York City), while others such as the National Museum of Play (Rochester, New York), the Computer History Museum (Mountain View, California), the National Video Game Arcade (Nottingham, United Kingdom), and the Powerhouse Museum (New South Wales, Australia) have several exhibits (or in the case of the National Museum of Play, an entire floor) dedicated to games and gaming. The most recent brick-and-mortar museum committed solely to video games is the National Video Game Museum in Frisco, Texas. The first video game–only museum, however, is in the heart of Rome: Vigamus.

Vigamus, Rome's Video Game Museum

Most people when they visit Rome head immediately to St. Peter's or the Roman Forum, especially if they can only spend a few brief hours in the Eternal City. For others (including myself), the first stop is Vigamus, Rome's video game museum, and the first museum in the world to exclusively focus on interactive games (see Figure 4.1). Vigamus is about a half mile from the Lepanto stop on the Metro A-line just off the Piazza Mazzini on Via Sabotino. The museum's unassuming orange sign gives a hint of what treasures lie one story below street-level. The

Figure 4.1. Inside Vigamus, Rome's video game museum. Photo by the author.

joyful noise bubbling up the steps is a mix of chiptunes, shouts, and laughter. Upon entering, the visitor is met by life-size figures of Lara Croft and a Templar from *Assassin's Creed.*

Vigamus is divided into several sections, all of which have incredible things on offer. The first cases highlight the hardware and first video games ever created, many of which are hand-signed by their creators. The earliest Atari consoles are on view, as are various Commodore and Amiga computers. First-generation consoles from every major manufacturer are here as well as a selection of the games that defined genres. The signage is in English and Italian, and many of the cases feature looping video interviews with video game luminaries.

Copies of *Zork* sit across from boxed copies of *Monkey Island* and *King's Quest.* There is a case dedicated to *Doom.* Other cases include hardware from Atari and Intellivision and others, the earliest consoles on the top shelf. Handheld game systems of every variety are positioned next to sample games: back then one could not play the games without the appropriate gear. The pairing of hardware with software gives context to younger visitors and reminders to older ones.

The next room is dedicated to the fabled "crash" of the video game industry in 1983 that saw the fall of Atari and the rise of Nintendo. The centerpiece contains several cartridges, manuals, hardware, and comics, as well as dirt from the Alamogordo landfill, site of the Atari Burial Ground that I helped excavate (see chapter 1). Being reunited with that material felt good, and I am glad that Vigamus is one of a few museums that has this material on display. The exhibit explains the myth of the crash, the story of the *E.T.* burial, and that of its recovery.

Down the hall and around the corner is a room of playable games on original systems. One can play *Doom* on an original first-generation PlayStation (even though my first experience with the game was via MS-DOS on a PC clone). In the connecting hallway are cases full of *Mario Bros.* cartridges, a history of that franchise behind glass. Other cases contain other favorites of mine, including the *Half-Life* series of games.

Ubisoft sponsors the next room, which is full of *Assassin's Creed* game art as well as several stations for playing the games, a constant LAN party. The room is full of kids, all wearing museum-provided gaming headphones. The sense of enjoyment is palpable.

The biggest room contains a setting for traditional lectures, and off to the side are several arcade cabinets, including the very first cabinet for *Space Invaders* with the instructions in Japanese. Playable history.

Vigamus sports an Oculus Rift room, which has state-of-the-art OR hardware donated prior to the Facebook buyout. The room contains two complete OR setups with chairs and hardware, as well as screens to show others what the player is seeing. The applications for archaeogaming with OR and augmented reality are quite real.

Although Vigamus was the first video game museum to open, it is not representative of other museums' approaches to collecting and displaying video games. At the Henry Ford Museum, the Atari artifacts are displayed as an example of twenty-first-century archaeology within the context of the history of technology in which this museum specializes. The National Museum of Play features video game cabinets in an arcade-style context to encourage engagement and interaction. Representative artifacts of video game history populate cases surrounding the interactive space, reminding visitors of the evolution of play in the late twentieth and early twenty-first centuries. Behind the scenes, however, is an extensive archive to video game history, and hardware in various states of restoration. The museum is a gathering place for sharing oral history and knowledge, for conservation and preservation, as well as communication of history and research to the public. Museums such as the Strong and Henry Ford are not just one-dimensional avenues of public-facing displays of gaming technology and art. Robust research is at the heart of the permanent collections. So do museums created within video games do the same thing?

Museums within Video Games

Seeing video games within a museum context, with traditional vitrines, signage, and interactive displays containing artifacts less than sixty years old led me to wonder about the reception, use, and interpretation of museums within the games themselves. What did they look like? What artifacts would they contain and why? Do these museums have another function other than presenting artifacts to visitors?

The *Play the Past* blog features games with museums in them, but museum presence in the gaming world past and present remains relatively small.[1] In *Uncharted 2* and *3* and *The Last of Us* (all from Naughty Dog), museums act as spaces to further each game's narrative. The museum in *Bioshock 2* is used as a political device to indoctrinate young visitors into believing the Utopian ideals of their city, Rapture. The museum in *Wildstar* provides game lore along with a sense of civic pride tied to a player's faction.

Museums in other games fit neatly into one or more categories of setting, politics, lore:[2]

Lands of Lore: Guardians of Destiny

Gabriel Knight 2 and 3

Call of Cthulhu: Shadow of the Comet (with its Lovecraft Museum)

Ultima games (including VII)

The Dagger of Amon Ra

Blood 2

Still Life

Fallout 3

Runaway

Ghostbusters: The Video Game

Ghostbusters 2

Batman: Arkham City

Planescape: Torment

Shivers

Turok 3

Vampire The Masquerade: Bloodlines

Parasite Eve

Sly Cooper

Sly 2

The Messenger (aka Louvre: The Final Curse)

Ripley's Believe It or Not!

The Riddle of Master Lu

Secret Files: Tunguska

MediEvil 2

Re-Volt

Wario Land: Shake It!

The Simpson's: Bart vs. The Space Mutants

John Saul's Blackstone Chronicles: An Adventure in Terror

Chex Quest 2

Tomb Raider: The Angel of Darkness

The DaVinci Code

Mystery at the Museums

There are two museums in the unmodded, vanilla version of *Elder Scrolls V: Skyrim*. The first is the Dwemer Museum, located in Understone Keep in Markarth. In the game's lore, the Dwemer are an extinct (vanished) race of dwarves adept at mechanical devices and engineering. The museum is owned and managed by an NPC named Calcelmo who is a scholar and archaeologist specializing in Dwemer history, collecting artifacts for the museum from Dwemer ruins and from his excavation at Nchouand-Zel. Museum guards are present. Admission is free.

The museum's collections that are on display are largely under glass on tables spread throughout the vaulted underground chambers, showcasing rare and interesting Dwemer artifacts as well as a display of kitchenware (bowls, cups, cooking pots, utensils). This is in keeping with real-world archaeological museum displays that feature not only the "shinies" but also examples of artifacts used in everyday life. As a departure from other games, though, players are able to pick the locks of the display cases to either level up their lockpicking skill or to steal the museum objects to either use or sell, leaving the player with an ethical choice.

In the vastness of Skyrim, there is only one other museum, a small collection in the hamlet of Dawnstar. The quest "Visit the Museum at

Dawnstar" leads the player to a thatched, lakeside house. The curator, Silus Vesuius, is still assembling items for the museum's permanent collection and gives the player a quest to find pieces of Mehrune's Razor, a Daedric (dark elf) artifact of great historical importance. The museum, which is also Vesuius's house, contains several locked display cases containing artifacts of the Daedric cult, the Mythic Dawn. There is a complete set of Mythic Dawn clothing, a scabbard, books, and a manuscript leaf. As the player approaches each case, the curator narrates a history of what the case contains. Following the conclusion of the tour, the player can opt to kill (or incapacitate) the curator in order to access the artifacts via lockpicking.

If the player decides to undertake the "Pieces of the Past" quest, three pieces of the dagger must be located and either looted or purchased at various locations within the game, prompting further ethical questions about the nature of museum acquisition, in this case via money or bloodshed. It is not a far cry from some real-world private collectors, or from nineteenth-century private museums where the public was admitted for a fee to view artifacts collected by a wealthy patron.

The most recent addition to the series (although published by Zenimax instead of Bethesda) is *Elder Scrolls Online.* The open world is huge, requiring months to explore in real-time, yet it only has a single museum: the House of Orsimer Glories, which is in Wrothgar. This museum is run by the NPC curator Umutha and specializes in Orcish history. While she does not collect relics herself for display, she does ask adventurers to help her find more to fill the cases. This common quest type is not unique to this edition of the game but follows the tradition set at least fifteen years earlier in prior volumes.

The Museum in Godsreach (*Tribunal*) finds the player asked by the curator to find artifacts that she will buy to fill her empty display cases. The Museum of Oddities (*Shivering Isles*) also features a curator in need of artifacts ("oddities"), and the player must quest for twelve of them, including a "Soul Tomato," a "Ring of Disrobing," and a pelvis. The function of museums in the *Elder Scrolls* universe is to collect and to display while also serving as a source of increasing player experience and possibly wealth.

In considering video game museums in both the real and virtual worlds, there is one element that is relatively new: in-game or online museums of artifacts, relics, collectibles, and other items found by players. With games such as *Destiny* creating procedurally generated armor and weapons, players are asking for repositories for this data, managed by the game publishers, perhaps for online, in-game view. Such museums would also include items pertaining to the lore of the game side by side with newly discovered artifacts. With games now culturally ubiquitous in the real world, and with millions of players spending millions of hours in-game each year, it stands to reason that these requests for transposing cultural institutions from real to virtual spaces is a logical next step. Some people go to the Metropolitan Museum of Art to spend hours ogling the collection of arms and armor. An in-game equivalent exists for players of *World of Warcraft* in the hyper-detailed Armory, a robust database of items that can be referenced at any time.[3] While not quite a museum for the casual visitor, it does utilize similar kinds of data used by most museums behind the scenes to catalogue and maintain information about the collection, which is arguably more important to the serious player than traditional displays and didactic signage. Players of the *BioShock* franchise were rewarded in the *Ultimate Rapture Edition* by a special level containing the "Museum of Orphaned Concepts," which contained the concept art and abandoned ideas for the first two games in the series. Fans of the games could now spend time learning more about the backstory of Rapture while at the same time learning about game creation and narrative. In *BioShock Infinite,* the Columbia Archaeological Society museum contains concept art that can be viewed after players complete various "Blue Ribbon Challenges." The *Ratchet & Clank* games featured similar content in their "Insomniac Museum," a secret space that only opened at a certain place during a certain hour.

This leads one into a possible paradox where players can research in-game artifacts prior to actually discovering them—in *Destiny,* players need to take their artifacts to the archaeologist for identification (similar to *Diablo* players asking the NPC Deckard Cain to identify magic items). However, one can go to any number of community forums or game websites to learn about these items, determine what the best ones are, and obtain their locations (either fixed, or as random drops). It is a kind of meta-archaeology, reading the context before finding the item. At the same time, it is not so different than an archaeologist looking at past evidence and findspots, using that data to determine where to look next.

With video game museums, we have virtual spaces for recording virtual objects with real context and real data, and real spaces for the same.

Virtual Artifacts and Their Real-World Manifestation

We are all heretics, at least those of us who play video games. We seek to communicate with that which we cannot see, but to do so we have to interact with objects. When that communion concludes, players take it on faith that the invisible remains accessible, and event present.

Video games embody a paradox that stems from centuries of creating things to give people access to the unknown or the unknowable. Victor Buchli, in the preface of his book *An Archaeology of the Immaterial,* states that "the production of the immaterial has been and always will be an important operation in human social life. To intervene materially, to reject the materiality of the world, is at the heart of the productive paradox of the immaterial" (Buchli 2016: vii). Raiford Guins seconds this, noting that "video games are object-information composite by design . . . they are already objects of and for information" (Guins 2014: 47). The physical device contains the ephemeral data.

As described in chapter 1, a video game is a complex site-artifact, created through an interdisciplinary mix of creativity, coding, and manufacturing, all within a sociopolitical context of when and where the game was made, and still even beholden, as Guins relates, to government standards for electronic devices and patent functionality (and non-functionality) (Guins 2014: 7–8). The thing though—the game-as-artifact—continues the physical/metaphysical paradox when one thinks of the vessel and what it contains. With video games, as Buchli describes, the physical container is actually the more fragile and fugitive of the two components, with the underlying code able to outlive its vessel (Buchli 2016: x). The code is kept somewhere else, in other physical copies, as well as on backups, servers, and master disks, practically immortal (when care is given to its preservation). Games are ideas that require physical media in order to reach their intended audiences. Even if a disk is defective, there is always another way to communicate the idea of the game to the player.

So what does this mean for gameplay? Someone writes code that becomes a game. That code lives on media somewhere: a cartridge, a smartphone, a server. The code waits to be activated by the player who then works within the rules established by that code in order to play the game. Upon completion of play, the player disengages with the code wherever it lives, unseen, by removing contact with the hardware used to play it. The code remains, waiting to be accessed again, or not. Code is amoral. It exists until it does not, and it does not care if it is accessed zero, one, or one million times. The code itself is immaterial, albeit manipulated by its maker for the player to interact with, but on another plane, that of gameplay. Playing the game, the player is conscious of one world while unconscious of the world above it. It is another dimension. Glitches in the game give fleeting, frustrating access into that other plane, although the interpretation of why a glitch happened remains beyond most understanding. We see the fallibility of the maker but not the exact reason for that mistake.

Buchli continues with the paradox: "An . . . aspect of the immaterial's paradoxicality is its profound visuality. This paradox is more an 'artefact' of our received visualist sensorium which requires the decorporealization of sight for its efficacy" (Buchli 2016: 19). In other words, with video games, seeing is believing. We hold a world on a disk. We place the disk in the drive/slot. The world is either created or accessed, or it is created upon being accessed. This leads us to consider how the world is created in the first place, and I do not think it matters if the game is static (e.g., *Donkey Kong*), or procedural (e.g., *No Man's Sky*). Is the world waiting for us like some amusement park at dawn, or is it created for us on the fly, the code generating the world as fast as we can explore it? And when we are done exploring it, does it reset to a zero-state, or does it continue to exist with or without us? As players, are we creating the artifacts of the world just by interacting with the environment, working within the rules of algorithms to create it? Are we then in turn makers and producers of what we see, the code itself lying dormant until played with?

It is video games as embodiments of the Heisenberg Principal. And not only that, but when we start to pay attention to how and where and when and why things are created based on our observations, we might begin to recognize patterns, and when we recognize patterns, we can begin to create our own rules to quantify them, and when we begin to combine those rules of creation, we approach a Grand Unified Theory (GUT) of a particular game, which operates on its own set of rules separate from other games, which have their own GUTs. In effect, each game is its own universe with its own physics governed by rules that can be clean or messy, strict or arbitrary, really reflecting the state of the maker responsible for the code itself.

William Sims Bainbridge in his ethnography of *World of Warcraft* observed that the boundary between the real and game world is porous, and it is difficult to cleanly separate the two. Play takes place in its own environment (Bainbridge 2010: 222). The crossover from the real to the virtual, however, continues to be pursued by game developers who wish to inject realism into their games. This is perhaps best illustrated in war games that are either set in a particular place and time or attempt to mirror current weapons, armor, and vehicles. After filming *Saving Private Ryan*, director Steven Spielberg wanted to see a war game that was as accurate as possible with locations, history, and weapons, marking the first case of this kind of realism in video games (Stanton 2015: 154–55). This has been taken to the extreme in the *Call of Duty* series, where the makes and manufactures of guns are licensed by Infinity Ward/Activision for use in the game. Players could conceivably go out into the real world to buy the weapon they favored when playing the game (Stanton 2015: 354). It is only a matter of time before the line between material and immaterial is blurred with the active use of 3D printing (Buchli 2016: 144–60). Players will be able to print the creatures and/or items they find or, conversely, 3D scan something to import directly into the game (as has already been done in virtual worlds such as *Second Life* with the import of buildings created in *Unity, Maya,* or similar.

The code, however, is the supreme artifact, which can itself be broken down further into its grammar, syntax, and orthography. Think of code as you would an ancient (or modern) clay pot. The pot is an artifact, a thing. But the pot might be glazed. The clay of the pot can be examined; we can learn about its crystals and structure. That data in turn can inform where the clay was sourced, and we can deduce who might have sourced it, where it went for production, and ultimately where it went for use. The pot can be interacted with and can serve multiple functions desired by the user. The pot was not spontaneously generated. It was designed and then made, in most cases by an unseen hand. So it is with video games, made by people most of us will never see, comprised of syntax and grammar most of us will never understand or even notice, creating something we can manipulate to get at the sweetness of fantasy, or a world not of this one but of one or more imaginations.[4] The game has become a metaphysical artifact/object occupying two states at once, a thing in the real world and a visual space in another.

So what happens when we reach Iconoclasm in video games? In certain interpretations of Christianity and Islam, the faithful must eschew the material in order to approach the divine. How will we as players interact with these immaterial worlds post-media, post-hardware? What then becomes the archaeological artifact of the game, and how will that be defined when the artifact cannot be counted or weighed, when we shift between worlds without console, controller, keyboard, or mouse? How do we conduct an archaeological investigation of a thing we cannot touch?

Experimental Archaeology

Experimental archaeology focuses on testing hypotheses of how things might have been done in the past: everything from construction to transport and more, attempting to recreate methods using materials as suggested by primary sources and the archaeological record. Famous examples of experimental archaeology include Thor Heyerdahl's *Kon-Tiki* voyage to demonstrate trans-Pacific trade[5] and Janet Stephens's work in recreating ancient Roman hairstyles on living models.[6]

Reconstructions of ancient sites can serve as a kind of experimental archaeology within games such as those in the *Assassin's Creed* series. The natural world (and its data) translates into the virtual by way of engines such as *Unity* and *Maya,* as well as in sandbox software such as *Minecraft.*

Within the framework of archaeogaming, experimental archaeology works backward as well, beginning with the game. Take food for example, mainly because it is arguably the most accessible way for someone to try to recreate something from a game in the real world. Rosanna Pansino's YouTube channel, "Nerdy Nummies," with nearly seven million subscribers, includes video game–themed sweets (e.g., *Warcraft* Cookies and *Undertale* Spider Donuts),[7] but nothing that attempts to recreate or interpret actual recipes from games that include a cooking skill. While there are few YouTube channels dedicated to video game cookery (and none approaching Pansino's popularity), there are some websites that include sections on recreating the food featured in games. *The Geeky Chef* currently features seventeen game-recreations, including Seheron fish sandwich (*Dragon Age: Inquisition*), Yeto's superb pumpkin and goat cheese soup (*The Legend of Zelda: Twilight Princess*), sweetroll (*Skyrim*), and other favorites.[8] The recipes are posted online, and the community troubleshoots them to come as close as possible to the perception of the virtual food. Other sites such as Eat Game Live,[9] Eat a Byte,[10] and Gourmet Gaming[11] also regularly publish food-from-the-game recipes, which include narratives of what inspired the recipe, selection of ingredients, and the outcomes, some good, some not. For *Final Fantasy XV,* its development team actually camped and cooked in order to get the in-game recipes correct (and believable).[12]

The experimental archaeology within the context of food recipes tests the possibility of a virtual world recipe actually working in the real one. The amounts and names of ingredients can be inexact within a game, much like reading real-world recipes from history, making best guesses, and then revising to try again.[13] For example, a fifteenth-century onion tart recipe from Italy states to boil onions and scallions, mash them, then beat with lard, eggs, cheese, and saffron, and "make the tart."[14]

The trick, in games just as in interpreting old recipes, is in measuring the ingredients. In games that have a cooking component, all rely on finding a cooking pot, fire, or hearth, and also wild (or purchased) ingredients, but not measures. For example, in *Skyrim,* players can make apple cabbage stew with a salt pile, a red apple, and cabbage. In *World of Warcraft,* players can make a "tasty cupcake" with two units of simple flour and a Northern egg. Players depend on recipes either found or bought that can be learned when a player gets to an appropriate level. But for the experimental chef in a real-world kitchen, mixing flour and an egg and then baking over a fire will yield something less-than-tasty.

Lore and Lore Communities

One of the elements of any culture is that its people maintain a shared narrative, a shared history. Combine culture with a constructed environment and you have the makings of a civilization. Many games contain ready-made lore, a historic and often racial narrative of the cultures (playable and not) created by the developers from scratch or inherited from earlier media (books, films, etc.), with the game tying into that history, sometimes becoming "canon." Even in historical games such as *Battlefield 1942,* players use lore from World War II to inform their own historical reenactments within the game (Chapman 2016: 211). Lore does not confine itself to fantasy.

As with other aspects of video games, particularly with MMOs, we not only experience lore through art, architecture, books, and even artifacts that are all provided in-game, we also inherit (or become part of) the lore created by the in-game player community. For example, one particular five-person instance group in *World of Warcraft* filmed their elaborate preparations only to be completely annihilated (wiped) by the enemies (mobs) within the instance (dungeon) after the headstrong lone wolf, "Leeroy Jenkins," rushed in before the party was fully prepared. That single act of bravado became an instant classic, not tied to any race or class within the game but as part of the lore of the game itself.[15]

Lore is a game's own mythology, stuffed with gods, monsters, and heroes, both supernatural and human, passed down through generations of players either by other players or by the words crafted by the developers themselves. Consider Greek mythology, its lore recorded and distributed in part by Hesiod in *Theogony.* These initial communications are not unlike Blizzard Entertainment's foray into the first *Warcraft* games and related books, which created a story-empire that ultimately resulted not only in the most popular MMO ever played but also in a Hollywood blockbuster film, *Warcraft,* based on the game lore of the ancient conflict between orcs and humans.

Lore inevitably begets lore communities comprised of players with a serious academic interest in the minutiae of all of the elements of these parent tales to the point of excessiveness. This is no difference between the arguments of those deeply invested in canon lore and its representation and deviations in a game, and those dealing with the academic details of archaeological desiderata of pottery chronology. The same scholarship, attention to detail, and passions exist.

Sometimes the archeological record produces evidence to overturn previous theories, creating a new narrative. The burden of proof falls to the discovering archaeologists, which is then vetted (or refuted) by the community through research and dialogue. A notable recent example features the resting place of King Richard III, whose burial place at Greyfriars Friary in Leicester was lost to time after its sixteenth-century demolition. In 2012 archaeologists from the University of Leicester began their excavation in a public parking lot. A skeleton of a man in his thirties with a curved spine and head injury from a bladed weapon seemed to point to the identification of the remains as belonging to King Richard III. DNA and radiocarbon testing followed, as did an osteological analysis of the bones, which ultimately concluded in the positive identification of the remains. The body, its disposition and injuries, confirmed the lore surrounding the king's death and burial, and the tests satisfied scientists and the public. The body was reinterred in 2015, a royal burial.

With game lore communities, sometimes new lore introduced as canon (or into the game whether or not it is canon) causes as much debate (or more) as that seen in professional archaeological circles. When Blizzard announced that it was releasing its *Mists of Pandaria* patch for *WoW,* the lore community reeled. Blizzard introduced a panda NPC as part of an April Fool's joke in 2002. *Warcraft* had no race of panda-inspired humanoids. Ten years later, Blizzard introduced a playable region filled with pandas, their art, architecture, and philosophy inspired by ancient China. It was as if Blizzard created new lore out of thin air, something that is within a developer's power, but at the same time shocked the students of the lore of Azeroth. Culture doesn't spring fully formed from the earth, absent one day and then fully present the next. But it can (and does) in video games, especially when the developer needs to create new content to keep the game interesting/relevant, and to cater to emerging markets. Chinese players of *WoW* number in the millions, so perhaps it made sense to Blizzard to create Chinese-themed lore to cater to this massive group of players. Blizzard created *WoW,* after all, to make money. Tara Copplestone recognizes this cynical fact: "The epistemological assumptions of videogame developers can and do—whether knowingly or not—play a significant role in how history or cultural-heritage is produced in the games that they craft through code, art, sound and narrative" (Copplestone 2016: 6).

With games, developers have full control over what appears in the game-space (and what doesn't). Sometimes, as in the above case with Blizzard, the decision to proceed with game-defying lore is made unilaterally. In other cases, as with Bethesda and their wildly popular *Elder Scrolls* series, the lore community is consulted. As games within this series were developed, the lore communities online were asked to help with continuity between titles so that the games all tied in to the shared lore of Tamriel. The stories and cycles approach a depth and sophistication rivaling any real-world saga, making the gameplay inseparable from the story that crafted this environment.

With both lore community examples above, one sees how they reflect the actual, real-world practice of mythmaking. On the one hand, one receives canon lore directly from the primary texts created by the developer. On the other hand, a community of people continue to spread the myths while adding to them or modifying them. Myth, derived from canon, changes with time and voices, recalling the original while adding to it like so many layers of sediment. We have an archaeology of storytelling.

These stories can inform the production of artifacts and monuments in both the real and virtual worlds. One can build a plain structure, or one can infuse that structure with meaning by including iconography derived from myth. Adding that imagery creates clues to the archaeologist about the structure's function, although the archaeologist must take care to note if these symbols and references are added as easy, ready-made tropes or if they are indeed imbued with deeper meaning and intended purpose. The lore community can spot fraud easily and can be vocal with the developer about deviations from the story and from the use of iconography in nontraditional ways either by design or accident.

Keith Stuart, a writer for Eurogamer.net, wrote about the problem with video game lore:[16] developers equate volume with depth. They also equate obfuscation with depth. To many developers, their games merit and promote byzantine backstory and hundreds or thousands of pages of faux history to justify why the games and game-worlds are what they are. He argues, though, that most lore does not serve gameplay and provides little benefit to players. Adding some lore and some backstory can work to imbue a bit of mystery, and including some occasional cues can create ambience. For some players, though, the lore is crucial to the game. One can enjoy the *Star Wars* universe as a player, but knowing that depth of detail and depth of overarching narrative adds meaning and can also carry emotional resonance, especially when playing an MMO such as *Star Wars: The Old Republic.* The lore of *Star Wars* (films, books, games) approaches the sacred. That attitude is present in other series as well. For example lore complaints about *Fallout 4* run rampant in online forums,[17] citing discrepancies with everything from base in-world currency to the intelligence of mutants to the fate of the Institute. For games such as those in the *Fallout* series, the lore is not just the developer-created backstory of how the world came to be. The lore is created in the first game, which becomes canon. The rules set up in the first game must carry through to future games in the series, and those games must not deviate from those rules unless there is a very good reason as explained in later titles. Complexity shows up again when considering game lore. With complexity, a base set of rules can be used to generate future rules and scenarios that create more information about a world without violating the initial rules of creation. Disregarding those rules is considered to be bad form (and even laziness) on the part of the game studio.

Lore-transition (or disregard for lore) can come when a game franchise is handed off to another publisher. For example, Bethesda Softworks handed of the wildly popular *Elder Scrolls* series to Zenimax Online for *Elder Scrolls Online.* The hardcore community of players was greatly concerned about how the lore would be handled in this change of studios.[18] Zenimax attempted to sidestep the lore issues by setting the world of *ESO* over one thousand years in the past, before the world of the first *Elder Scrolls* title, *Arena* (2004). That setting does avoid many continuity issues, but it cannot get around introducing others. Because the world of Tamriel is so old and is so tied to its own traditions and contains literal libraries of lorebooks for players to consume, any new, core elements to that world must jibe with what has come before. The example taken from the link above in note 18 is that of the "anchors," evil sites that tie Tamriel to the demon-haunted world of Oblivion. In all of the books of Tamriel lore, in all of the antiquity-theme quests, and in all of the dialogues with antiquarian NPCs, these anchors (which are gigantic and which leave a massive footprint on the land even after destruction) are absent from the literature and from the Tamriel that appears in the five earlier games. It is as if the Singularity happened, and two different Tamriels collided. Retrofitting lore failed, at least in this instance.

Compare game lore to real-world lore in the form of Classical mythology. Myths and origin stories have always enjoyed flexibility, with geographic variations serving as canon in their parent regions while being acknowledged as myths evolved. Perhaps one of the greatest differences between the lore of the real and of the virtual is that in the real world, lore is expected to grow and change; we cannot define for absolute certainty the first time a story was told, and we rely on secondary sources that can and do conflict with one another. In the case of video game lore, players can point to the first appearance of something and can readily follow the thread forward in time, pointing out when a game franchise breaks with tradition.

In Greek mythology, we get most of our origin stories from Hesiod's *Theogony*. Later authors spin their own interpretations of myth. For example, in Zeus's origin story, Callimachus writes two versions, one having Zeus raised on honey on Crete by nymphs, while another story says that Zeus spent his infancy in a cradle suspended in the air. Athenaeus, however, writes that as a baby Zeus was sustained by doves and an eagle that fed him nectar and ambrosia. Antoninus Liberalis writes another account, where Zeus comes of age in a cave of bees along with three friends. In *Theogony*, Zeus is the child of Kronos and Rhea, but his upbringing is not mentioned. All of these stories contribute to the overall lore surrounding the king of the Greek gods, but none are as specific or verifiable as any lore from a video game. With games, there is an Ur-moment, unless the developer has decided to deliberately shroud parts of a game's history/mythology.

What then is the role of the archaeogamer when studying lore? One can certainly compare and contrast the lore shared between titles within a series. One can study the player community reactions (both positive and negative) to in-game lore. Perhaps the most interesting element on the horizon of lore-heavy games is lore that is procedurally generated. Can code create culture, or at least a backstory of culture, through art, monuments, and language, and what will that culture look like? Will different players see different cultures created within the same game, and how is complexity involved in the process? Procedural lore will mix the lore of the real and virtual worlds, following the rules of both, where players can discover the origins of something, which can then be open to interpretation based on variations across all players and their copies of the games. We see player agency and a randomness of creation in games by Sid Meier (the *Civilization* series), but there is no real underlying story as to the "why" of the buildings. Allowing the game to create its own culture to be explored by players after its creation would seem to be the next—and certainly most vital—stage of video game archaeology. This is what we have been training for.

Lore Realized: Video Game Cosplay

In my home: a scale model of the Parthenon (purchased in Greece), a replica clay lamp (purchased in Italy), an imitation Viking coin (purchased in Sweden), a TARDIS (made of Lego), an iron sword (purchased at Hot Topic in the mall). The iron sword is actually made of foam and is an officially licensed *Minecraft* product. Surprising no one, you can buy artifacts from video games in the real world to play with/display.

Acquiring things seems to be a human need, and depending on your interests/obsessions, that stuff can be meatspace-manifestations of your favorite pop culture escapes, or of your favorite ancient civilizations. Sometimes both. We crave souvenirs. We want what we cannot touch in video games. So we make them. Virtual artifacts of cultures that exist only within games become real through independent or corporate creativity and industry. That *Minecraft* sword serves the exact same purpose as a wooden gladius purchased at a Renaissance Faire. It is a fun reminder of another place and time, and it allows us to feel connected to the media we love. The official term for this is "participatory culture."[19]

This intersection of tchotchkes and entertainment is nothing new. Kids in the 1950s could send away for decoder rings from their favorite radio programs, or ray guns from their favorite comics or science fiction serials, or replica props from TV and movies. It was only natural that video games would follow suit. It fills a fundamental need of belonging or of feeling close to a culture (pop or ancient or other).

This need is perhaps most visibly manifested in cosplay (an abbreviation of "costume play"). The material culture of comics, television, film, and games is robust and deep, evidenced at Comic Cons (comic book conventions) worldwide and at special events such as BlizzCon where cosplayers create true-to-life clothing, armor, weapons, accessories, and more, as students of the games created by Blizzard Entertainment. Think of serious restoration specialists and conservators, but for games. Some people will authentically recreate what George Washington wore when crossing the Delaware as depicted in great detail in Emanuel Leutze's 1850 painting. Others will invest just as much time and as many resources into recreating Grom Hellscream's clothing and arms from *World of Warcraft: Warlords of Draenor*. In meatspace, we sometimes call these people "historical reenactors." In the virtual world, they are "cosplayers." Both take what they do very seriously, and their attention to their craft is often professional-grade and accurate down to the last stitch.

With video games we see two levels of material culture: intra-game and extra-game. In the game, the artifacts are literal, to be collected and used by players for combat, crafting, or commerce. In meatspace, these replica artifacts represent what is real in-game, absent any magic. But these objects can still be used in combat (always mock so far as I know), crafting, or commerce (search for "Etsy" and "*Skyrim*" together for examples).

For costumes, the reproductions are intended for play, or for outward representations of the characters they exemplify, and for signaling to other people their affection for a particular game. This is more of a practical consideration for the cosplayer for ease-of-movement without sacrificing visual/emotional impact. Take Harrison Krix's design and creation of the Big Daddy character from *BioShock* (see Figure 4.2).[20] It took Krix seven weeks to build the costume of the giant, anonymous monster, with a multi-eyed diving helmet, suit, and boots, and rotating drill-arm. In the real world, such a suit would be made of fiber and metal. For cosplay, Krix used insulation foam, cardboard, expanding foam, stretch fabric, Ureshell, resin, fiberglass, a ready-made smoked security camera dome, PVC, MDF wood, a real cordless drill (housed inside the arm), PVC pipe, paint, gouache, iron powder, and computer case fans to keep the wearer cool. The end result was a life-size, wear-

Figure 4.2. *Left: BioShock*'s Big Daddy (image 2K Games). *Right:* Cosplay at MCM London Comic Con 2015. Photo by Pete Sheffield, CC BY-SA 2.0.

able, functional costume straight out of the video game, fulfilling its creator's intention of making something incredibly realistic in the natural world while remaining as true as possible to the synthetic. Creating the costume required years of experience in working with the above materials and tools, an understanding of the construction process, and a deep devotion to the subject matter as well as to its intended audience. Such a perfect representation is not at all rare for serious cosplay/cosplayers as they create and showcase their knowledge of material science and their skill in execution to fellow fans and makers. The participatory culture creates the material culture, extrapolating intellectual content from media, transposing it into real-world representation.

Fast-forward five hundred years to when archaeologists are excavating us and all of our junk. Out of the rubbish heap comes a shattered helmet . . . of Master Chief. Will we know enough then to recall and understand the connection to the *Halo* universe? I can imagine pop culture and video game specialists on-site who were trained for this very moment of discovery.

Thinking back two thousand years, was there any evidence of cultural kitsch, of souvenirs in antiquity? The majority of existing/preserved Greek painted pottery was actually found on Italian archaeological sites (albeit largely in the Greek colonies). When did humanity begin to collect representations of things and places they loved? And in this second Golden Age of video games, who were the first to create real-world artifacts of items found originally in games? Atari comes close with its *Swordquest* prizes, the virtual made real.[21]

Atari published *Swordquest: Earth World* in 1982 as the first of a never-completed series of games, which were the heirs to 1980's *Adventure.* As a marketing ploy, Atari's parent company, Warner Communications, paired Atari with DC Comics and the Franklin Mint to create a crossover, real-world adventure featuring hidden clues in the game and comic book series, plus in-person tournaments and fully realized artifact-prizes encrusted in real precious metal and gemstones. The final prize, the Sword of Ultimate Sorcery, was pictured in the contest's print advertising, a real-world manifestation of the eponymous *Swordquest* prize. With the cancellation of *Swordquest: Air World,* the sword (and the Philosopher's Stone) was never found/awarded. It remains a mystery as to what happened to these two artifacts, although there are a number of rumors surrounding their fate (Vendel and Goldberg 2012). Now in 2018, players with means can purchase video game replica weapons and jewelry outright without the need to complete any quests. Online storefronts such as Badali Jewelry offer 14k gold earrings with Vault symbols on them, licensed from Gearbox Software, creators of

Borderlands. Australia's Epic Weapons is licensed to create real, metal replicas of swords and other offensive weapons found in games such as *World of Warcraft.* These sell for hundreds into the thousands of dollars, which possibly translates into the equivalent time a player spends in-game to acquire similar, virtual weapons.

Archaeological Re-Creations

All games build worlds, and those built environments can be studied by archaeologists. Colleen Morgan defines this research as "encompassing the modeling of landscapes, excavations, buildings, cities, and environments built with a variety of computer applications in order to test scientific questions, communicate impressions of the past to others, and invite outside participation in the construction of the past" (Morgan 2009: 471). Archaeologists can also contribute to the creation of those environments, working hand in glove with game developers who need environments in which to set and tell their stories. This marks the major difference between virtual worlds such as *Second Life,* which is not a game, and open worlds such as those of *Assassin's Creed: Unity, Skyrim,* and *No Man's Sky.* In these examples, built environments do not exist simply for the sake of being built environments but contribute to the gameplay experience/ambience and to advancing (or hosting) the games' narratives.[22] Completing a 1:1 reconstruction of an ancient house or of an entire city is admirable in its own right but gains additional depth and use when integrated with player action. In a virtual world, visitors can explore nooks and crannies, much like visiting a real-world site. In a game, however, this exploration can be part of something bigger that adds additional layers to the structure with which a player is interacting. The built space becomes a theater and becomes something more than what it was. For archaeogaming then, it is important to understand why a feature (such as a temple) was built, and also to understand why it is photorealistic or why it seems sketched, and to what narrative purpose the feature serves.

Archaeological reconstruction allows archaeologists to visualize possibilities of how artifacts, buildings, and settlements/towns might have looked based on existing evidence. Archaeologists should be just as interested in the process of digital reconstruction as they are in the outcome (Morgan 2009: 478). The *Rome Reborn* project created a 3D scale model of ancient Rome as it existed in the fourth century CE, tying it to Google Maps as a layer.[23] At the artifact level, archaeologists such as Sebastian Heath are pushing the envelope with 3D scanning and reconstruction, going beyond the re-creation of real things in digital space, opting instead to visualize artifacts as they are in perfect clarity.[24] What can we learn from re-making these ancient things in digital formats?

The purposes of imaging (either by drawing or through digital reconstruction) in archaeology include (1) communicating to the public and to peers what things might have looked like and (2) testing theories based on known archaeological evidence. For digital games, however, the reasons behind historic reconstruction are different: (1) they create a play-environment; (2) they add a sense of authenticity; (3) they create a sense of time and space.

Classical reception of architectural tropes by game developers has created a kind of digital shorthand, where fluted columns and armless statues communicate Western antiquity, immediately bringing a player into a time and place for a particular level. Ruins mean "old." Columns mean "civilization." With a few broad strokes by the developer, a player can switch from columned Greece/Rome to Egypt (drop a pyramid and some sand) to Mexico (drop a different kind of pyramid and jungle).

For some games (e.g., *Mario* or *Temple Run*), it is enough to make environments that support side-scrolling action and jumping that do not add much to the story or to characters. For other games, the environment exists in support of these major elements. The *Assassin's Creed* series takes increasingly bold, labor-intensive measures to recreate a city and its buildings as accurately as possible while still keeping the landscape manageable and the game fun to play. *Assassin's Creed: Unity* recreates ancient Paris at the time of the French Revolution and boasts a scale reproduction of the Notre Dame cathedral, which took over two years to create. Compromises were made, however, by compressing the city to make it easier to navigate and to jump across rooftops. The purpose of the recreation of the city and its structures is to add realness and believability for the player and an immersive environment in which several narratives can unfold. That Paris is a wonder to behold while still being fun to play in.

The developer, when choosing to create a historical game or a game that is set in the real world in real places either in the present or in the past, is faced with the choice of how "real" to make the world.[25] While archaeological illustration strives to be exact in its detail, the developer cannot afford the time and materials needed for that level of accuracy when creating the game-space. It is not practical from a business standpoint, and it could be argued that a constant level of hyper-realism adds little to the story and to the emotion of gameplay.

Developers such as Ubisoft or Naughty Dog aim for a certain level of texture and detail, some of it quite high, letting the immersion in the world fool players' brains into believing that they are there. This is of course boosted by sound design, something typically lacking from archaeological reconstructions.

In game development, the detail/accuracy must justify the story, and vice versa. How does the environment advance the narrative, character development, and gameplay? Retro-looking games such as *Minecraft* and *Undertale* provide exceptionally rewarding gameplay experiences without looking like photorealistic versions of anything (even though in the case of *Minecraft* players attempt to make accurate representations of things, but with blocks). In archaeogaming then, one can study game-spaces to compare the built environment there against the one in the real world. How are they different, and why? Why choose to represent one building over another? Why choose a lower (or higher) level of detail/accuracy? How do these built environments change over time between versions? Copplestone writes, "These ideas, that historical representation is subjective and that inaccuracies might actually provide a space to explore the past in different ways, mark a significant departure from understandings of history as authoritative and direct accounts of a recoverable past, thus shifting more towards a deconstructionist understanding/way of playing" (Copplestone 2016: 19). In other words, it is OK if games are historically inaccurate as it gives the audience a chance to consider those incongruities and anachronisms in a wider dialogue about the past. Adam Chapman argues that questions about historical accuracy in video games (whether in the visuals or in the way history is presented) "aren't particularly useful or indeed are even rather irrelevant. After all, these popular forms haven't waited for the outcomes of these debates and are already working as history out in the world, because they are treated as history by audiences who use them as a resource for establishing an understanding of the past" (Chapman 2016: 11–12).

When thinking about the above questions, one addresses the game as an archaeological site. The questions are no different from those asked of structures in the real world. The Parthenon we see in Athens now is not the original one built before Pericles initiated his building program on the Acropolis. And the fifth-century version we do see has changed over the past two thousand years through time, theft, and explosions. The versions of the Parthenon were built primarily to house the holy of holies, the original wooden statue of Athena, and were used secondarily as a place of not necessarily worship, but certainly as a divine space to visit. The level of detail communicated the wealth and power of Athens, the piety of the city and the leader-builder, as well as a storytelling device about the founding of the city itself. In the real world as well as in the digital, these built environments serve a practical purpose, but they are also devices for communicating many levels of messages to all who care (and have the ability) to read and comprehend them.

Thinking about communication, one of the reasons games feature ancient architecture and environments is that they are set within that period of history. As such, they become historical simulations, spaces for play that reimagine history in ways that are more speculative than accurate, or that strive for accuracy in presentation within which players can experiment with creations of alternate histories. These games and spaces project many of the values that are stereotypically associated with modern Western society into the past (Gardner 2007: 265). When looking back on many of the older world-building and history games (e.g., *Civilization*), visions of the past are modernized, globalizing, homogenized. Games endorse the primacy of the nation-state (Gardner 2007: 270). For Sid Meier, the godfather of historical simulations, it is less important to get the environments picture perfect than it is to focus on playing around with history itself, saying that "a game is a series of interesting decisions" (Rouse 2014: 83). Will Wright, creator of the *Sims* series, agrees, saying that "games are about exploring sets of possibilities. When you're designing a game, you're doing the same thing" (King and Borland 2004: 26). Andrew Gardner notes that the *Praetorians* game stereotypes non-Roman cultures and turns a basic game into a fascinating exercise in orientalist cultural politics (Gardner 2007: 260). *Age of Empires* focuses on the "struggle for technology," flattening of cultural diversity (Gardner 2007: 262). When studying games like these, it can reveal more about the beliefs and zeitgeist of the time in which a game was created. This cultural artifactual approach aims to reveal how video games are constructed and what they can teach us about contemporary society (Sotamaa 2014: 7).

Throughout the history of video games, designers have had to make the decision of how much detail to add to the visuals of their games. As computer graphics have improved, the need has increased for game developers to create photorealistic environments in which to set the action. This comes at a cost: the more time and energy spent in creating believable spaces, the less time and energy can be devoted to story and level design. "As much as level designers will try to emulate the design of the real world, we spend just as much time trying to work around the limitation those rules impose" (Johnston 2015: 179). "Successful level design is the antithesis of successful architecture" (Johnston 2015: 169). One approaches a quantum state, then, of being able to read a quark's location or spin, but not both at the same time of observation. Developers need to decide when enough is enough regarding graphics. How much detail is needed for the space to become believable, and what can we get away with without sacrificing the quality of the story or of the emotions players feel while playing? Do players get just as much of a thrill in shooting each other from behind monotone, textureless walls as they would when set in a more realistic environment? Is the hide-and-seek mechanic enough? For designer David Johnston, there is a shorthand that can be used to satisfy both requirements of immersion and action. In his "Dust" level for *Counter-Strike,* he focused on "adopting a visual framework inspired by African and Turkish architecture, but without sharing any of the same goals or values" (Johnston 179). That is to say, he gave the map a certain modern "Near Eastern" feel without incorporating the Islamic underpinnings of those designs. Players react to that shorthand and interpret it on the fly. All of a sudden they are fighting in a place that does not exist in the real world but has real-world flavor added. That shorthand is enough for PvP (player-vs-player). For cities requiring rooftop chases (every *Uncharted* and *Assassin's Creed* title), more detail is required. This includes the visual as well as the audible, recreating past sounds, a whole other branch of archaeology.

When studying the physical media of video games as built environments (and the built environments contained within the games themselves), the gaming archaeologist must attempt to determine why a level of reality was settled upon in service to the story, how that vérité was reached, why it appears in the game at all, and who created the representations of various structures. If archaeologists are to participate in the creation of video games, this is one area in which to get involved. Assist with the creation of a ruin, a place of worship, a marketplace, a city. Consult with game studios on why it might not be the best idea to situate the Colosseum (built CE 72–80) in the Rome ruled by Nero (CE 37–68).[26] Aside from this anachronism, *Ryse* bases its Roman feel on paintings from the Renaissance as opposed to actual reconstructions of archeological and architectural evidence.[27] The Rome of *Ryse* is Impressionistic, evoking the feeling of Roman antiquity without dedicating itself too hard to a time period (see Figure 4.3). When played, the game does feel like Rome, but it is certainly not Rome. For most game developers, that is exactly what they are aiming for.

Figure 4.3. *Ryse Son of Rome* (Crytek). Screen capture by author.

Conclusion

Just because we cannot see material culture doesn't mean that it's not there. With video games, it is possible to consider developer- and player-made artifacts as "intangible heritage" because they leave no trace in the natural world (see Vecco 2010). But as with the study of dance and ceremony, archaeologists and ethnographers can do meaningful work within synthetic worlds, asking all of the same research questions as their Earth-bound counterparts. In re-creating built environments in digital spaces, archaeologists can work through archaeological problems in a kinesthetic way. The digital is ever increasingly part of the human experience and cannot be ignored by archaeologists. As elements of games appear in the natural world by way of reproduction clothing, armor, weapons, and other artifacts, it is up to archaeologists to determine their origins, the worlds from which these things came, who produced them, and why.

Notes

1. See *Play the Past*, http://www.playthepast.org/?p=4717 (retrieved December 8, 2016).
2. This list is from http://www.mobygames.com/forums/dga,2/dgb,5/dgm,15 9789/ (retrieved December 8, 2016).
3. http://wow.gamepedia.com/Armory (retrieved December 8, 2016).

4. Professor John Aycock (University of Calgary) is leading the way with re-verse-engineering older video games to understand and deconstruct their underlying code.

5. Read Heyerdahl's first-person account in *The Kon-Tiki Expedition: By Raft across the South Seas* (George Allen and Unwin 1950).

6. https://en.wikipedia.org/wiki/Janet_Stephens (accessed December 8, 2016).

7. "Nerdy Nummies" (Rosanna Pansino), https://www.youtube.com/playlist ?list=PLABDF3052CBF1B195 (retrieved December 8, 2016).

8. The Geeky Chef (Cassandra Reeder), http://www.geekychef.com/search/label/video%20games (retrieved December 8, 2016).

9. Eat Game Live, http://www.eatgamelive.com (retrieved December 8, 2016).

10. Eat a Byte, http://www.eatabyte.com/ (retrieved December 8, 2016).

11. Gourmet Gaming, http://gourmetgaming.tumblr.com/ (retrieved December 8, 2016).

12. https://www.geek.com/games/final-fantasy-xvs-developers-cooked-all-of-the-delicious-food-you-see-in-the-game-1683645/ (retrieved September 17, 2017).

13. See the ongoing work of Grace Tsai at Texas A&M University concerning recreating food from seventeenth-century recipes used aboard seafaring vessels: http://mentalfloss.com/article/503719/archaeologists-are-recreating-recipes-17th-century-ships (retrieved September 17, 2017).

14. http://www.medievalcookery.com/helewyse/libro.html#CII (retrieved February 20, 2018).

15. Watch the Leeroy Jenkins video here, which has been viewed over forty-five million times: https://www.youtube.com/watch?v=LkCNJRfSZBU (retrieved December 10, 2016). To further add to the lore, on December 27, 2017, the original poster of the video declared that the event was staged: http://www .ladbible.com/technology/gaming-interesting-technology-the-answer-is-finally-here-the-leeroy-jenkins-video-was-staged-20171227 (retrieved February 20, 2018).

16. http://www.eurogamer.net/articles/2016-04-23-against-the-lore (retrieved December 10, 2016).

17. See https://steamcommunity.com/app/377160/discussions/0/458606877310719380/ for a good example (retrieved December 10, 2016).

18. For a representative sample, see http://www.shadowlocked.com/201205082608/features/8-reasons-why-the-elder-scrolls-online-has-had-its-time.html (retrieved December 10, 2016).

19. Archaeologist Paul Mullins writes about archaeology and material culture on his blog by the same name (paulmullins.wordpress.com), including entries on participatory culture, namely Japanese anime cosplay. For more on participatory culture (including video game cosplay), see H. Jenkins, *Fans, Bloggers, and Gamers: Exploring Participatory Culture* (New York: NYU Press, 2006), and A. Delwiche and J. J. Henderson, eds., *The Participatory Cultures Handbook* (New York: Routledge, 2012).

20. The complete, step-by-step creation of the costume may be found at http://volpinprops.blogspot.com/2009/09/big-daddy-bioshock.html (retrieved October 6, 2016).

21. For a full recounting of this *Swordquest* contest, see E. Grundhauser, "The Quest for the Real-Life Treasures of Atari's *Swordquest*," http://www.atlasobscura.com/articles/the-quest-for-the-real-life-treasures-of-ataris-swordquest (retrieved October 6, 2016).

22. Shawn Graham (2016: 17) argues, however, that *Assassin's Creed* has beautiful reconstructions that "make no real difference to the gameplay or the story."

23. Rome Reborn Project: http://romereborn.frischerconsulting.com/ (retrieved December 10, 2016).

24. See Sebastian Heath, "Closing Gaps in Low-Cost 3D," in *Visions of Substance: 3D Imaging in Mediterranean Archaeology*, ed. B. Olson and W. Caraher (Grand Forks: The Digital Press at the University of North Dakota, 2015), 53–62.

25. For a full analysis of accuracy in reconstruction in video games, see Copplestone 2016.

26. See this reddit thread for more historical inaccuracies in *Ryse:* https://www.reddit.com/r/xboxone/comments/1q5dtf/historical_inaccuracies_in_ryse_son_of_rome/ (retrieved December 10, 2016).

27. For examples see http://www.crytek.com/blog/work-of-art-ryse-features-in-a-major-new-renaissance-exhibition (retrieved December 10, 2016).

Further Reading

Castronova, E. 2003. "On Virtual Economies." *Game Studies: The International Journal of Computer Game Research* 3(2): 1–14.

———. 2005. *Synthetic Worlds: The Business and Culture of Online Games.* Chicago: University of Chicago Press.

———. 2007. *Exodus to the Virtual World: How Online Fun Is Changing Reality.* New York: Palgrave MacMillan.

Chapman, A., A. Foka, and J. Westin. 2016. "Introduction: What Is Historical Game Studies?" *Rethinking History.* DOI: 10.1080/13642529.2016.1256638.

Ingold, T. 2007. "Materials against Materiality." *Archaeological Dialogues* 14(1): 1–16.

Jones, A. M. 2015. "Meeting Pasts Halfway: A Consideration of the Ontology of Material Evidence in Archaeology." In *Material Evidence: Learning from Archaeological Practice,* edited by R. Chapman and A. Wylie, 324–38. New York: Routledge.

Mol, A., et al. 2017. "From the Stone Age to the Information Age: History and Heritage in Sid Meier's *Civilization VI.*" *Advances in Archaeological Practice* 5(2): 214–19.

Strauven, W. 2011. "The Observer's Dilemma: To Touch or Not to Touch." In *Media Archaeology: Approaches, Applications, and Implications,* edited by E. Huhtamo and J. Parikka, 148–63. Los Angeles: University of California Press.

Sunden, Jenny. 2010. "A Sense of Play: Affect, Emotion, and Embodiment in *World of Warcraft*." In *Working with Affect in Feminist Readings: Disturbing Differences,* edited by Marianne Liljestrom and Susanna Paasonen, 45–57. New York: Routledge.

Conclusion

Video game archaeology is not really all that different from the archaeology of other things, materials, places, and cultures. The modern approach is the same: study with research questions in mind and focus on understanding systems, how everything interrelates. Because we are dealing with the archaeology of the recent past, and even of current history, we are in the unique position of being able to talk to developers and players as we conduct our research. Video games and their players should be approached as a network of actors that work together and influence each other (Sotamaa 2014: 7) as well as their environment. Nardi concurs, stating that "we must study the subject position of designers and corporate managers, carefully scrutinizing their products and actions. In virtual worlds we see just how very much technology is anything but neutral" (Nardi 2015: 25).

Video games are archaeological sites, and many of these games create their own environments or synthetic worlds in which players operate. One can argue that any game-space is a world; it does not necessarily have to have recognizable landscapes (with rocks and trees) or even notions of up and down or east and west. As Wolf describes in his essay on worlds, they are defined by the objects and events that compose them, and these in turn are defined by what is considered canonical for a given world (Wolf 2014: 127). Presented with a world and its rules, archaeologists can begin to ask and answer questions about any digital game and the space it contains, ultimately drawing parallels and perhaps even universals to the archaeological study of games. Are there macro-level rules that can be applied across all games, a kind of Grand Unified Theory of gaming? And can these top-level rules, as Edward Castronova posited in 2008, reveal macro-level behavioral trends (Wolf 2014: 130)? We can use games as simulations, MMO worlds as sandboxes in which we can test theories, either by active intervention or passive observation of player-, community-, and game-behavior. From the long-term study of player behavior, we can mine the data to identify aggregate trends, what Wolf calls "inherent complexity" (Wolf 2014: 130).

William Sims Bainbridge conducted an ethnography in *World of Warcraft* in 2009 that became the book *The Warcraft Civilization: Social*

Science in a Virtual World. In it, he notes that *WoW* is so complex and offers so much scope for action that it transcends the game category to become a virtual world. It is a game, a synthetic world, and an online community (Bainbridge 2010: 4). *WoW* merges art, design, technology, and economics, plus social and cultural aspects, into a truly vibrant, bustling, online existence. The world comes ready-made with lore, the history of all that happened before the game. There are quests for knowledge of the past. One can even read books in-game (as one can now in other series such as *Elder Scrolls* and *Dragon Age*) (Bainbridge 2010: 39).

WoW is so popular that hundreds of servers (called "shards" and named "realms") each hold one complete instance of *WoW*, hundreds of identical worlds but populated by millions of different players. It is a model of the presumed multiverse, where several versions of our own world exist in the same space and time but on different planes. Players can opt to move their characters (toons) to other realms, leaving old alliances and guilds behind, making new ones, albeit in familiar regions and capital cities. There are hundreds of copies of Thunder Bluff, the Tauren capital. The cities all look the same. Their NPCs are all the same. The quests are identical. But the people moving through the town are different, yet they have the same needs and goals in their gameplay. They create the same in-game social structures with the in-game city as a backdrop. It remains to be seen what archaeologists can accomplish when studying the archaeology of hundreds of copies of the same city but populated with different people. The servers are clustered by real regions of the Earth: North Americans play together in one cluster, while the Chinese play in another. What are the trends? What player cultures emerge in identical in-game environments peopled with Europeans, Chinese, Americans who control Tauren, Blood Elves, Orcs? And does the game behave in the same way (or differently) across all of the server instances?

Getting beyond the in-game social elements, archaeologists can also explore virtual worlds from the outside. We can explore issues relating to emerging technology, intellectual property rights, socio-technical implications of online misbehavior, cultural boundaries, gender-specific norms, and the meaning of virtual life and death (Bainbridge 2010: 12). Bainbridge's research methods should be emulated when studying other games and virtual worlds both large and small. He first created several toons on several servers, and over the course of his study took over twenty-two thousand time-stamped screenshots. He also visited lore websites, guild websites, and the Armory (for guild and player data collected from across all realms in the game) (Bainbridge 2010: 18). To crunch the numbers he used *Statistical Package for the Social Sciences* (*SPSS*) for world-created data analysis (Bainbridge 2010: 152). We must consider contexts and usage, reception of the games in the specialized press and online communities, statistical information about player's preferences and rituals, etc. (Therrien 2012: 26). Archaeology is nothing but the collection, analysis, and interpretation of data no matter what is being studied.

As with the spread of civilization thousands of years ago, over the past forty years we have seen the proliferation of digital entertainment in the form of games and hardware on which to play them. This universe continues to expand, leaving behind the detritus of progress, again no different from abandonment levels of cities or trash dropped off the back of an Oregon Trail wagon train. "New media, like the computer technology on which they rely, race simultaneously toward what we might call the 'bleeding edge of obsolescence'" (Chun 2011: 184). As a culture, we constantly rediscover the old-as-new, the media serving as both storage and memory (Chun 2011: 184). Games contain data, and we remember that data. We interact with the material culture of video games; we play what is new and what is old, and in playing older games for the first time, they are still new to us as players. It is an act of nostalgia that can be recreated again and again given the right hardware and software. It is no different than seeing a '57 Chevy on the road as you drive your '17 Toyota or choosing to drive that '57 Chevy in 2018. The old and the new coexist.

The archaeological study of video games is, as Pias describes, "a plea in favor of the material intransigence of the concrete found in 'games' and for the rehabilitation of the excluded 'perversion' and 'corruptions' (after Callois) of the game, offering the chance for a critical examination of the genealogy of anthropological game theories whose concept of play merely disguises the fact that their purpose is to remove the paradox from the social organization. Games should be taken seriously" (Pias 2011: 181). Games are ultimately human creations. They are built environments, possibly the newest type of built environments as people continue to explore the making of things in infinite, digital space. This new construction (and modification of old construction)—think new games and modding older ones—leads to the creation of new social institutions, which, as Shennan writes, "produce novel ecologies for human action and exist at the boundary of cultural and ecological inheritance" (2012: 31).

Do built environments create and/or influence human behavior? Do new environments (such as games) create new behaviors in people, how they relate to these synthetic environments, and how they interact with each other when a game contains a social element? How do the things within the game-space influence the actions of players, and vice versa? Will the conclusions archaeologists draw from studying video games overlap with those who study cultures in the natural world? Where might differences lie, and are we seeing the emergence of "post-human" thought? What does the archaeology of blended space look like?

Archaeologists consider the material evidence both of the past and of the present. Holtorf, quoting John Barrett from 1994, states that "our knowledge is not grounded upon the material evidence itself, but arises from the interpretation strategies which we are prepared to bring to bear upon that evidence" (Holtorf 2005: 72). In our interpretation of the material evidence, we reveal "secret truths that undo the status quo and cause change, not just in Western academia and for the explorers concerned, but also at the sites of discovery" (Holtorf 2005: 50). Any good science challenges old assumptions, putting those to the test while building upon them. Archaeogaming is just another level on the way to understanding the interrelationships of people and things, and the interrelationships between things and other things. We try to extrapolate meaning. Instead of "archaeology of the contemporary past" we need to do "an archaeology of emergent processes" (Yaneva 2013: 122). It is not just the things we study but what those things produce. We are studying verbs instead of nouns. Everything is in the act of becoming something else.

Communication professor Christopher Paul finds meaning in the sociocultural frame tied to games' roles as cultural objects and media products: the role of games in society and the role of games in people's lives (Paul 2014: 460–61). But the meaning of games is also found in play (Bogost 2006), and in the game's reaction to player expression within the game (Rouse 2014: 88). This is archaeology in motion, and it is a way of thinking about the past and the present affected by elements of the past that surround us daily. There is action and interaction both outside video games and within governed by actual and synthetic time, physics, logic, and emotion.

The future of archaeogaming must include elements from all of the preceding chapters in this book, but the video game archaeologist should feel free to specialize. There is more than enough work for everyone as the discipline grows. Video game art historians, historians, archivists, and ethicists can all support the archaeological work at hand. Archaeogaming requires a foundation in archaeological theory, from positivism through post-processualism and beyond, taking from each to create a hybrid theory from which we can operate. We also need, according to Bogost, "procedural literacy that helps scholars grapple with the essence of computational media," including how to understand procedural rhetoric, which he defines as "the practice of using processes persuasively . . . through the authorship of rules of behavior" (Bogost 2007: 28–29). The hardware runs the software, which executes the rules/processes to generate the game-space. As archaeologists, we need to understand how those processes work as the fundamental underpinnings of any digital world we explore. The video game archaeologist is first and foremost an archaeologist, at the bare minimum one with basic survey/excavation/ conservation/documentation training/experience in the natural world at a field school or other site, supplemented by work in computer science and informatics, artificial intelligence, coding, and complexity science and tempered by varied humanities interests in game studies, media studies, history, art, economics, anthropology, sociology, philosophy, and linguistics. As David Byrne and Gill Callaghan wrote in *Complexity Theory and the Social Sciences,* "The future of useful social science is at the very least interdisciplinary and probably post-disciplinary" (Byrne and Callaghan 2014: 3). We are magpies.

We are at the beginning of an exciting era in new media, exploring synthetic, habitable places, the groundwork laid in the early 2000s and finally given a name—"archaeogaming"—in 2013.[1] Dozens of archaeologists internationally are now at work on understanding video games as artifacts, built environments, archaeological sites, and objects of material culture. The current epicenters of academic archaeogaming research are the University of York's Centre for Digital Heritage and the University of Leiden's department of archaeology (in the form of the VALUE Project). Independent scholars and hobbyists continue to contribute and publish, and there are now sessions of academic papers dedicated to video game archaeology at professional conferences such as the Society for American Archaeology, the European Association of Archaeologists, and the Society for Historical Archaeology. Archaeogaming started with curious individuals finding each other to create an informal collective, which is now coalescing into a community of practice, something akin to the Theoretical Archaeology Group (TAG) in the US and UK. The more we work together as a community, the more we share our work with each other, and the more we actively communicate our work to an interested, curious public, the better our discipline will become. It is my hope that this is only one book in what will become many on the subject of video game archaeology so that we can hear from a diversity of voices on a multitude of topics. This brief introduction is only the opening chapter, which I hope fuels future discussion and argument and growth. In the archaeology of video games, there is no such thing as "game over."

Note

1. "Archaeogaming" fits hand in glove with the study of historical video games (games set in a historical period). While we have "archaeogamers," history has "developer-historians" and "player-historians" (Chapman 2016: 283).

Appendix

No Man's Sky Archaeological Survey (NMSAS) Code of Ethics

By Catherine Flick
with L. Meghan Dennis and Andrew Reinhard

Preamble

No Man's Sky is a procedurally generated artificial universe in which the *No Man's Sky* Archaeological Survey ("the Survey") takes place. For the purposes of the Survey, the universe ("in-universe" or "in-game universe") is considered a simulation of a real, existing universe, and thus incursions into and exploration of this universe will raise ethical and social issues. This Code attempts to address potential ethical and social issues by presenting six Principles ("the Principles") relating to the behavior of those involved in the Survey within the game universe ("archaeonauts"), and in dealing with the data collected about the in-game universe. While this Code of Ethics has been written for the *NMS* project, the authors urge that similar projects in other video games and virtual worlds use this in a modified form, or create their own set of ethical standards for researchers to adhere to.

Some of these Principles are not as realistic as we would like: in-game mechanics prevent us from making real choices about how we interact with the in-game universe. Currently we are suggesting that archaeonauts spend their first few days upgrading their tools and ships and getting to grips with the game mechanics, however, in a sustainable way that adheres to the Principles as much as is possible.

These Principles are not intended to be followed in a dogmatic way but to guide in a thoughtful way: to allow those encountering ethical tensions guidance in reasoning through the potential impact of decisions they make. The Code provides an ethical foundation, which can support decision-making and to which one can appeal. Survey team members should bring any queries or complaints to the Ethics Board, which consists of the authors of this Code. Breaches of the code could result in disciplinary procedures, up to and including removal from the Survey team. In brief, the Principles require archaeonauts to:

1. Act consistently with the in-universe public interest, protecting worlds, human and nonhuman people and animals, and their societies and cultures and, where possible, not interfering with the normal development of societies and cultures by introducing knowledge, strength, or technologies more advanced than their current levels.
2. Advance the integrity and reputation of the Survey consistent with the public interest.
3. Maintain integrity and independence in their professional judgment.
4. Release data publicly and publish in the public interest, in line with open-access principles, unless this conflicts with Principle 5.
5. Ensure the integrity of archaeological sites, humans and nonhuman people and animals, and archaeological artifacts where possible; work to ensure good stewardship of sites, peoples, and artifacts; and avoid and discourage activities that enhance the commercial value of archaeological artifacts. Interaction with artifacts in order to progress according to game mechanics is permissible; destruction or sale of artifacts for profit is not.
6. Only act against another human or nonhuman person or animal in self-defense where no other option is available (including avoidance of and/or escape from potentially hostile situations, and self-terminate with respawn).

Principles

1. The Public

Archaeonauts have a responsibility toward the worlds, people, animals, and other living beings found upon these worlds, and whose lives and cultures are studied. These obligations can supersede the goal of seeking new knowledge and can lead to decisions not to undertake or to discontinue a research project when the primary obligation conflicts with other responsibilities, such as those owed to sponsors or clients. These ethical obligations include:

a. To avoid harm or wrong, understanding that the development of knowledge, strength, or technologies can lead to change that may be positive or negative for the sentient beings or animals worked with or studied.

b. To respect the well-being of human and nonhuman people and animals.
c. To consult actively with the affected individuals or group(s), with the goal of establishing a working relationship that can be beneficial to all parties involved.

2. The Survey

Archaeonauts shall advance the integrity and reputation of the Survey consistent with the public interest. In particular, archaeonauts shall, as appropriate:

a. Help develop an organizational environment favorable to acting ethically.
b. Promote public knowledge of the Survey.
c. Extend Survey knowledge by appropriate participation in meetings and publications.
d. Support, as members of the Survey, other archaeonauts striving to follow this Code.
e. Obey all laws governing their work, unless, in exceptional circumstances, such compliance is inconsistent with the public interest.
f. Express concerns to the archaeonauts involved when significant violations of this Code are detected unless this is impossible, counterproductive, or dangerous.
g. Be alert to the danger of compromising ethics as a condition to engage in Survey research, yet also be alert to proper demands of good citizenship or host-guest relations.

3. Judgment

Archaeonauts shall maintain integrity and independence in their professional judgment. In particular, archaeonauts shall, as appropriate:

a. Temper all professional judgments by the need to support and maintain human values.
b. Maintain professional objectivity in the evaluation of any collected data.
c. Disclose to all concerned parties those conflicts of interest that cannot reasonably be avoided or escaped.

4. Data

Data collected shall be released publicly where in the public interest and not in conflict with Principle 5a. In particular, archaeonauts shall, as appropriate:

a. Seriously consider all reasonable requests for access to their data and other research materials for purposes of research. They should also make every effort to insure preservation of their fieldwork data for use by posterity. This is enabled for the purposes of the Survey through the Open Context/NMS Archaeology database.
b. Ensure that their data is of high quality and follows the Survey protocol.
c. Where species encountered in the process of data collection are sentient, determine in advance (if possible) whether they wish to remain anonymous or receive recognition, and make every effort to comply with those wishes. [This principle will be revised based on actual gameplay experience.]
d. When working in conjunction with other archaeonauts, ensure all involved in the data-collection activities receive appropriate levels of recognition.

5. Artifacts and archaeological record

Archaeonauts have a responsibility to act professionally as regards the exploration, collection, and documentation of archaeological sites and artifacts. Archaeonauts are expected to recall that:

a. The archaeological record—that is, in situ archaeological material and sites, archaeological collections, records, and reports—is irreplaceable. It is the responsibility of all archaeonauts to work for the long-term conservation and protection of the archaeological record by practicing and promoting stewardship of the archaeological record. Stewards are both caretakers of and advocates for the archaeological record for the benefit of all people; as they investigate and interpret the record, they should use the specialized knowledge they gain to promote public understanding and support for its long-term preservation.
b. Trading use of or interaction with archaeological artifacts to increase the archaeonaut's capacity is only permitted where the artifact is artificially placed by another technologically advanced race solely in order for said capacities to be increased. That is: interaction with

crates (particularly Neutral crates which often give artifacts as rewards) is permitted, as is trade of these items. Interaction with in situ items such as Vortex Cubes, however, is not permitted.

6. Self

Archaeonauts are responsible for their own safety and security when conducting research for the Survey. It is reasonably expected for archaeonauts to:

a. Ensure their bodily and psychological integrity where possible in the "real world."
b. Within the game, avoid potentially hostile situations, even if the potential for research is high.
c. If hostile situations cannot be avoided or cannot be escaped, self-termination and respawning is preferred. Violence in self-defense against human or nonhuman entities should always be a last resort when all other possibilities have been exhausted.

Help! I've crashed on a planet and I want to get off! (Practical suggestions on beginning the game.)

1. Don't panic.
2. It's okay to mine natural resources in a sustainable way (e.g. plutonium, gold, copper, nickel)—don't completely strip a planet of its gold, for example. Where possible, try to avoid extracting iron from plant life. There should be rock formations from which you can get iron.
3. It's okay to interact with plant life to extract resources (e.g. platinum, zinc). These plants seem to continue existing after the extraction process.
4. It's okay to interact with cargo drops/chests, etc., and take the resources from those.
5. It's okay (and encouraged) to interact with monoliths, beacons, knowledge stones, and other interactable-with things that provide you with information.
6. It's *not* okay to pick up (interact with) non-natural items that alert Sentinels, such as Vortex Cubes or Gravitino Balls for farming purposes if they have been left about on a world. Within this world these are considered precious by the Sentinels, so archaeonauts should respect them and leave them in situ.

7. If you upset Sentinels (by overmining or farming on hostile worlds) it is best to hide until the chase is dropped (you will be notified) rather than shooting the Sentinels. However, rare exceptions can be made if you need to progress in the game by entering a hostile world (i.e., where Sentinels are aggressive) where it would be impossible to progress without engaging with Sentinels (e.g., getting hyperdrive blueprints). Hostile engagement with Sentinels is absolutely a last resort.

8. Breaking into locked buildings is only permissible when explicitly requested to by the story mechanics (e.g., for getting hyperdrive blueprints). We acknowledge that this is a limitation of the game and if there were other options we would recommend those instead.

9. Please, unlike in real life, feed the (friendly) animals.

10. If you encounter hostile creatures, you should not engage. Yes, it sucks to die, but you will respawn and be given the opportunity to find your "grave" and retrieve your stuff.

11. If you are scanned by hostile ships, you should not engage. You will respawn at a space station and be given the opportunity to go and collect your stuff from your "grave."

12. Try to pick ethical responses (where applicable) to the challenges offered to you by aliens.

13. Some archaeologically significant structures are able to be physically manipulated. Moving and examining items is okay as long as they are returned to the location and position they were originally in. Before interacting with an artifact or features, take screengrabs and video (if possible). Also, if possible, take video of your interaction with artifacts (excluding monoliths).

14. These suggestions are not the be-all and end-all and are a work in progress. There will be edge cases and difficult decisions to make. It will be challenging to follow all of these guidelines all of the time. You will be tempted to engage with that ship, or pick up that cube, play football with artifacts, or zap that annoying bug (or bear-butterfly-cat-thing) biting your leg. Try as much as you can to be sensible and thoughtful in your adventures in the universe. For more details on the specifics of the principles that guide these suggestions, read above.

Catherine Flick is a senior lecturer in Computing and Social Responsibility at De Montfort University.

L. Meghan Dennis is a PhD candidate in archaeology at the University of York specializing in ethics and the archaeology of digital spaces.

Notes

Reproduced here by permission of the authors.

Input into this code has come from the ACM Software Engineering Code of Ethics, the Society for American Archaeology (SAA) Code of Ethics, the Code and Standard of the Register of Professional Archaeologists, and the American Anthropological Association (AAA) Code of Ethics.

Glossary

This brief glossary contains definitions of the video game terms used in this book with which archaeologists might not be familiar, and archaeological terms from the text that video game player-scholars might not know.

agent-based modeling (ABM): A method of testing hypotheses within a digital environment where one parameter is changed in order to see how it affects the actions and interactions of autonomous agents (e.g., NPCs) within that environment in order to assess their effects on the entire system.

Anthropocene: A designation given to our current geological period, which is dominated by the presence and activities of humans.

archaeogaming: The archaeology in and of games, including the application of archaeological tools and methods to investigate them as landscapes, sites, and artifacts, and to understand how archaeology and archaeologists and their ethics are both portrayed and perceived by game developers and players.

assemblage: A collection of objects—either objects of the same kind spread across a site or, more typically, objects of different kinds of materials found in the same place.

augmented reality (AR): Technology that merges the natural world with digital data that simultaneously occupies one's senses (audio, visual, or both) in real-time through a device such as a smartphone or tablet computer (and their cameras, GPS functionality, and speakers/headphones).

avatar: A player's proxy within a digital game, where the player serves as its homunculus that animates and drives the character through the synthetic world.

built environment: A space or place constructed by people for the use and habitation of other people. A digital built environment is one in which people's use and habitation is mediated by computer hardware.

chiptunes: Music composed/played to emulate video game soundtracks of the 1980s.

complexity: How rules combine to create emergent behavior in a system.

cosplay: "Costume play" in which fans of media create clothing and accoutrements in order to dress as their favorite characters.

diegetic games: Games where players learn about how the game is played by actually playing the game.

emergent behavior: The resulting effect(s) when rules underlying a system combine to create something one rule alone cannot produce.

eSports: Competitive video gaming in front of a live audience, usually with corporate sponsorship and cash prizes.

gamifact/glitch: An unintended, unexpected in-game artifact created from chaos in the underlying code and observed by the player, disrupting gameplay.

griefing: The act of intentionally hazing other players for personal pleasure in a video game.

guildie: A fellow member of the same guild (group/clan) within a video game.

Harris matrix: A two-dimensional, visual representation of a site's stratigraphy, as invented by archaeologist Edward Harris based on geological principles.

intangible heritage: Elements of cultural heritage that leave no material remains (e.g., dance, ceremonies, etc.).

Late Capitalism: The current period of history, which is post-Industrial and focuses on the consumption and disposal of mass-produced goods.

machine-created culture (MCC): Digital built environments or elements of digital material culture directly created by algorithms/code authored by other code routines instead of being written directly by a person.

massively multiplayer online game (MMO): A game played simultaneously over the internet by a large group of people in a shared space.

material culture: The story of a group of people as defined by the things they use regularly.

mechanics: The rules or operations within the game that allow players to navigate and engage with the synthetic world.

meatspace: The space in which people reside corporeally. Also known as the natural world.

metaspace: The digitally enabled space in which people reside as mediated by hardware. Also known as the synthetic world.

mods/modding: Player-created modifications to commercially produced video games; the act of creating game modifications.

non-player character: A character in a game with whom a player interacts but does not overtly control.

n00b: Abbreviation for "newbie," someone who is just beginning to play a particular video game.

open-world game: A game containing a massive landscape for players to explore on their own terms and at their own pace.

platform game: A classic, two-dimensional video game where players move left or right and can often jump up or down to reach other areas of the game.

point-and-click game: A game in which the player uses a pointing device to select hidden objects or to advance the game's action/narrative.

procedural content generation (PCG or ProcGen): The use of algorithms in software code to speedily create detail in a video game, serving as development shorthand and to keep computing resources to a minimum during play.

player-vs-player (PvP): A game (or part of a game) where players can battle each other for pride or in-game rewards.

reception studies: An academic approach to understanding how an audience perceives something.

respawn: An automated resurrection of a player-character in a game.

retrogames/retrogaming: Games (and the act of engaging with them) from the early periods of video game history (1970s until the mid-1990s), and games specifically designed as throwbacks to that time.

roguelike game: A digital role-playing game containing a procedurally generated dungeon with tile-based graphics, turn-based gameplay, and perma-death (permanent death) for the player's character. The term is derived from the 1980 game *Rogue*.

role-playing game (RPG): A game in which the player adopts the persona of their avatar in order to adventure within realms/worlds, often fantasy based.

seriation: The arrangement of a collection of artifacts into a chronological sequence based on characteristics such as shape, color, material, etc.

Steam: Online marketplace for purchasing and playing computer games from independent and major commercial video developers.

stratigraphy: Layers of soil (strata) when viewed as a whole in order to understand the chronology of an archaeological site.

synthetic world (née virtual world): A born-digital space with which users can engage as mediated by hardware.

Twitch: A live-streaming video service for gameplay.

virtual reality: Technology used to fully immerse a user within a synthetic world that is separate from the natural one.

Works Cited

Aldred, J. 2012. "A Question of Character: Transmediation, Abstraction, and Identification in Early Games Licensed from Movies." In *Before the Crash: Early Video Game History,* edited by M. J. P. Wolf, 90–104. Detroit: Wayne State University Press.

Bainbridge, W. S. 2010. *The Warcraft Civilization: Social Science in a Virtual World.* Cambridge, MA: MIT Press.

Barad, K. 2007. *Meeting the Universe Halfway: Quantum Physics and the Entanglement of Matter and Meaning.* Durham, NC: Duke University Press.

Barrett, J. C. 2012. "Agency: A Revisionist Account." In *Archaeological Theory Today,* 2nd ed., edited by I. Hodder, 146–66. Cambridge: Polity.

Bird, D., and J. F. O'Connell. 2012. "Human Behavioral Ecology." In *Archaeological Theory Today,* 2nd ed., edited by I. Hodder, 37–61. Cambridge: Polity.

Boellstorff, T., B. Nardi, C. Pearce, and T. L. Taylor. 2012. *Ethnography and Virtual Worlds: A Handbook of Method.* Princeton, NJ: Princeton University Press.

Bogost, I. 2006. *Unit Operations: An Approach to Video Game Criticism.* Cambridge, MA: MIT Press.

———. 2007. *Persuasive Games: The Expressive Power of Videogames.* Cambridge, MA: MIT Press.

———. 2012. *Alien Phenomenology, or What It's Like to Be a Thing.* Minneapolis: University of Minnesota Press.

Brittain, M., and T. Clack. 2007. "Archaeology and the Media." In *Archaeology and the Media,* edited by T. Clack and M. Brittain, 11–65. Walnut Creek, CA: Left Coast Press.

Buchli, V. 2016. *An Archaeology of the Immaterial.* New York: Routledge.

Byrne, D., and G. Callaghan. 2014. *Complexity Theory and the Social Sciences: The State of the Art.* New York: Routledge.

Carver, M. 2009. *Archaeological Investigation.* New York: Routledge.

Castronova, E. 2005. *Synthetic Worlds: The Business and Culture of Online Games.* Chicago: University of Chicago Press.

Chapman, J. 2008. "Object Fragmentation and Past Landscapes." In *Handbook of Landscape Archaeology,* edited by B. David and J. Thomas, 187–201. Walnut Creek, CA: Left Coast Press.

Chapman, A. 2016. *Digital Games as History: How Videogames Represent the Past and Offer Access to Historical Practice.* New York: Routledge.

Cheetham, P. N. 2008. "Noninvasive Subsurface Mapping Techniques, Satellite and Aerial Imagery in Landscape Archaeology." In *Handbook of Landscape Archaeology,* edited by B. David and J. Thomas, 562–82. Walnut Creek, CA: Left Coast Press.

Chun, W. H. K. 2011. "The Enduring Ephemeral, or the Future Is Memory." In *Media Archaeology: Approaches, Applications, and Implications,* edited by E. Huhtamo and J. Parikka, 184–203. Los Angeles: University of California Press.

Cole, T. 2013. "The Place of Things in Contemporary History." In *The Oxford Handbook of the Archaeology of the Contemporary World,* edited by P. Graves-Brown, R. Harrison, and A. Piccini, 66–81. Oxford: Oxford University Press.

Copplestone, T. 2016. "But That's Not Accurate: The Differing Perceptions of Accuracy in Cultural Heritage Videogames Between Creators, Consumers, and Critics." *Rethinking History.* DOI: 10.1080/13642529.2017.1256615.

Cubitt, S. 2013. "Global Media and Archaeologies of Network Technologies." In *The Oxford Handbook of the Archaeology of the Contemporary World,* edited by P. Graves-Brown, R. Harrison, and A. Piccini, 133–48. Oxford: Oxford University Press.

Darvill, T. 2008. "Pathways to a Panoramic Past: A Brief History of Landscape Archaeology in Europe." In *Handbook of Landscape Archaeology,* edited by B. David and J. Thomas, 60–76. Walnut Creek, CA: Left Coast Press.

David, B., and J. Thomas. 2008a. "Preface." In *Handbook of Landscape Archaeology,* edited by B. David and J. Thomas, 19–22. Walnut Creek, CA: Left Coast Press.

———. 2008b. "Landscape Archaeology: Introduction." In *Handbook of Landscape Archaeology,* edited by B. David and J. Thomas, 27–43. Walnut Creek, CA: Left Coast Press.

DeMarrais, E., C. Gosden, and A. C. Renfrew, eds. 2004. *Rethinking Materiality: The Engagement of Mind with the Material World.* Cambridge: McDonald Institute for Archaeological Research.

Dennis, L. M. 2016. "Archaeogaming, Ethics, and Participatory Standards." *SAA Archaeological Record* 16(5): 29–33.

Dormans, J. 2014. "Emergence." In *The Routledge Companion to Video Game Studies,* edited by M. J. P. Wolf and B. Perron, 427–33. New York: Routledge.

Ducheneaut, N., N. Yee, E. Nickell, and R. J. Moore. 2007. "The Life and Death of Online Gaming Communities: A Look at Guilds in *World of Warcraft.*" *CHI 2007 Proceedings,* 839–48.

Edgeworth, M. 2014. "From Spade-Work to Screen-Work: New Forms of Archaeological Discovery in Digital Space." In *Visualization in the Age of Computerization,* edited by A. Carusi et al., 40–58. New York: Routledge.

Ellison, C., and B Keogh. 2015. "The Joy of Virtual Violence." In *The State of Play: Creators and Critics on Video Game Culture,* edited by D. Goldberg and L. Larsson, 141–56. New York: Seven Stories Press.

Ernst, W. 2011. "Media Archaeogeography: Method and Machine versus History of Narrative Media." In *Media Archaeology: Approaches, Applications, and Implications,* edited by E. Huhtamo and J. Parikka, 239–55. Los Angeles: University of California Press.

Eve, S. 2012. "Augmenting Phenomenology: Using Augmented Reality to Aid Archaeological Phenomenology in the Landscape." *Journal of Archaeological Method and Theory* 19(4): 582–600.

Fabian, J. 2002. *Time and the Other: How Anthropology Makes Its Object.* New York: Columbia University Press.

Fewster, K. 2013. "The Relationship between Ethnoarchaeology and Archaeologies of the Contemporary Past: A Historical Investigation." In *The Oxford Handbook of the Archaeology of the Contemporary World,* edited by P. Graves-Brown, R. Harrison, and A. Piccini, 27–39. Oxford: Oxford University Press.

Foucault, M. 1972. *The Archaeology of Knowledge.* Translated by A. M. Sheridan Smith. New York: Pantheon.

Gardner, A. 2007. "The Past as Playground: The Ancient World in Video Game Representation." In *Archaeology and the Media,* edited by T. Clack and M. Brittain, 255–72. Walnut Creek, CA: Left Coast Press.

Goldberg, D., and L. Larrson. 2015. "Introduction: Post-Escapism: A New Discourse on Video Game Culture." In *The State of Play: Creators and Critics on Video Game Culture,* edited by D. Goldberg and L. Larsson, 7–14. New York: Seven Stories Press.

González-Tennant, E. 2016. "Archaeological Walking Simulators." *SAA Archaeological Record* 16(5): 23–28.

Graham, S. 2016. "The Archaeologist Who Studies Video Games and the Things He Learned There." *SAA Archaeological Record* 16(5): 16–18.

Guins, R. 2014. *Game After: A Cultural Study of Video Game Afterlife.* Cambridge, MA: MIT Press.

Harrison, R., and J. Schofield. 2010. *After Modernity: Archaeological Approaches to the Contemporary Past.* Oxford: Oxford University Press.

Harvey, P. 2013. "Anthropological Approaches to Contemporary Material Worlds." In *The Oxford Handbook of the Archaeology of the Contemporary World,* edited by P. Graves-Brown, R. Harrison, and A. Piccini, 54–65. Oxford: Oxford University Press.

Heaven, D. 2015. "What Digital Trash Dumped in Games Tells Us about the Players." *New Scientist,* November 18, https://www.newscientist.com/article/dn28505-what-digital-trash-dumped-in-games-tells-us-about-the-players/ (accessed August 28, 2016).

Heilen, Michael P., Brian Schiffer, and J. Jefferson Reid. 2008. "Landscape Formation Processes," 601–608. In *Handbook of Landscape Archaeology,* edited by Bruno David and Julian Thomas. Walnut Creek, CA: Left Coast Press.

Hernandez, P. 2016. "YouTuber's Journey into Abandoned MMO is Creepypasta Material." Kotaku, March 28, 2016, kotaku.com/youtubers-journey-into-abandoned-mmo-is-creepypasta-mat-1767500088 (accessed August 28, 2016).

Hill, R. A. 2008. "Nonhuman Primate Approaches to Landscapes." In *Handbook of Landscape Archaeology,* edited by B. David and J. Thomas, 95–101. Walnut Creek, CA: Left Coast Press.

Hodder, I. 1982. *Symbols in Action: Ethnoarchaeological Studies of Material Culture.* Cambridge: Cambridge University Press.

———. 2005. "Reflexive Methods." In *Handbook of Archaeological Methods,* edited by H. D. G. Maschner and C. Chippindale, 643–72. Lanham, MD: AltaMira Press.

———. 2012. *Entangled: An Archaeology of the Relationships between Humans and Things.* London: Wiley-Blackwell.

Holtorf, C. 2005. *From Stonehenge to Las Vegas: Archaeology as Pop Culture.* Lanham, MD: Altamira Press.

———. 2007a. *Archaeology Is a Brand! The Meaning of Archaeology in Contemporary Popular Culture.* Oxford: Archaeopress.

———. 2007b. "An Archaeological Fashion Show: How Archaeologists Dress and How They Are Portrayed in the Media." In *Archaeology and the Media,* edited by T. Clack and M. Brittain, 69–88. Walnut Creek, CA: Left Coast Press.

———. 2011. "Imagine This: Archaeology in the Experience Society." In *Contemporary Archaeologies: Excavating Now,* 2nd ed., edited by C. Holtorf and A. Piccini, 47–64. Frankfurt: Peter Lang.

———. 2012. "Popular Culture, Portrayal of Archaeology: Archaeology on Screen." In *The Oxford Companion to Archaeology,* 650–51. Oxford: Oxford University Press.

Huggett, J. 2017. "The Apparatus of Digital Archaeology." *Internet Archaeology* 44.

Huhtamo, E., and J. Parikka. 2011. "Introduction: An Archaeology of Media Archaeology." In *Media Archaeology: Approaches, Applications, and Implications,* edited by E. Huhtamo and J. Parikka, 1–21. Los Angeles: University of California Press.

Johnson, M. 2010. *Archaeological Theory: An Introduction.* 2nd ed. London: Wiley-Blackwell.

Johnston, D. 2015. "The Making of Dust: Architecture and the Art of Level Design." In *The State of Play: Creators and Critics on Video Game Culture,* edited by D. Goldberg and L. Larsson, 169–82. New York: Seven Stories Press.

King, B., and J. Borland. 2004. *Dungeons and Dreamers: The Rise of Computer Culture from Geek to Chic.* New York: McGraw-Hill/Osborne.

Knoblauch, W. 2015. "Game Over? A Cold War Kid Reflects on Apocalyptic Video Games." In *The State of Play: Creators and Critics on Video Game Culture,* edited by D. Goldberg and L. Larsson, 183–210. New York: Seven Stories Press.

Kocurek, C. A. 2015. *Coin-Operated America: Rebooting Boyhood at the Video Game Arcade.* Minneapolis: University of Minnesota Press.

Kohler, T. A. 2012. "Complex Systems and Archaeology." In *Archaeological Theory Today*, 2nd ed., edited by I. Hodder, 93–123. Cambridge: Polity.

Kramer, M. J. 2016. "Distorting History to Make it More Accurate." April 3, 2016. http://www.michaeljkramer.net/tag/glitch-art/ (accessed August 28, 2017).

LaMotta, V. 2012. "Behavioral Archaeology." In *Archaeological Theory Today*, 2nd ed., edited by I. Hodder, 62–92. Cambridge: Polity.

Latour, B. 2005. *Reassembling the Social: An Introduction to Actor-Network Theory.* Oxford: Oxford University Press.

Lolos, Y. 2012. *Land of Sikyon: Archaeology and History of a Greek City-State.* Athens: American School of Classical Studies at Athens.

Lowe, D. 2013. "Always Already Ancient: Ruins in the Virtual World." In *Greek and Roman Games in the Computer Age,* edited by T. S. Thorsen, 53–90. Trondheim: Akademika Publishing.

Manon, H. S., and D. Temkin. 2011. "Notes on Glitch." *World Picture* 6, http://worldpicturejournal.com/WP_6/Manon.html.

McFadyen, L. 2008. "Building and Architecture as Landscape Practice." In *Handbook of Landscape Archaeology,* edited by B. David and J. Thomas, 307–14. Walnut Creek, CA: Left Coast Press.

Meskell, L. 2012. "The Social Life of Heritage." In *Archaeological Theory Today,* 2nd ed., edited by I. Hodder, 227–50. Cambridge: Polity.

Meyers, K. 2011. "The Adventuring Archaeologist Trope." *Play the Past.* http://www.playthepast.org/?p=1635.

Mol, A. 2014. "Play-Things and the Origins of Online Networks: Virtual Material Culture in Multiplayer Games." *Archaeological Review* 29(1).

Mol, A., et al. 2016. "Video Games in Archaeology: Enjoyable but Trivial?" *SAA Archaeological Record* 16(5): 11–15.

_____. 2017a. *The Interactive Past: Archaeology, Heritage, and Video Games.* Leiden: Sidestone Press.

———. 2017b. "From the Stone Age to the Information Age: History and Heritage in Sid Meier's *Civilization VI.*" *Advances in Archaeological Practice* 5(2): 214–19.

Moore, L. 2006. "Going Public: Customization and American Archaeology." *SAA Archaeological Record* 6(3): 16–19.

Morgan, C. 2016. "Video Games and Archaeology." *SAA Archaeological Record* 16(5): 9–10.

———. 2009. "(Re)Building Çatalhöyük: Changing Virtual Reality in Archaeology." *Archaeologies: Journal of the World Archaeological Congress.* DOI 10.1007/s11759-009-9113-0.

Moshenska, G. 2014. "The Archaeology of (Flash) Memory." *Post-Medieval Archaeology* 48(1): 255–59.

Murphy, S. C. 2012. "Every Which Way But . . . : Reading the Atari Catalogue." In *Before the Crash: Early Video Game History,* edited by M. J. P. Wolf, 105–18. Detroit: Wayne State University Press.

Nardi, B. 2015. "Virtuality." *Annual Review of Anthropology.* (44): 15–31.

Olivier, L. 2015. *The Dark Abyss of Time: Archaeology and Memory.* Translated by A. Greenspan. Lanham, MD: Rowman and Littlefield.

Olsen, B. 2010. *In Defense of Things: Archaeology and the Ontology of Objects.* Lanham, MD: Rowman and Littlefield.

———. 2012. "Symmetrical Archaeology." In *Archaeological Theory Today,* 2nd ed., edited by I. Hodder, 208–28. Cambridge: Polity.

Pangburn, D. J. 2014. "There's Not Much 'Glitch' in Glitch Art." *Motherboard,* March 4. https://motherboard.vice.com/en_us/article/wnj5aq/theres-not-much-glitch-in-glitch-art.

Parikka, J. 2012. *What Is Media Archaeology?* Cambridge: Polity.

Paul, C. A. 2014. "Meaning." In *The Routledge Companion to Video Game Studies,* edited by M. J. P. Wolf and B. Perron, 459–65. New York: Routledge.

Perry, S., and C. Morgan. 2015. "Materializing Media Archaeologies: The MAD-P Hard Drive Excavation." *Journal of Contemporary Archaeology* 2(1): DOI: 10.1558/jca.v2i1.27083.

Pias, C. 2011. "The Game Player's Duty: The User as the Gestalt of the Parts." In *Media Archaeology: Approaches, Applications, and Implications,* edited by E. Huhtamo and J. Parikka, 164–83. Los Angeles: University of California Press.

Piccini, A., and C. Holtorf. 2011. "Introduction: Fragments from a Conversation about Contemporary Archaeology." In *Contemporary Archaeologies: Excavating Now,* 2nd ed., edited by C. Holtorf and A. Piccini, 9–29. Frankfurt: Peter Lang.

Renfrew, C. 1994. *The Ancient Mind: Elements of Cognitive Archaeology.* Cambridge: Cambridge University Press.

———. 1987. *Archaeology and Language: The Puzzle of Indo-European Origins.* Cambridge: Cambridge University Press.

Renfrew, C., and P. Bahn. 1991. *Archaeology: Theories, Methods, and Practice.* London: Thames and Hudson.

Reno, J. 2013. "Waste." In *The Oxford Handbook of the Archaeology of the Contemporary World,* edited by P. Graves-Brown, R. Harrison, and A. Piccini, 259–72. Oxford: Oxford University Press.

Richards, T. 2008. "Survey Strategies in Landscape Archaeology." In *Handbook of Landscape Archaeology,* edited by B. David and J. Thomas, 551–61. Walnut Creek, CA: Left Coast Press.

Roberts, R. G., and Z. Jacobs. 2008. "Dating in Landscape Archaeology." In *Handbook of Landscape Archaeology,* edited by B. David and J. Thomas, 347–64. Walnut Creek, CA: Left Coast Press.

Robinson, James. 2014. *Being and the Past: An Investigation into the Archaeological and Historiological Implications of the Thought of Martin Heidegger, Affected through an Examination of Past Approaches to the Study of Roman Urbanism.* University of York BA Dissertation.

Roskams, Steve. 2001. *Excavation.* Cambridge: Cambridge University Press.

Rouse III, R. 2014. "Game Design." In *The Routledge Companion to Video Game Studies,* edited by M. J. P. Wolf and B. Perron, 83–90. New York: Routledge.

Schut, K. 2014. "Media Ecology." In *The Routledge Companion to Video Game Studies,* edited by M. J. P. Wolf and B. Perron, 324–30. New York: Routledge.

Sewell, W. H., Jr. 1997. "The Concept(s) of Culture." In *Beyond the Cultural Turn: New Directions in the Study of Society and Culture,* edited by V. E. Bonnell and L. Hunt, 35–61. Berkeley: University of California Press.

Shennan, S. 2012. "Darwinian Cultural Evolution." In *Archaeological Theory Today,* 2nd ed., edited by I. Hodder, 15–36. Cambridge: Polity.

Sotamaa, O. 2014. "Artifact." In *The Routledge Companion to Video Game Studies,* edited by M. J. P. Wolf and B. Perron, 3–9. New York: Routledge.

Stanton, R. 2015. *A Brief History of Video Games: The Evolution of a Global Industry.* Philadelphia: Running Press.

Strong, V. 2008. "Uncommon Ground: Landscape as Social Geography." In *Handbook of Landscape Archaeology,* edited by B. David and J. Thomas, 51–59. Walnut Creek, CA: Left Coast Press.

Summerhayes, G. R. 2008. "Sourcing Techniques in Landscape Archaeology." In *Handbook of Landscape Archaeology,* edited by B. David and J. Thomas, 530–35. Walnut Creek, CA: Left Coast Press.

Therrien, C. 2012. "Video Games Caught Up in History." In *Before the Crash: Early Video Game History,* edited by M. J. P. Wolf, 9–29. Detroit: Wayne State University Press.

Tilley, C. 2008. "Phenomenological Approaches to Landscape Archaeology." In *Handbook of Landscape Archaeology,* edited by B. David and J. Thomas, 271–76. Walnut Creek, CA: Left Coast Press.

Vendel, C., and M. Goldberg. 2012. *Atari, Inc.: Business Is Fun.* Carmel, NY: Syzygy Press.

Watrall, E. 2002. "Interactive Entertainment as Public Archaeology." *SAA Archaeological Record* 2(2): 37–39.

Whalen, Z. 2012. "Channel F for Forgotten: The Fairchild Video Entertainment System." In *Before the Crash: Early Video Game History,* edited by M. J. P. Wolf, 60–80. Detroit: Wayne State University Press.

Wolf, M. J. P. 2012a. "Introduction." In *Before the Crash: Early Video Game History,* edited by M. J. P. Wolf, 1–8. Detroit: Wayne State University Press.

———. 2012b. "The Video Game Industry Crash of 1977." In *Before the Crash: Early Video Game History,* edited by M. J. P. Wolf, 81–89. Detroit: Wayne State University Press.

———. 2014. "Worlds." In *The Routledge Companion to Video Game Studies,* edited by M. J. P. Wolf and B. Perron, 125–31. New York: Routledge.

Vecco, M. A. 2010. "A Definition of Cultural Heritage: From the Tangible to the Intangible." *Journal of Cultural Heritage* 11(3): 321–24.

Yaneva, A. 2013. "Actor-Network Theory Approaches to the Archaeology of Contemporary Architecture." In *The Oxford Handbook of the Archaeology of the Contemporary World,* edited by P. Graves-Brown, R. Harrison, and A. Piccini, 121–34. Oxford: Oxford University Press.

Games Cited

This list—a "ludography" if you will—contains all of the games mentioned in this volume, as well as the primary publisher and date of first release. For games that are part of a series (e.g., *Tomb Raider*), I have listed the series name only and publication year of the first game in that series.

Active Worlds (ActiveWorlds, Inc., 1995)

Adventure (Atari, Inc., 1980)

Age of Empires (Ensemble Studios, 1997)

Amanthine Voyage: The Tree of Life (Big Fish, 2013)

ARK: Survival Evolved (Studio WildCard, 2017)

Assassin's Creed (series) (Ubisoft, 2007–)

Asteroids (Atari, Inc., 1979)

Baal (Psygnosis, 1988)

The Ball (Teotl Studios, 2010)

Battlefield 1942 (EA DICE, 2002)

BioShock (series) (2K Games, 2007–)

Black and White (Lionhead Studios, 2001)

Borderlands (series) (2K Games, 2009–)

Buried (Tara Copplestone and Luke Botham, 2014)

Call of Duty (series) (Activision, 2003–)

Can U Dig It! (Dig-It! Games, 2014)

Centipede (Atari, Inc., 1980)

Civilization (series) (Sid Meier, 1991–)

Counter-Strike (Valve, 2000)

Destiny (Bungie, Inc., 2014)

Diablo (series) (Blizzard Entertainment, 1996–)

Donkey Kong (Nintendo, 1981)

Doom (id Software, 1993)

Dragon Age: Inquisition (BioWare, 2014)

Eden (Kingly Software, 2016)

Elder Scrolls (series) (Bethesda Softworks, 1994–)

Elite (Acornsoft, 1984)

E.T.: The Extraterrestrial (Atari, Inc., 1982)

Eve Online (CCP Games, 2003)

EverQuest (Daybreak Game Company, 1999)

Eye of the Beholder (Strategic Simulations, 1990)

Fable (series) (Lionhead, 2004–abandoned 2016)

Fallout (series) (Bethesda Softworks, 1997–)

Final Fantasy (series) (Nintendo/ PlayStation, 1987–)

Glowgrass (Nate Cull, 1997)

Halo (series) (Bungie, Inc./Microsoft, 2001–)

Hearthstone: League of Explorers (Blizzard Entertainment, 2015)

Half-Life (Valve, 1998)

Hunt the Ancestor (BBC, 2014)

Indiana Jones (series) (multiple, 1982–)

Ingress (Niantic Labs, 2012)

Jet-Set Willy (Software Projects, 1984)

Joust (Atari, Inc., 1982)

King's Quest (series) (Sierra, 1980–2016)

The Last of Us (Naughty Dog, 2013)

The Legend of Zelda: Twilight Princess (Nintendo, 2006)

Lego Indiana Jones (series) (LucasArts, 2008–)

Loot Pursuit: Tulum (Dig-It! Games, 2013)

Mario Bros. (Nintendo, 1985)

Mario Kart (series) (Nintendo, 1992–)

Mass Effect (series) (Electronic Arts, 2007–)

Mayan Mysteries (Dig-It! Games, 2014)

Minecraft (Mojang, 2009)

Monkey Island (LucasArts, 1990)

MUD (Roy Trubshaw, 1980)

Myst (Brøderbund, 1993)

NiBiRu: Age of Secrets (The Adventure Company, 2005)

No Man's Sky (Hello Games, 2016)

Pac-Man (Namco/Midway, 1980)

Paper Mario (Nintendo, 2000)

Pokémon Go (Niantic, 2016)

Pong (Atari, Inc., 1972)

Praetorians (Eidos Interactive, 2003)

Quake (id Software, 1996)

Raiders of the Lost Ark (Atari, Inc., 1981)

Red Dead Redemption (Rockstar Games, 2010)

Riddle of the Sphinx II (Omni Creative, 2013)

Roman Town (Dig-It! Games, 2010)

Ryse: Son of Rome (Crytek, 2013)

Space Invaders (Taito, 1978)

Sphaira (Ubisoft, 1989)

Star Wars (cabinet) (Atari, Inc., 1983)

Star Wars: The Old Republic (BioWare, 2011)

Super Meat Boy (Team Meat, 2010)

Swordquest (series) (Atari, Inc., 1982)

Temple Run (Imangi Studios, 2011)

Tomb Raider (series) (Eidos Interactive, Square Enix, 1996–)

Ultima Ratio Regum (Mark Johnson, 2012–)

Uncharted (series) (Naughty Dog, 2007–17)

Undertale (Toby Fox, 2015)

Wolfenstein 3D (id Software, 1992)

World of Warcraft (Blizzard Entertainment, 2004–)

Zork (series) (Infocom, 1977)

Index

CPSIA information can be obtained
at www.ICGtesting.com
Printed in the USA
JSHW021148281220
10572JS00015B/180